THE
AIR FORCE ACADEMY CANDIDATE BOOK

HOW TO PREPARE • HOW TO GET IN • HOW TO SURVIVE

FIFTH EDITION

SUE ROSS

Silver Horn Books
Monument, CO

Cover photos courtesy USAFA.

Copyright: © 1988, © 1990, © 1995 by William L. Smallwood
© 2007, © 2012 by Sue Ross

All rights reserved. No part of this book may be reproduced or transmitted in any form or by any means without permission of the publisher, except in the case of brief quotations embodied in critical articles and reviews. For information contact Silver Horn Books, c/o Sierra Consulting, 20030 Silver Horn Ln., Monument, CO 80132.

First Edition 1988; Second Edition 1990; Third Edition 1995; Second Printing 1997; Fourth Edition 2007; Second Printing 2009; Fifth Edition 2012; Second Printing 2016.

Although the authors and publisher have exhaustively researched all sources to ensure the accuracy and completeness of the information contained in this book, we assume no responsibility for errors, inaccuracies, omissions, or any inconsistency herein. Any slights of people or organizations are unintentional.

ISBN 978-0-9797943-4-6

Printed and bound in the United States of America

TABLE OF CONTENTS

A Word From The Author v

1. THE ACADEMIC INSTITUTION 1
2. THE MILITARY INSTITUTION 5
3. GRADUATES SPEAK: WHAT THE AIR FORCE ACADEMY DID FOR ME 10

HOW TO PREPARE
4. MENTAL PREPARATION IS ESSENTIAL 35
5. WHY YOU SHOULD EXPECT ACADEMIC SHOCK 45
6. WHAT THE PROFESSORS SAY ABOUT ACADEMIC SHOCK 56
7. HOW TO PREPARE PHYSICALLY 67
8. OTHER TYPES OF PREPARATION 72

HOW TO GET IN
9. THE FIRST STEP: APPLYING TO THE ACADEMY 79
10. THE SECOND STEP: GETTING THE NOMINATION 88
11. TIPS FROM CONGRESSIONAL STAFFERS 95
12. INTERVIEWS: ADVICE FROM THOSE WHO CONDUCT THEM 101
13. ALTERNATE ROUTES TO THE ACADEMY 114

HOW TO SURVIVE
14. THE RUGGED DOOLIE YEAR 123
15. SURVIVAL ADVICE FROM DOOLIES 131
16. SURVIVAL ADVICE FROM UPPERCLASSMEN 143
17. GETTING ALONG WITH CLASSMATES AND ROOMMATES 150
18. ACADEMIC SURVIVAL 157
19. REACH OUT FOR HELP 167
20. ADVICE FOR INTERCOLLEGIATE ATHLETES 174
21. DIVERSITY AND TOLERANCE 187
22. HAVE FUN 196
23. LIVING WITH THE HONOR CODE 200
24. AFTER GRADUATION: AIR, SPACE, AND CYBERSPACE 209
25. ADVICE FOR PARENTS 215

ACKNOWLEDGEMENTS 246
INDEX 248

A Word From The Author

Are you thinking about applying to the Air Force Academy? Then I congratulate you on considering this excellent opportunity, and being willing to serve your country. Because you have this book in your hand, you probably realize that applying to an academy is a whole different ball game compared to applying to other colleges. And if you are not sure if the Academy is right for you, I hope this book will help you decide.

First, visit the Academy web site and study it. You will learn the history of the institution, the kinds of courses you can take, the physical examinations that you must pass and the names and background of all the professors. The admissions web address is www.academyadmissions.com. You can find additional information about every aspect of the Academy at www.usafa.edu.

This book has almost none of that material, although it will tell you where to find some of the more detailed information. This is above all a "how to" book.

It will tell you how to *prepare* for the Academy, how to prepare to be competitive so you can get an appointment, and how to prepare to be a cadet if you get in.

One chapter, which is probably the most important one in the book, tells you how to prepare mentally. Other chapters tell you how to prepare academically, physically, and in other important ways.

This book will also tell you how to *get into* the Academy.

One chapter describes all the procedures. Another chapter describes how to get a congressional nomination and some of the pitfalls of that process. Other chapters give you guidelines on how to conduct yourself during interviews, and how you might be able to get into the Academy by alternate routes if you are now unqualified or have failed to get in by the regular procedures.

This book will tell you how to *survive* the challenging first year when you get to the Academy.

Throughout the book, cadets, graduates, staff, and faculty members tell you what you must do to survive, and special advice is given to intercollegiate athletes, women, and others who will be in the minority at the Academy. Later, if you decide to go and receive an appointment, I recommend that you read and reread these chapters.

Parents: the final chapter is for you, with advice gleaned from interviews with a wide variety of parents from around the United States who have had sons and daughters at the Academy and who believe some of the hard lessons they learned should be passed on to parents who are about to go through the experience. This chapter offers advice on how to survive the experience yourself, cadets and staff members' suggestions on what to do to support your son or daughter, and perhaps more importantly what NOT to do!

You are advised to read through this book if you're only thinking about going to the Air Force Academy. You are advised to STUDY it if you decide to apply.

If the latter is your choice, you will be one of many competing for a very limited number of openings. Besides meeting all the qualifications and having good information and advice, you need one other thing, something that no one else can give you: You need *desire*. You need a burning and focused desire that will drive you over all the hurdles that may be thrown in front of you and keep you on track through all the steps of the application process. If you're easily discouraged or don't feel that burning desire, take some friendly advice and apply to State U—and save yourself lots of headaches.

A final word: Thousands upon thousands of young men and women have made it into the Air Force Academy and managed to graduate. Practically all of them will tell you that it was one of the greatest experiences of their life—that it made them into something they would never have become without that experience. If you really want to be all that you are capable of being, go for it!

SCR

ONE
The Academic Institution

The United States Air Force Academy is located just north of Colorado Springs, Colorado. Most of its modernistic, steel and glass buildings are perched on a ridge 7,258 feet above sea level at the base of the Rocky Mountains.

Looking toward the south from a classroom, you can see a panorama of the 14,110-foot Pikes Peak and the city of Colorado Springs, including scorched hillsides damaged by recent wildfires. To the east is an endless stretch of prairie that reaches across the eastern one-third of Colorado and into Kansas and Oklahoma.

Looking north, you see the Rampart Range disappearing behind ridges of foothills covered with scrub oak and scattered stands of Ponderosa Pine. These broken foothills begin with Jack's Valley, where much of the field training takes place, and extend northward for about 50 miles where they meet the sprawling metropolis of Denver, the state capital.

The students, called cadets, are usually too busy to admire the view from their rooms, but many do keep an eye to the southeast. The Academy airfield lies in that direction, and if the cadets are not stealing glances at their friends swinging beneath the canopies of their parachutes, their eyes are on the many sailplanes and single-engine trainers flying overhead.

The first thing you should know about the Air Force Academy is that it is designed to develop young men and women into leaders of character, to serve as career officers in the United States Air Force.

HOW GOOD IS THE ACADEMIC PROGRAM?

But what of the "college" itself, the books and professors, the required and elective courses, the majors and minors? Does the military and athletic training take away from the academic standards? Is the education at the Academy comparable to other universities?

Those who know the most about college academic standards, the accrediting associations, speak for the quality of the Academy's academic program. The Bachelor of Science Degree that is awarded to its graduates is accredited by the North Central Association of Colleges and Schools. The Engineering Accreditation Commission has accredited all of the specialized engineering majors. These are the majors in aeronautical, astronautical, civil, and electrical engineering, and engineering mechanics and engineering sciences. In addition, the chemistry, computer science, and management degrees are accredited by their respective accreditation boards.

In the minds of some, being accredited is about the same as getting a "B" grade. Accreditation says that the college or program is good. If you are the quality of student who could be accepted into the Academy, you are probably seeking an *outstanding* education, not one that is just satisfactory.

Much of a college's reputation is based on more subjective criteria or the enthusiasm of its graduates. However, there are some meaningful clues. For example, in 2012, *U.S. News and World Report* ranked the Academy's undergraduate engineering programs #5 in the nation, undergraduate business management #1, and the school overall as the #3 Public Liberal Arts College in the country. *Forbes* ranked it #35 of the 650 best colleges in the nation and #2 as "best value."

Another example is the number of graduates who have been selected to receive the prestigious Rhodes Scholarship. These scholarships, which are for graduate study at Oxford University in England, are awarded to just 32 graduating seniors in the United States each year. Graduates of the Air Force Academy have won nearly one per year, which is a relatively large number considering that thousands of graduating seniors are in competition for these scholarships.

Air Force Academy graduates have also received a relatively large number of Guggenheim, National Science Foundation, and other prestigious fellowships—enough to indicate that the academic program has indeed earned widespread respect.

What is the academic program like? If you are thinking it is solely technical and scientific, you are mistaken. Every cadet must complete 102 semester hours of courses in the core curriculum—the equivalent of more than three years of study in a typical college. This curriculum is designed to give future Air Force officers a broad education so they can function in a high-tech military and also operate in a globalized world. To achieve this breadth and balance, core credits are divided across four general areas: humanities, basic sciences, social sciences, and engineering.

Most cadets will take 40 - 50 credit hours in a specific academic major, although some will get approval to pursue a general "Bachelor of Science" degree. Some will also choose an academic minor, often in a foreign language. The admissions web site lists the academic majors offered, and more detailed information about the curriculum can be found by selecting "academics" on the web site www.usafa.edu.

PROFESSORS DEDICATED TO TEACHING

What about the professors? Most of the professors (about 75 percent) are Air Force officers, for the most part captains and majors

The Academy sits at the base of the Rampart Range.   *Courtesy USAFA*

in their late twenties or thirties. All of them have master's degrees and over half have doctorates. Note that these professors are regarded as "teaching professors." Unlike their counterparts at most universities, they are not under the gun to perform research and publish papers in their specialty, a burden that often places teaching lower in their priorities. In many universities, professors spend most of their time with their research duties, resulting in huge classes of 300-400 students. They often hand over some of their classroom and grading duties to teaching assistants, students who may be just a few years ahead of the class they are assisting with.

But none of that will be found at the Air Force Academy. Classes are small, averaging about 20 students for core courses. It is not unusual for major's classes to have only eight to ten students. The professors' number one priority is to teach cadets, period. They also must make themselves available for Extra Instruction. In 2012, the *Princeton Review* ranked the Air Force Academy the #5 college for the Most Accessible Faculty, and Academy professors have won the Colorado Professor of the Year Award 8 of the last 10 years. The role of professors at the Air Force Academy is drastically different than at most universities. They are there to teach.

Over two hundred cadets were interviewed during the research for this book. Rarely were officials present, so there were many opportunities for the cadets to complain about their professors, especially as they discussed their problems with the rigorous academic program. They had surprisingly few complaints.

Most cadets commended the enthusiasm and dedication of the faculty. They spoke favorably of faculty attitudes, the professors who say, "I am determined that you are going to get through this course, and I don't care how much time we have to spend together outside of class. If you are willing to put in the effort, I will help you pass this class!"

The Academy's official policy is to counsel students with academic problems. Often such counseling leads to the assignment of tutors or remedial sessions conducted by the faculty or learning skills coaches. Never are cadets left to flounder on their own. This policy saves many cadets who might otherwise have flunked out of the Academy or a civilian college.

USAFA professors are dedicated to teaching. *Courtesy USAFA*

Of course, some students fail to maintain a 2.0 average, and this will eventually cause them to be disenrolled. But most cadets who were interviewed believe that those who fail are largely those who lack the motivation to succeed. "If they select you for this place," commented one cadet, "you know you can make it through. You don't have to be smart. You just have to be determined." The Dean of Faculty echoed this thought: "We believe that if you get through the rigorous admissions process and get an appointment, you have what it takes to succeed. It's a partnership"—a partnership between the student and the faculty.

In summary, the educational program at the Air Force Academy is equally good as, if not better than, those at most colleges and universities. The success of the graduates has proven that many times over. You get a bonus when you go to the Air Force Academy. You are not just a number in the database. You are not a faceless body trekking along with tens of thousands of others at a large university, sitting in the back of a crowded lecture hall, with your papers and tests graded by teaching assistants.

If you go to the Air Force Academy, your professors will know your name on the first day of class. You will develop a close personal relationship based on mutual dedication, and they will go to great lengths to see that you get the best education you can.

That is a deal that would be hard to beat anywhere.

TWO
The Military Institution

If you are mainly looking for a way to get a really good college education, totally free, do not go to the Air Force Academy. If you do, you will be sorry and so will the Air Force.

Why? Because the primary mission of the Academy is to produce high quality, career oriented officers for the Air Force.

The Air Force Academy's goal is not to educate the youth of America. It is not to produce leaders in business and the professions. It is neither to win football games for the alumni nor to produce players for the NFL. Its mission is to produce leaders of character to serve as officers in the Air Force.

If you are thinking about applying for the Air Force Academy, it is very important that you understand what the Air Force expects of an officer. That philosophy, when translated into action, has a profound effect on every cadet at the Academy.

In the case of nearly all cadets who survive more than a week or two at the Academy, almost without exception they become different people. Literally. They become so different, in fact, that their parents often look at them with awe and wonder as they try to understand what happened to the son or daughter they used to know.

The Air Force wants their officers to have a wide variety of attributes. They want them to be intelligent, well educated and enthusiastic about flying or some other career field in the Air Force. They want them healthy and physically strong, able to handle high levels of stress, and to

Remember the Air Force Academy is a military institution, not just a college.
Courtesy USAFA

have good moral character. Most important, they want officers who are good leaders.

They want the kind of leaders who thrive on new and difficult challenges. They want leaders who can withstand the incredible pressures of warfare—the kind who can remain cool and effective when surrounded by chaos or under fire.

Finally, they want leaders who understand and believe strongly in the American concept of government and freedom. Air Force officers must be willing to go to war and, if necessary, die in the line of duty.

What all of the above means for the cadet is quite simple. "College life" at the Air Force Academy is not anything like it is at State U.

At the Academy there are a few parties, jokes, and laughs behind closed doors, some great clandestine pranks. But generally the atmosphere is military: formal, restrained, and serious. One does not see the traditional college-type activities—campus politics and protest marches, staying out late and Saturday morning sleep-ins, class ditching and CliffsNotes, beer and loud music. If you believe that one of the goals of your college years is to have as much fun as possible, the Academy will surely disappoint you.

BASIC CADET TRAINING:
THE FIRST LESSONS IN LEADERSHIP

The first step in the program of officer development begins when the new appointees arrive. That is the beginning of Basic Cadet Training, or BCT—appropriately (but not officially) pronounced "beast." This is a rigorous six-week program that has many goals. One is to begin a growth process, a process that forces the basic cadets to begin stretching their personal limits. These include limits of all kinds—limits of stress endurance, physical stamina, patience, tolerance, commitment, mental

During BCT, the upperclassmen are looking for commitment and perseverance.

Courtesy USAFA

concentration, and character.

Another goal is to make basic cadets truly believe one of the most important of all military truths: YOU CANNOT DO IT ALONE.

Many who come to the Academy are strong-willed individualists. Often they have had hard-driving high school careers and are used to going it alone to achieve their goals. They are used to succeeding at nearly everything they do, and standing out as exceptional. This tendency has to be eliminated early in officer development. In BCT the basic cadets are given tasks that are impossible to do without the cooperation and help of others. Often this aspect of the training is the most frustrating for those who excelled during their high school careers.

The basic cadet also begins to learn one of an officer's most important skills, the skill of time management. In wartime, and even in many peacetime assignments, there is never enough time available for an officer to do everything that is supposed to be done.

The difference between success or failure, or even survival and death, often depends upon an officer's ability to set priorities. Quickly, and often under conditions of extreme stress, he or she must decide which things must be done first, second and third—and which things can be put off to a later time.

Basic cadets start learning how to make the same kind of decisions under mild stress and non-life threatening conditions. They are continually given too much to do with too little time to do it.

During BCT, the basic cadet also receives instruction on the Cadet Honor Code. This code states, "We will not lie, steal, or cheat, nor tolerate among us anyone who does." All cadets must accept and learn to live by the Honor Code. (Chapter 23 covers the Honor Code in detail.)

BCT also includes a number of traditional military training exercises such as weapons training, how to march and salute, and small-force combat tactics.

One of the overall goals of BCT is not appreciated by the basic cadets until they finish the six-week program. But as they march to the formation where they will receive their fourth-class shoulder boards, signifying their formal acceptance into the Cadet Wing, they feel pride for having the guts to stick it out through the rigorous BCT program. They feel a greatly increased sense of confidence from knowing they had the strength to master what was probably the most difficult challenge of their life. And they feel a strong bond with their classmates from having survived that challenge together.

That is just what the Air Force wants. An officer has to have a unique kind of personal pride, confidence, and sense of teamwork in order to lead others, especially in warfare. That confidence has to be real and it has to be felt inside, the way the new cadets feel it after BCT.

BCT begins around the end of June when the new cadets arrive at the Academy. It ends in early August. But the military training continues, although in a less concentrated manner.

THE FOURTHCLASS YEAR: A LONG, HARD CLIMB

During the academic year, all cadets must take courses in military science in addition to their regular academic courses. This is an extra burden and is one reason why graduates of the Air Force Academy often have 40 percent more credit hours than graduates from civilian colleges.

The Academy will teach you how to perform under stress. *Courtesy USAFA*

In addition to the demands of extra course work, there are also unique physical demands placed upon the cadet. Participation in athletics is mandatory. Twice a week, in the afternoon after classes, every cadet not participating in an intercollegiate sport must participate in an intramural sport.

Cadets also must maintain specific levels of physical fitness while they are at the Academy. Weight checks and fitness tests are administered twice a year throughout the four years. Those who do not meet the standards for fitness or weight must enter rehabilitation programs and are disenrolled if they do not come up to standards.

Without doubt, the fourthclass or "doolie" year is very, very demanding.[1] The rigor of the academic load, for most cadets, requires a drastic change in study habits. There is the usual homesickness, which for some is much worse than for others. Most of all, there is the persistent, dawn-to-dusk supervision and training of the doolies by the upperclassmen.

The latter, though frustrating, stressful, and tiresome, is a necessary test for potential officers. Are there doolies in the class who are likely to give up and quit under pressure? Are there doolies who cannot control their temper and emotions? Are there doolies who think only of themselves and put their own needs above those of their classmates? Are there doolies who get flustered under pressure and cannot learn to remain calm? Are there doolies who are attending the Academy for reasons other than becoming Air Force officers?

The upperclassmen have the duty to answer such questions for each fourthclass cadet under their supervision by putting the doolies through a constant series of hurdles. Those hurdles are designed to expose the kinds of weakness that the Air Force cannot have in its officers. (The specific kinds of hurdles are described throughout this book.)

But the doolie year always ends, and with it comes "recognition," the ritual where the doolie is accepted by the upperclassman. With this new status comes new privileges and almost a new way of life. The recognized doolie is now accepted as a friend by the other cadets and can even call them by their first names.

Equally important, the cadet is now considered to have true officer potential. In military science classes and in a variety of summer activities, the cadets start thinking of themselves as potential officers. Of course, over the next three years, they still must face challenges designed to extend their personal limits and improve their officer skills.

With the end of the doolie year, however, the worst is over. But there are still three rigorous years ahead. Is it all worth it? The next chapter provides an answer to this question from the perspective of some graduates who have succeeded in a wide variety of military and civilian career fields.

---

1. *Freshman cadets are officially known as "Cadet Fourthclass Smith" and so on. The more common, cadet slang for a freshman is "four degree." "Doolie" is used less often by cadets, but is used in this book for brevity.*

THREE
Graduates Speak:
What The Air Force Acadamy Did For Me

Every college and university has a dedicated group of alumni supporters, eager to share what made their college experience worthwhile—education, sports, clubs, friends, sororities and fraternities.

When Air Force Academy graduates look back on their four years as a cadet, they share some of these same memories. They also share a bond that comes from overcoming the unique challenges they faced at the Academy. And all of them will tell you those challenges shaped the rest of their lives, no matter what career path they chose or how long they stayed in the Air Force.

This chapter offers the perspectives of a diverse group of graduates, with a diverse set of career experiences. These accounts offer insight into the value of an Academy education, and helpful advice for all of you, in their own words.

Gregg Popovich, Class of 1970

Coach Popovich was the Academy basketball team's captain and leading scorer his senior year. After graduation, he was a special services officer and also toured with the US Armed Forces basketball team. He was assistant varsity basketball coach at the Air Force Academy and head basketball coach for USAFA Prep School. As general manager and then head coach for the San Antonio Spurs, Coach Popovich has led his team to four NBA championships, and was named NBA Coach of the Year in 2003 and again in 2012. He is also known for extensive community service, earning the Daily Point of Light Award from President George Bush.

Gregg Popovich, Class of 1970.
Courtesy Gregg Popovich

I didn't grow up in a military family, and I never thought about being in the military or flying. I went to the Air Force Academy because I wanted to play Division I basketball. I was recruited by exactly zero Division I schools, and the Academy offered the combination of academics and other challenges that really appealed to me. Before I got there, I didn't give the military aspect a second thought.

During the first summer [in BCT], I was very homesick. I spent more than one evening tearfully wondering what I'd gotten myself into. But all the competitive aspects of BCT took my mind off being homesick—the morning runs, intramural sports, the obstacle course—that got me through. Being a naturally competitive person, I enjoyed the competition.

Once academics started, that took my mind off being homesick, too. You're just too busy. Juggling all the demands requires discipline. The number of courses cadets take is much more than students at other colleges, but once you're in the routine, the competitiveness kicks in. And then when you find a specific interest, the Academy becomes much more enjoyable.

What did I take from the Academy? The first thing that strikes you, especially in the civilian world, is how much discipline and attention to detail inform your life. You're never late; you respect other peoples' time. The second thing is the great relationships you form with other people, and the trust and integrity that go with it. Also, you can multitask without being anxious about it—at the Academy you really learn that in spades.

My advice to high school students, especially athletes, who are considering the Academy: Number one is to be objective about yourself—make sure you really desire a competitive experience, a challenging situation where you will be tested and find out your strengths and weaknesses.

Number two is try to visit the Academy and get a mental image of the layout. Learn what day–to-day life is like so you aren't so shocked. If I hadn't been so naïve I wouldn't have been so shocked! The constant criticism [from upperclassmen] is a real shocker—when you first get there, you won't be used to all that criticism.

Also, make sure you come in the best shape of your life; if you're not in shape you'll be resented for it. Study as much as you can—read books, build your vocabulary, take extra math to get a head start. And try to acquaint yourself with what the military is all about. I showed up not knowing the most basic facts about the services, and they were asking me to memorize facts about Pratt and Whitney engines [on Air Force aircraft]—I had no clue!

During that first year, you need to seek out someone to talk to about the things that bother you. My AOC [commanding officer] was a Marine pilot who'd been shot down four times. Flying makes me sick, so he wasn't someone I could express my doubts, concerns, and worries to. I sought out nobody—I was trying to figure out the world all by myself.

Finally, I'd say try to take advantage of the leadership opportunities presented. I sort of hid from it, I think because I didn't understand it. I fought the system. You need to embrace the system and understand what's going on around you. You have to understand it's a marathon. You need day-to-day persistence. Bear down mentally for the long stretch.

After all is said and done, the experience will be one that sets you up for life. You will have accomplished a great deal, know who you are, and be ready for *anything*.

General Edward A. Rice, Jr., Class of 1978

General Rice is currently commander of Air Education and Training Command.   USAF

General Rice went to pilot training after graduation and ended up flying B-52 bombers. He did that for four years, then went to the Pentagon for a one-year internship, where he worked with the Air Staff. He then went back to B-52s as an aircraft commander and flight commander. He was selected for a White House Fellowship, where he served in the U.S. Health and Human Services Department. He has commanded flying units at the squadron, group, and wing level. He commanded 13th Air Force in the Pacific theater, and is U.S. Forces Japan, and is now commander of the Air Education and Training Command.

Going to the Air Force Academy was a lifelong dream for me. My father was an Air Force officer and I grew up seeing the kind of people who served with him. From the time I was nine years old I wanted to be one of them, so it was the biggest day of my life when I got accepted at the Academy.

Before I went, I talked to a lot of people who gave me advice and I was probably as knowledgeable and as prepared as anyone could have been. When I got there, the physical part was not real difficult because I had lettered in football and track and had good upper-body strength. It was the mental part that was tough, especially all the memorizing when my mind was stressed with all the other demands that were placed upon us.

I remember one night at Jack's Valley [an area north of the Academy where part of BCT is conducted] when one of the guys in my element challenged the twelve or thirteen others in our tent to match SAT scores. Several others did and beat the guy. I had very good grades in high school and good, but not exceptional SAT scores. That experience didn't do anything for my confidence, and I began to wonder how well I was going to do when I started competing academically with guys like that.

Well, as it turned out, that same guy who challenged the others that night ended up failing math because of poor study habits. That was a good lesson for me, and for anybody who reads this book, because it shows that it really doesn't matter who you were before—you're going to be equal with everybody else when you arrive at the Academy. You're going to have to start fresh and prove yourself again with another group of people.

In my own case, I started the academic year highly motivated, but leery of how I would be able to compete with so many outstanding students. I studied extremely hard every night and every weekend. But then, when I got the first midterm progress report, I was extremely disappointed; I had "B's" and one "C." My goal was to be on the Dean's List so I buckled down and really worked the last half of the semester. Well, I made it, and then I set a goal of 3.5 for the next semester and made that. The third semester I tried for a 4.0, but missed it with "A's" and one "B." Finally, at the end of the four years I ended up as a distinguished graduate and only failed to make the Dean's List one semester, which was during the fall semester of my senior year when I was Cadet Wing Commander [highest ranking cadet in the wing]. I'm not telling you all of this to be bragging; I'm saying it to point out a lesson for others who might go there feeling a little bit threatened like I was. My advice is to forget about the competition and concentrate on what you, personally, are going to do. And don't set your goals too low; set them high and you'll make yourself try to achieve them.

I majored in engineering and was considered a good student.

> *You're going to have to start fresh and prove yourself again.*

However, in my years in the Air Force I have used very little if any of what I learned in that academic field. On the other hand, every cadet is also exposed to a military education at the Academy, which is designed to teach you how to be an effective leader. Besides working hard at academics, I also tried to take advantage of every opportunity to get leadership experience. The summer after my sophomore year I was a Group Sergeant Major for SERE [survival, evasion, resistance, escape] training and a Group Sergeant Major for BCT. During my junior year I was Group Sergeant Major and Wing Sergeant Major—the latter the highest office that a cadet can hold as a junior. During the final year I was BCT commander at Jack's Valley and Cadet Wing Commander during the fall semester.

I'm not trying to impress anybody by reciting these accomplishments. What I am trying to do is make a point: Even though I have not used my academic major in the Air Force, I have used the leadership experiences and techniques many times. Also, what I learned from those leadership experiences has contributed much more to my success in the Air Force than anything I achieved by my academic standing.

The cadet leadership experiences are especially valuable because cadet leaders really don't have much authority. What they have is lots of responsibility. For example, as Cadet Wing Commander I was responsible for 4400 cadets. In the Air Force there are generals who don't have that many people under them.

In the Air Force if you supervise someone, you usually write that person's performance reports. So you have some leverage in getting that person to perform the way you would like. But as a cadet commander you have none of that authority so you have to rely on more personal techniques. What I learned was that if you want people to respond to you, you must make it clear to them that you are interested in their welfare and not your own. That's a cardinal principle and probably the most important thing we learned about leadership. To be a good leader you must take care of the people working for you.

If I had just one bit of advice to give a candidate, what would it be?

I would say this: If you have what it takes to get into the Academy, you have what it takes to be as successful as your attitude will let you be. When you get there, your instructors will help you academically and the military officers will help you militarily. And if you have the attitude—the good strong positive attitude and the willingness to work hard—there is really no limit to the success you can achieve. Those who have problems are the people who don't want to be there, or the people who aren't willing to put forth much effort to stay out of trouble.

Lieutenant General John Hesterman III, class of 1983

As a cadet, General Hesterman completed an exchange semester at the United States Naval Academy, was captain of the judo team, and served as Cadet Wing Commander his senior year. After graduation, he attended pilot training at Sheppard AFB, Texas and then flew the F-4. He has been an instructor pilot in the F-16C, F-117A, F-15E and T-38C. Hesterman has commanded the 494th Fighter Squadron, the 4th Operations Group, the 12th Flying Training Wing, and the 48th Fighter Wing. He is currently the Military Deputy for Readiness to the Under Secretary of Defense for Personnel and Readiness at the Pentagon.

Lieutenant General Hesterman and his family.
Courtesy John Hesterman

I decided I wanted to go to the Air Force Academy when I was ten. My father was an Air Force officer, and I grew up around Air Force bases, so it seemed like a natural goal. I spent a lot of time in high school trying to make sure I'd be competitive for an academy appointment. I had started doing judo at a young age and met the Academy judo coach, who was also the Olympic coach, so I was also excited at the opportunity to compete there.

I thought I was in pretty good shape physically, so didn't prepare as seriously as I should have. I underestimated the effects of the high altitude, and for the first few days of BCT I thought I might collapse, but adapted after a week or so. Since I grew up in a military family, the military aspect of training was not much of a surprise. Some of my classmates who didn't have that experience were a little overwhelmed. What I remember most about BCT was bonding with my classmates, and learning quickly this was not something I was going to be able to do by myself. We needed each other.

During the fourthclass year, life was full. There just wasn't enough time, at least for the naps I wanted to take. I think the hardest part, for me, was that I'm not a morning guy. Having to be up and alert at reveille was difficult, knowing my friends back home were sleeping until 11. But it was a good thing; having the opportunity to travel for judo and visiting my friends at regular colleges made me realize that the discipline at the Academy was something I needed. If they didn't help me with a regimented program and make me go to class, I don't know how long it would have taken me to graduate from college. The Academy provided the structure I needed to succeed.

The Honor Code was something we all had to get used to. Although I came from a family that taught and valued integrity, in my high school we often shared homework and test notes. I had to pay attention to the higher standard for academic integrity, because it came with very real consequences. You have to adhere to this strict standard or they won't let you stay.

One of the best things about Academy academics is that the teacher to student ratio is so favorable. A lot of folks didn't ask for help, but I did; sometimes because I needed help with the work, and often just for an explanation or clarification. The instructors were always so good about it. A judo principle is maximum efficiency with minimum effort. I visited my instructors often, I think, just to make sure I didn't do any accidental extra work! They were always helpful.

I realized from travelling for judo that the Academy can be an intense place; you can forget what normal life is like. It is a very good idea to get involved in a sport or an activity. Everyone feels some stress and those opportunities give you an outlet. If you only go to class and do your military duties, it can be more of a grind than it is for those who have a place to unwind and vent a bit of that stress. Get out, go play a bit.

The most important thing the Academy gave me was a ready supply of lifelong friends. I have never gone anywhere where I didn't have someone close by that I went to school with. Even if I hadn't talked to them for 15 years, we still shared a bond, friendship, and trust. I could trust them to look after my house or my kid or my dog; and they happily would as I would for them. When I was deployed during the first Gulf War, another grad took care of my house and even did my taxes! Every assignment brings me in contact with someone from the Academy, and it always only takes a few moments to catch up. Like most graduates, I am blessed with so many dear friends, all of whom have done something relevant and worthwhile with their lives while serving so many and our great nation.

The Air Force Academy is a wonderful opportunity. The Air Force paid me to go to school, taught me to fly high performance airplanes, and gave me a fascinating job and lots of leadership opportunities. They sent me to 85 or so different countries. You can get out of the Air Force after the initial commitment, or stay in. Either way you will have contributed a great deal to your country and will make any community better. My friends are doctors and lawyers and pilots and space and cyber experts, to name just a few of their talents and occupations, both in and out of the Air Force. You give up a few choices and liberties while you're in, but the payback is immense.

As you prepare for and before you go through the application process, you can figure out what you can do to be more competitive as the whole person (student, athlete, leader, and communicator) that our Academies seek. Even if you decide to go somewhere else, preparing for Academy admission will make you more competitive for admission anywhere. I know I did some things I might not have done otherwise, just to be sure I was a well rounded candidate. They gave me a broader perspective, and I learned from and genuinely enjoyed the experiences. As an added benefit, you may find something that you love doing!

During that first year, your days are going to seem long, but really the whole Academy experience goes by very quickly. Remember, don't try to do it alone. You will want to work closely with your classmates and you will learn to take care of each other. It will make the year much easier and will make you a better cadet and officer later. In the end, you will have friends for life.

Finally, don't take cadet life too seriously, you can try hard and do well and still smile about it all. It can sometimes seem like life at the Academy is the center and focus of the universe, but always remember, there's a big world out there. I think the folks who see the humor in the place, enjoy their friends, and laugh a lot just do better.

The Air Force Academy gives you an exceptional opportunity to be with so many high quality, immensely talented, and very thoughtful people. I played intramural sports with guys and gals who where high school All-American athletes. I could always find someone who knew more than I did about any subject I picked. You get to know and love people from all over the country with all kinds of amazing stories. And even those who were big fish in small ponds in high school, and found themselves squarely in the middle or even the bottom of their class at the Academy, all graduated and started even again. They all did and continue to do well.

At the end of the day, the Air Force Academy experience is an amazing opportunity to do a lot of very cool things that most people just don't get to do. Good luck!

Colonel Tamra Rank, class of 1983

After graduating from the Academy with a degree in computer science, Colonel Rank attended pilot training in Texas and became a T-38 instructor pilot. She also flew KC-10s and T-1s as an instructor. She has commanded a pilot training squadron, attended war college in Australia through an exchange program, and served as vice commander

Colonel Rank and her daughter at an Academy graduation banquet. *Courtesy Tamra Rank*

of the 375th Air Mobility Wing. She is currently the vice superintendent of the Air Force Academy.

I went to the Academy because I wanted to do something different. I didn't want to stay in Iowa, even though I love Iowa. I knew nothing about the Air Force Academy or the military. I had visited as a senior in high school—my first time on an airplane—and I thought the facilities were awesome. That's what I took from that visit.

I actually liked BCT—the assault course, fighting with pugil sticks. I was physically fit, I was a runner, and I was pretty tough. I liked being in the tent with the other girls in the squadron. I really didn't think it was bad.

The academic year was hard. I had never had to work at academics before, and I didn't adjust well. I regret that I didn't do better. I should have gotten some help on how to study, because I didn't know how to work at learning.

At the time, if you weren't in serious trouble, no one would help you. Now we're more in tune with people who aren't performing to their potential. The professors and AOCs put more effort into looking at everyone, not just those who are failing.

Every once in awhile I would call home and tell my mother I was going to quit, and she would say "fine." But I'm not a quitter. Most cadets are type As who have never quit at anything or failed at anything. Interesting how at every other university, if you leave you "transfer," but at the Academy when you leave, you "quit." The Academy was very compatible with the atmosphere I grew up in. I was taught to do the right thing and see things through. I got more than my share of attention, good and bad. But I'm not one to back down.

Your roommate makes a huge difference. We laughed a lot when the door was closed. You'll have lots of friends there who are all going through the same things you are. The people who were my friends there are still my friends. If you don't see them for 20 years, it won't matter. You still have that trust and common respect. You'll still be friends and become friends with their families. The Academy teaches you how to get along with other people and make the most of those relationships. It's important that men and women can be friends, and the Academy also teaches you how to figure that out.

If you go to the Academy, you have to know what kind of person you are; you have to be comfortable and confident in who you are.

You are constantly being told what to do, and you have to be able to understand that it's not because they're treating you like a kid. They're teaching you discipline. Discipline means being able to accept "because I said so" as an answer. Running on the marble strips may not have an exact purpose, but why doesn't matter. The purpose is just about discipline, which is a good thing. It's not a democracy, but we serve so there can be one for everyone else.

The Air Force is a good life. Some of the days aren't good, but the years are good. The friends you'll have, the bonds, flying airplanes—that's about the coolest thing you can do. I would also tell the women cadets, don't think you can't be a pilot and a mom or an officer and a mom, because there are plenty of examples of people like me who have done both.

Chad Hennings, class of 1988

While Hennings was at the Air Force Academy, he won numerous honors for his football prowess: As a senior, he was unanimously elected to the college All American first team, won the Outland Trophy, and was voted the Defensive Player of the Decade by the Western Athletic Conference. After graduation he went through pilot training, transitioned to the A-10 Warthog and flew combat missions in Iraq. After the Gulf War, as the Air Force began to downsize, he elected to pursue another dream: playing professional football. He played nine seasons with the Dallas Cowboys and earned three Super Bowl rings before becoming a successful businessman, author and public speaker. He was inducted into the Colorado Sports Hall of Fame in 2005, the College Football Hall of Fame in 2006, and the Air Force Academy Athletic Hall of Fame in 2007.

I went to the Air Force Academy for the complete experience: a first-class education, the chance to play Division I college football, and the military life—the esprit de corps, the service. My senior year in high school, I went to the Academy on a recruiting visit, and had opportunity to eat at Mitch's [Mitchell Hall, the cadet dining hall], see the dormitory, go to classes, and talk to some cadets and instructors. The visit gave me a fairly decent feel for the Academy and cadet life.

BCT was a challenge, mentally, physically, spiritually, and emotionally. Since it was my first time away from home, it gave me

Former Dallas Cowboy Chad Hennings is tackling new challenges as a businessman.
Courtesy Dallas Cowboys

the chance to mature in all these areas. Of course I had been on athletic teams before, but it wasn't until I was under so much stress and duress that I felt part of a team the way I did with my classmates in BCT.

BCT was a challenge, with memorizing quotes and military terminology and military history, but then it's out of the frying pan into the fire. The academic year is about balancing and time prioritization. You have to balance military duties such as calling minutes [yelling out the uniform and time remaining to the next required event], academics and football practice.

It's like drinking from a fire hose. You have to absorb so much information, sort it out, and prioritize it. I got a 3.2 grade point average my first semester, so I got off on a great start and laid a great academic foundation.

Sometimes I contemplated leaving the Academy, but I fought the mental temptation to quit, and just took it day by day. I remember sitting in the chapel, looking out the stained-glass windows to the east toward Iowa, thinking, "Someday I will drive back down the road toward home as a graduate of the Air Force Academy."

But at some point, everyone needs to get help. When I needed help, I went to upperclassmen for advice. Not every technique they offered was something I could use, but I picked and chose what worked for me and "hybridized" it into my own method for balancing everything.

Football at the Academy was very competitive. I felt even more pressure to perform since I was traveling with the varsity team as a fourthclassman. I got some playing time and a good taste of Division I football, playing schools like Virginia Tech and other service academies. I got an appreciation for what Falcon football was all about, the legacy and the tradition. Going to a bowl game that first year was just icing on the cake.

The big lesson for getting along as an athlete was balance. When my squadron mates were getting ready for a SAMI [Saturday morning room inspection] I was at a hotel before a game or at spring practice. I usually couldn't march in the parades with them, or march to lunch with them. But I tried to make up for the military training I missed when I was in the squadron. I made a real effort to be part of the squadron. I think they understood that when they finally had some free time, I was at practice.

What I learned at the Academy helped when I was flying fighters, when I was playing for the Cowboys, and now in my business career. My Academy experience helped me make the transition from the Air Force to the NFL: being able to handle training camp for 6 weeks when it's 95 degrees and 75 percent humidity in Austin, Texas. Training camp was reminiscent of BCT with the mental and physical grind. But I knew how to follow through; how to think strategically and tactically; to take it day by day with a diligent attitude, hard work, attention to detail, and flexibility.

What I learned at the Academy also contributed to the *length* of my football career. I don't think I would have been able to do nine years in the NFL without the experience gained from the Academy and active duty. That experience helped give me a sense of how to define success, how to balance my life: taking care of yourself physically, mentally always trying to improve, balancing family, giving back to the community, character, spiritual values. Spiritual values are the glue to maintaining your lifestyle; they give you the stick-to-itiveness to stay in the fight and do what's right, and be the best you can be.

I still believe in the Honor Code. Character and integrity are so important—particularly now that I'm in business. I'm so much more at ease dealing with people I know I can trust. I remember when I was a cadet, we heard a speech from a West Point graduate who was a Medal of Honor recipient and a successful businessman. He said, "All we have is our word. Once you compromise that you can't get it back." That lecture was very impactful. There are no gray areas when it comes to honor; you can't cross that line.

My final word of advice is to expect pressure and duress. Most cadets are overachievers and already put pressure on themselves. You have to know that you won't be able to accomplish everything. You have to prioritize and take it one day at a time.

Also, get involved. Be a sponge with classes, intramural sports, and extracurricular clubs. Take full advantage of all the opportunities the Academy has to offer.

Christopher B. Howard, PhD, Lieutenant Colonel (retired), Class of 1991

After winning a Texas state high school football championship, Dr. Howard played football at the Air Force Academy, winning the Campbell Trophy as the player with the best combination of academics, community service, and on-field performance. After graduation, he attended Oxford University as a Rhodes Scholar, earning both a master's and doctorate degree. He attended pilot training and became a helicopter pilot, then joined the Air Force Reserve as an intelligence officer, and served as Reserve Air Attaché to Liberia. He also earned an MBA with distinction from the Harvard Business School and has held positions in the corporate, non-profit, and academic sectors. Dr. Howard is now president of Hampden-Sydney College, a top ranked private, liberal arts college for men in Virginia.

Dr. Howard is president of Hampden-Sydney College.   *Courtesy Chris Howard*

In 7th grade, I saw a picture of a West Point cadet, and said "That's what I want to do." I wrote a letter to my congressman right away, saying I'm a good student, an athlete, and a leader. I need a nomination to West Point. He wrote back and said, "I'm not your congressman"! But West Point remained my goal. In high school, I was commander of our award-winning Army JROTC battalion, a strong student, and an all-conference football player. So I was recruited by all three service academies. I actually had an appointment to West Point already, through the JROTC program.

I visited all three academies, and when I came to the Air Force Academy, I fell in love with the physical environment, the community, and the coaching staff. I decided that was where I wanted to go, and I never looked back.

The physical aspect of BCT wasn't easy for me, even though I was a football player. BCT is more like cross-country or track than football. And at an altitude of 7528', "far above Annapolis and West Point" as we had to say, the air is rare. I lost 20 or 25 pounds in BCT. It was a great challenge. I was well prepared for the military aspects. I knew drill and ceremony cold because of Army JROTC, I had commanded before, and I had learned discipline playing football in Texas.

I always carried a full workload in high school, but the Academy was that times four or five…or ten, much more intense. I was good at managing my time, and I found it enjoyable and rewarding.

One of the most effective coping strategies I learned was how to compartmentalize. Separate the academic duties from the military from the athletic. We had this blue line on the way out to the football field, and the coach said that once we crossed it, we had to leave everything else behind. You do the same during Ac Call [academic call to quarters, study time in the evenings] and with everything else. That's a skill officers have to have.

You also have to learn how to balance your short- and long-term goals. Don't live each day thinking about getting to the end of the four years. Live holiday to holiday, month to month, or even meal to meal. It's a great skill to be able to work hard and pace yourself while dealing with stress. This skill has made me effective throughout my career.

The Academy prepared me well for Oxford and Harvard. It teaches you the self-discipline to take on anything. I knew how to study, how to manage my time, to work smart and take it seriously. As a cadet, you've been running with the best people the country has to offer, you've experienced excellence, so you come out with a jet pack on your back. The professors at Oxford are always happy to work with the Academy grads because of those qualities. The Academy is really a liberal arts college masquerading as an engineering school, but they have the hybrid right. It's so critically important to do the technical work, leadership, and humanities all together. I can discuss great literature, communicate effectively and efficiently, and at the same time I'm not afraid of quantitative analysis. That will serve you no matter where you go.

Another skill the Academy teaches you is how to work together. It's one team, one fight—whether in football, the squadron, the classroom, or intramurals. You will find that if you're there trying to help a classmate, living for others and not yourself, great things can happen. You take care of the buddy whose butt is dragging, who's falling behind in class or can't iron his or her shirt. Then suddenly you forget about yourself, and you won't be so tired and gloomy. That selfless attitude will carry you a long way.

If you're considering going to the Academy, you need to prepare yourself spiritually. Be ready for some gut checks. (However, a sense of humor is a must!) What is your life all about, what's your purpose, and what sacrifices will you be willing to make? If you get an appointment, you've been blessed with the skills to succeed. But get ready mentally, because you know it's going to be tough. It will be like steel sharpening steel—it's a really cool place to be.

Ask yourself what's important to you. Is it service, honor, giving back? The Air Force Academy wants people who want to be excellent, and serve with honor. Leadership will become part of your DNA, organic to everything you do, second nature. I find that's not the norm in the world. We know how to unify people around a common goal, achieve a mission, respect people along the way, get things done in an ethical manner. That's leadership.

Doctor (Lieutenant Colonel) Ky Kobayashi, Class of 1991

Recruited by the Academy as a football player, Dr. Kobayashi also wrestled and played baseball as a cadet. After graduating, he attended medical school at the University of Colorado. He is a flight doctor and an orthopedic surgeon. Kobayashi has deployed to Iraq multiple times, operating on both wounded service members and members of the local population. He is currently stationed at the Air Force Academy.

I was pretty naïve about the Academy and the military. My father served in the Korean War and provided some insight on his experiences; however, there was a lot about the Academy I did not know. I knew the

Dr. Ky Kobayashi, left, with his brothers: Dr. Dayton Kobayashi, Class of 1993, and Dr. Todd Kobayashi, Class of 1992.   *Photo by Lewis Carlyle*

Academy offered a wonderful education and produced strong officers who were committed to service and leadership. I knew that the Academy offered an opportunity to experience many different interests of mine—a journey that I wanted to pursue. I was fortunate to have a wonderful family, good friends, mentors, and athletics—all factors that influenced my decision to pursue the Academy experience.

I remember in-processing in June 1987. I was amazed at the beauty surrounding the Academy for a brief moment. That moment was short lived when we were standing in formation taking verbal corrections from the upper classmen. We did an about face and I looked up and thought, "What am I doing here?" But I actually enjoyed BCT and the experience in Jack's Valley. The physical demands required on the assault course and obstacle course were more fun than work. Above all, I learned the importance of teamwork and collaboration.

I looked up and thought, "What am I doing here?"

After BCT, you get into the grind of Academy life. The first year is tough—getting yelled at, having to know what to do and where to be, and keeping up with the academic and military demands. I think we all get a little homesick—even if you are from Colorado. I still remember that depressing feeling you get when you're on the road coming back to school after a break. In my first year, I often wondered whether I'd made the right decision. I thought about quitting multiple times. But it's actually harder to quit than to stay. It's a team, and everyone wants you to succeed. Quitting means letting the team down.

I grew up being taught that success is not easy. You have to be committed and be willing to sacrifice. It's ok to fail, but you have to be able to get back up again. At the Academy, I wasn't fast enough to run the wishbone as a quarterback, as much as I wanted it, so I pursued my other interests and strengths. You need to adapt and find where you fit in.

Early in my education, I was interested in a lot of different majors at the Academy. I was always fascinated by the biologic sciences and decided to pursue a pre-med track. This decision was one of the best decisions I have ever made. The biology instructors were invested in me. They genuinely wanted all of us to succeed, and helped guide us in the right direction. And now I get to pay it back—many patients are former instructors who helped me when I was a cadet.

My experience in medical school was wonderful. I enjoyed independence after four years of the Academy. I was able to narrow my focus and study a field of science that I was passionate about learning. Everyone said medical school would be so hard, but it wasn't that difficult for me. The Academy teaches students how to budget time and study efficiently. You learn to be prepared, remain focused, and think critically. I was well prepared for my graduate education.

Twenty years later, I now enjoy a career in orthopaedic surgery at the Air Force Academy as a hand and upper extremity specialist. I have the "best patients in the world." My patients include cadets, instructors, coaches, wounded warriors, and retirees. I am currently the team physician for the hockey team and am enjoying the team experience – challenges, triumphs, and some defeats. I have a little different perspective on the Academy at this point in my life. I am very thankful for my experiences and am forever grateful to those who have helped me pursue my dreams and passions.

My advice to anyone thinking of applying to the Academy - I would first have them read [this] book. Then talk to someone who's lived the experience. It's not for everyone; it's meant for a few. It is a full ride scholarship, but you have to want it. You have to be a leader. You can't just excel in academics or be a great athlete. You have to balance it all.

The first year is difficult and challenging. You only fail when you let yourself down by taking shortcuts or compromising your integrity. Realize that at some point along the way you will stumble and someone will yell at you. You might have been the best in your high school only to realize you are just average at the Academy. But it's good for all of us to take a big bite of humility, because in life there will always be someone better. And you will have to learn that you can't do it alone. Even now, to take care of my patients I need a good team to be successful. I'm a quarterback in another way these days.

The Academy is an amazing experience that pushes individuals beyond their limitations and comfort zones. When you know you can do more, you won't settle. You learn that living outside your comfort zone is ok. Your degree is more than just a B.S.—it's a degree in leadership, in being a contributor to society. I'm very proud of the traditions and alumni that are part of our heritage and leadership of America. I am blessed and privileged to be a part of this select group of individuals.

Lieutenant Colonel Kim "K.C." Campbell, class of 1997

Colonel Campbell served as the Cadet Wing Commander her senior year at the Academy, and graduated first in her class militarily. She received a Marshall Scholarship and studied in London after graduation, earning two master's degrees. She then attended pilot training and trained in the A-10. In April 2003, her A-10 was severely damaged by a surface-to-air missile over Baghdad, resulting in a complete loss of hydraulic control. She successfully landed the plane by performing a manual procedure that is considered extremely difficult. She was awarded the Distinguished Flying Cross with Valor and eight Air Medals. She has commanded an A-10 squadron, and is now stationed at the Pentagon.

I wanted to go to the Air Force Academy since I was in 5th grade. My father graduated in the class of 1970.[1] But what really got me interested was the Challenger space shuttle disaster. Those astronauts were doing something they believed in. They were willing to give their lives for something important. My dad and I talked about that. I wanted to be a part of something bigger than me, I wanted to be a pilot, and I wanted to serve.

My dad had a hard time with my decision at first, because he knew exactly what I was getting into. But once he knew I had made my mind up, he helped me prepare. I had always been athletic, but had never done anything to build upper body strength. So my dad put

Major Kim Campbell inspects her battle damaged A-10 Courtesy US Air Force

a pull-up bar in my bathroom door, and I did pull-ups several times a day. I also ran in combat boots with my dad.

I struggled with the SAT. I took it five times and didn't score well enough to get into the Academy, even after taking an SAT preparation class. I finally took the ACT and did well. Then I got a rejection letter in April of my senior year. I had applied to other schools but I never wanted to go anywhere else. I refused to take no for an answer, so I wrote the Admissions Office every week with an update—a test score, how many more pushups I could do. It paid off when I got an acceptance letter on June 2nd. I think if I hadn't been accepted, I would have come to the Academy on the first day of BCT in case someone else didn't

---

1. *Her father, Chuck Reed, was also a Cadet Wing Commander; he is now the mayor of San Jose, California.*

show up and they had an extra slot! After the school year started, I was summoned to the Admissions Office. I thought I was in trouble, but they just wanted to meet this person who was so determined to get in.

You can never be 100% prepared for BCT, but in high school I was in the Civil Air Patrol, and I knew how to wear a uniform and how to march, so I knew a lot of things others had to learn once they got there. Being physically fit also helped. I didn't struggle athletically like some people did; in fact I could do everything the guys did. I scored 480 points [out of a possible 500] on the first Physical Fitness Test.

After BCT, it was nice to get a little more freedom once the academic year started. My biggest struggle was time management—trying to figure out how to be good at everything while being totally exhausted. I struggled in some of the core classes; some came easier than others. I spent a lot of time in EI [Extra Instruction]. Always being able to get EI or call instructors at home if I needed, I found I could get through any class.

I also leaned on my family and my friends at the Academy who were going through the same things I was, and I spent every Sunday at chapel. My sponsor was a classmate of my dad's. He and his family were amazing. They gave me the chance to get away, get a good meal, relax and regroup.

I was the Cadet Wing Commander fall semester of my senior year. It was very challenging but very rewarding. I learned a lot about myself, leadership, how to work with peers. I had the opportunity to work with enlisted staff as well as with generals. The experiences helped me as a person and as a leader.

The Academy also helped me learn to take it one day at a time, not get caught up in little things, how to keep things in perspective. I learned how to deal with challenging situations. The Academy teaches you how to maintain your composure under stress and still be able to react and respond, whether you're recalling Scholfield's quote [mandatory knowledge for all cadets] or an emergency checklist when the jet isn't responding.

A final word of advice: people need to understand the Academy is not for everyone. It's not a normal college. Don't go because your parents or your brother wants you to go. Make the decision on your own. For me, it was an awesome experience, but I wouldn't want to have to do it again!

Adam Grayson, class of 1999

Adam Grayson joined the financial services industry after graduating from the Air Force Academy in 1999 and serving as a military logistics officer. He earned an MBA in finance and is completing his PhD in Organizational Development and Leadership. Outside of the financial services industry, Grayson works as an Executive Coach at the Center for Creative Leadership and is a partner of a strategic management consulting firm. Grayson enjoys reading and spending time outdoors with his family.

Adam Grayson is a financial advisor and leadership coach. Courtesy Adam Grayson.

I grew up in a small Midwestern town and had little money for college. I read about service academies in a magazine about the best values in colleges, and applied to all three. No one in my immediate family had military experience, and I had no idea what the difference was between officer and enlisted, or even the difference between the services. But I had a sense that going to the Air Force Academy was something big.

BCT was shocking to me. It wasn't that difficult physically, but it took a lot of mental fortitude. I was used to being independent and in control of my life. I hated not knowing what was coming next. I took it very seriously, because I didn't know any better. I was also impressed by the upperclassmen. Even though they were only a few years older, they seemed so polished and confident in how they carried themselves.

Academics were a grind. My high school's vocational building the biggest building on campus, and you could get a B pretty much by just showing up. So I wasn't very well prepared academically. I had a 0.94 GPA first prog [progress report, about halfway through the semester]. So I stopped taking the military part of Academy life quite so seriously, and I learned to prioritize better. I went to see all the teachers whose class I was failing, and every one of them scheduled time to give me Extra Instruction. I also found a classmate who could tutor me, whom I ended up marrying! I think some of the instructors passed me out of pity, but I also know they realized I was showing progress and making the effort.

I never thought of quitting. Pride carried me a long way. I also realized from the beginning that the Academy provided a great opportunity to learn leadership. I saw that my squadron's cadet leadership, the seniors, weren't doing a very good job. But I understood that they were being allowed to make mistakes, they were allowed experiential learning, and they got better as the year went along. I knew that was important. After graduation, I went into the logistics career field. From the first day as a second lieutenant, I had a 100 people under me, a leadership immersion for which the Academy prepared me.

In 2005, I deployed with the Army to Iraq, providing gun-truck escort and security for convoys. The Academy taught me how to be adaptive, how to determine what's important very quickly rather than wait for perfect clarity and the perfect plan. Throw anything at me and I'll figure it out and execute, which is a hallmark of a good officer and leader.

I think Air Force Academy grads have a personal code for how to live your life, how to behave, how to treat others, things you just won't tolerate. It goes beyond the honor code. We learn how to confront our personal limitations, and make tough decisions—the ones that aren't black and white. When I got out of the Air Force in 2007, I became a financial advisor. Unlike in the Air Force where the guidelines are rather clear, in the business world you can work really hard and still fail miserably. But I think Academy grads do very well in business because of that personal code. It goes back to being a moral leader, which is rare in the real world.

I feel like I'm a step ahead in my industry. I'm able to deal with ambiguity, and to prioritize. In my field, there is information overload, but I learned how to quickly pick out what's important. I trust my instincts. What we learn at the Academy is very practical—how to put theory into practice and get results. You're not bound by a professor's personal agenda or latest research project. You're encouraged to pursue your ideas and think critically.

Be sure you are going to the Academy because you want to go there, not because your parents or someone else thinks it's a good idea. That's the only way you'll stay, because you're the one who has to do it. Go there if you want to learn about yourself. Accurate self-assessment is difficult—there's a whole industry built around it. But Academy grads have a better sense of themselves. And while you're there, you'll be surrounded by good people, which makes you a better person.

Remember that academics really matter. Everyone is pulling at your time, but in the end academics affect everything. I wish I had spent more time on academics. Also, I wish I had "owned" my cadet experience by finding a club, hobby, or sport early on and stayed with it. It seemed the cadets who were happiest were the ones who had that group of people with a shared interest. I should have had more fun, but I don't regret a thing. I owe my success and the person I am to the experiences and people I learned from at the Academy.

Captain Barry Crawford, class of 2003

After graduating from the Air Force Academy in 2003, Captain Barry Crawford became a Special Tactics Officer, also known as a Combat Contoller. He served as the air-to-ground interface for special operations teams from all the services. He has been a flight commander, assistant director of operations, and weapons and tactics officer, and deployed multiple times to Iraq, Afghanistan, and Africa. A highly decorated combat veteran, he was recently awarded the Air Force Cross for heroism (the second highest award someone in the Air Force can receive, second only to the Congressional Medal of Honor). During a day-long battle under intense fire from more than 100 insurgents, he called in airstrikes and allowed his special operations team to get out of the kill zone, saving numerous Afghans and Americans, many of whom were wounded. He is currently in pilot training at Columbus AFB, Mississippi, and will fly A-10s with the 104th Fighter Squadron, Maryland Air National Guard.

Captain Crawford in Afghanistan.
Courtesy Barry Crawford

I applied to the Air Force Academy because I knew I wanted to serve in the Air Force, and I was very interested in aviation. I didn't get into the Academy on my first try, but was offered and accepted a Falcon Foundation scholarship and went to Valley Forge Military College for prep school.[2] It was only 30 minutes away from home and they had a plebe system for the first several months. Valley Forge mirrored West Point, and the plebe system stressed team work, military discipline, and an introduction to the military way of life. Even though Valley Forge was geared more towards the Army, it definitely helped me out in terms of mental toughness, knowledge and personal confidence.

Still, BCT was eye opening and challenging. I showed up well prepared physically. I had done a lot of running and physical training. This enabled me to deal with the other stresses of cadet life much easier. I tried to remember that everything is done for a reason, to prepare you

---

2. *The Falcon Foundation and prep schools are discussed in Chapter 13.*

for the rigors of the academic year, being an officer, and eventually being deployed. The team concept is definitely stressed in BCT. You can't make it through on your own, and friendships naturally form because of the unique training environment. The guy who was in the cot next to me in 2nd BCT, was my roommate for all four years, best man in my wedding, and god-father to one of my sons. Relationships built from day one are lifelong!

The academic year was challenging, because you had to juggle many requirements all at the same time…academics, athletics, and the military demands. You have to find a way to relax. For me it was physical fitness and outdoor activity. I was on the Alpine ski team my four degree year, started a crew (rowing) club, attended Navy SEAL Mini-BUD/s, and competed on USAFA's first Sandhurst Ranger Challenge team in West Point.

The "Global War on Terror" kicked off my two-degree year and the devastating airpower that the Air Force possessed quickly became the main effort early on in the war. The Air Force Special Operations Command - Combat Control Team (CCT) career field was recruiting heavily, they said they only take the best of the best, and I wanted to be a part of it. It was an extensive application package, with two phases of the selection process. Out of 20 people who were invited to attend the physical assessment, only 4 were selected. Several weeks later, I started the nearly three year training pipeline. I've had the chance to do some really incredible things up to this point in my military career. I've served with sister service Special Operations Forces (Army Special Forces, Rangers, SEAL/s, MARSOC) in Africa, Iraq, and Afghanistan, as well as with Coalition and NATO Special Operators.

We've been at war my entire career, and I've found myself in many extremely stressful situations, whether in training or combat operations. The Academy instilled in me a systematic approach to tackling problems and coping with high stress environments. You learn task management and how to prioritize.

I learned to lead by example, not to ask someone to do something I wouldn't do myself. The first combat control team I led had 48 airmen, mostly bright-eyed and brand new. Everyone was looking at me for leadership and guidance, so I had to be able to take charge and do my best as the officer in charge.

I also learned never to quit. Even when your body is quitting, you rely on mental toughness. In combat, you have to, because your life and the lives of others are on the line. I was an astronautical engineering major; I wasn't the smartest guy, and a few times I would think, "What did I get myself into; why am I doing this?" But I kept looking at my goal, to get a commission, and I never really thought about quitting. If you have mental and physical toughness, anything and everything is achievable!

I think the Academy also helped me be more comfortable interacting with higher ranking officers. You might have a lieutenant colonel or colonel as one of your instructors. So as a lieutenant and captain, dealing with general officers or colonels, I wasn't afraid to speak up and give an answer when I knew it was right. You can be humble and confident at the same time.

If you get an appointment to the Academy, prepare physically, both running and weight lifting. You can't prepare 100% for everything you'll face there, but if you're in shape there's less stress, and you'll get more out of it in the end.

Be sure you have goals for what you want to do. Write them down. Know that it's going to be challenging, but try to keep those goals in mind. Keep an eye on getting your commission, the end state, graduation. Along the way, make smaller goals. "I'll make it through first BCT; I'll make it through the summer." Don't be content just to survive; try to excel.

I would tell anyone considering the Academy that it's one of the finest educational institutions in the country, and it will give you a great foundation for military service. I'll also mention that, having worked with all the branches of the armed forces, I know for a fact the Air Force will treat you and your family the best. It's a great place to serve.

HOW TO PREPARE

FOUR
Mental Preparation Is Essential

If you are underprepared for the Academy academically, and manage to get an appointment anyway, you can still succeed. It will be a tough road, but many have succeeded through raw determination and the generous help of sympathetic professors and classmates.

The same can be said if you are not well prepared physically. With determination and hard work you can grind it out and get in shape at the Academy. It will make your life much more difficult than it needs to be, but again through determination and the help of the physical reconditioning program you can probably make it.

What is MOST important is your mental preparation. If your mind is properly prepared, all of the stress and all of the challenges will be easier to endure. If your mind is not prepared, then you had better be prepared for mental misery and something worse: failure.

Those who fail are usually those who have not mentally prepared themselves for the Academy.

GOALS: THE RIGHT MOTIVATION TO SUCCEED

Those who lose sight of their goals, or who never had the right ones in the first place, are usually the first to fall. To survive, you MUST have unwavering goals. You must have reasons, *good reasons*, not to give up.

The reasons why anybody wants to do anything are complex and difficult to break down into things one can write down in a list. But there

Are you mentally prepared for this kind of pressure?   *Courtesy USAFA*

are some basic reasons that underlie the motives of most young people who apply for the Academy. We will examine each of them and see if any of them might create problems for you.

I WANT A FREE, QUALITY EDUCATION.

This is an understandable reason to go to the Academy, especially in the current economy. The Air Force Academy is considered an outstanding academic institution, receiving top ratings in nation-wide surveys and turning out a high number of Rhodes Scholars. Those who want a rigorous education, especially in engineering, are seldom disappointed. But even the most enthusiastic scholars have to divide their attention between academic, military, and physical demands.

So if you want to focus solely on your education, a traditional college may be a better choice. Also, if you want to be highly specialized in one field of study, you may find the Academy's large and diverse core curriculum is not for you. The Academy education is designed to prepare well-rounded leaders for military service.

You must also realize that the education really is not really free. You have to earn that education with hard work and the complete dedication of your body and mind. You will pay for it with sweat, tears, and the freedom to do what you want. Also, you become obligated for that "free" education.

If you graduate, you are obligated to serve on active duty in the Air Force for five years. If you go on to pilot training and earn your pilot's wings, you are obligated to complete ten years of active duty service after completing pilot training. Of course, you should also realize that these required terms of duty can change at any time, even while you are in the Academy. So the safest approach, if you want to be a pilot or navigator, is to plan on remaining in the Air Force for quite a few years after you graduate.

The Air Force gives you four years of education that you must pay back with at least five and perhaps more years of active duty service, possibly in dangerous or unpleasant deployed locations.

Of course, you will be compensated with money and benefits during all those years, and the pay could be about what you would make after graduating from a civilian college. But you will be expected to perform whatever job you are assigned to the best of your ability, and live wherever the Air Force assigns you.

I WANT A CHALLENGE.

Many cadets say they came to the Academy for the challenge, because they knew it would be tough. They are smart, capable, high achievers who never felt sufficiently pushed or challenged in high school.

They want to take on something difficult to prove to themselves they can do it, learn their strengths and limitations, and make themselves better.

For those cadets who come deliberately seeking a challenge, few are disappointed. Cadets must learn to use every minute wisely and juggle many tasks under constant pressure. If the basic requirements do not push them to their limits, they can take on a double major, become leaders within the cadet wing, or get involved in extra-curricular activities. Surrounded by other equally capable, equally competitive young men and women, they often find they push one other to work even harder. Those who enjoy a competitive environment, who want to test themselves and push themselves to the limit, typically thrive at the Air Force Academy.

I WANT TO PLAY DIVISION I SPORTS.

The Academy may offer an opportunity to play Division I varsity sports that a student would not have at a civilian college. The Academy must recruit candidates who are not only competitive athletes, but who also have strong academic records, demonstrated leadership ability, and a commitment to serve their country. Ohio State and UCLA have a much broader pool from which to recruit. One fourthclass football player described how he had always wanted to go to Notre Dame, but wouldn't have been able to play football there. Instead, he came to the Academy, and in his first season started in a game *against* Notre Dame, to the roar of fans in Falcon Stadium.

> *If you want to focus solely on sports, another school may be a better choice.*

Cadet athletes enjoy excellent facilities, coaches, and trainers as well as supportive fans. They also have the advantages of keeping their "scholarship" if they are cut from the team or injured. They receive a top-notch education, and have guaranteed employment when they graduate. But athletes must remember that, like all cadets, they are at the Academy to become officers in the Air Force. They must divide their time between military training, the rigorous academic load, and the long, grueling hours of practice.

If an athlete wants to focus solely on sports, another school may be a better choice. You can read more about intercollegiate sports at the Academy in Chapter 20.

MY FATHER/MOTHER/GRANDPARENTS WANT ME TO GO.

This is definitely a bad reason to go to the Academy. In fact, all the Admissions Liaison Officers interviewed for this book cited this problematic motive as the number one reason cadets decide to quit. Lots of cadets said the same thing. Many sad tales were heard during cadet interviews about cadets who went to the Academy because of pressure at home.

There were the stories of the cadets whose fathers said that they would never speak to their sons or daughters again if they quit the Academy. One such cadet, unhappy but unable to go home, simply began walking westward over the Rampart Range. Another was found washing dishes in the local Holiday Inn.

Perhaps the most poignant story was about the girl who was admitted to the Academy but could not bring herself to take the oath after she arrived the first day. Partly because of that stress she ended up in the hospital and, happily, she came to her senses. In the solitude of her hospital bed she developed the courage to face her father and tell him that she was going to take charge of her own destiny, and that did not include going to the Air Force Academy.

Then there were the stories of bribes. "Go to the Academy and as soon as you are allowed to have a car, I will buy you whatever one you want." That one was typical.

There also were the sympathy stories. "Oh, we are so proud of you and everybody in town knows what a smart daughter we have who can get accepted in the Air Force Academy. Quit? You can't quit; it would disgrace us. Why, your father would never be able to show his face again."

Wrong. The father *will* show his face again and it will not be scarred. The same cannot be said for the daughter if she keeps struggling. Like almost all cadets who are at the Academy because of parental pressure, she will endure against her wishes until her resolve breaks. Then she will leave the Academy, often with undeserved scars of failure marring her psyche.

Admissions Liaison Officers and congressional nomination panels are constantly on the lookout for overenthusiastic parents of underenthusiastic candidates. They will normally offer a private, one-on-one opportunity for the candidate to bow out—such a candidate will not be offered an appointment and the parents will never know why.

Be 100% sure you are the one who wants to go, because you are the one who has to persevere for four years.

I WANT TO GO FOR THE GLAMOUR AND RECOGNITION.

This is a bad reason, but who would admit to it? Nobody, probably. But young people can get caught up in their egos without ever realizing that it is happening. A typical example is the student who says to a teacher or counselor at school, "Oh, I'm thinking about the Air Force

Academy as a possible college."

"The Air Force Academy! Oh, that's a wonderful idea!" is the excited reply. "You are bright and have all the other qualities. Go for it. Now here's all you have to do to get the process started..."

One thing leads to another and the student gets swept up in the process—and all the new attention feeds the ego. Letters start arriving from the Academy. There are telephone calls from the local Admissions Liaison Officer, and perhaps even a call from the Academy itself. All that is heady stuff for a high school kid.

Then there is the contact with a congressman or senator and a follow-up letter. Now the pressure is mounting. Something that seemed like a good idea just to explore is now picking up momentum. And the student, while perhaps having doubts, does not want to disappoint those who are now working hard to help him. So the student's determination grows, because who wants to be a failure at this point?

And he (or she) makes it. Suddenly he really has the RIGHT STUFF because he is ACCEPTED! He knows he is amazing because he can read the local newspaper where his outstanding honor is reported, or watch the audience at graduation as they applaud the announcement of his magnificent achievement.

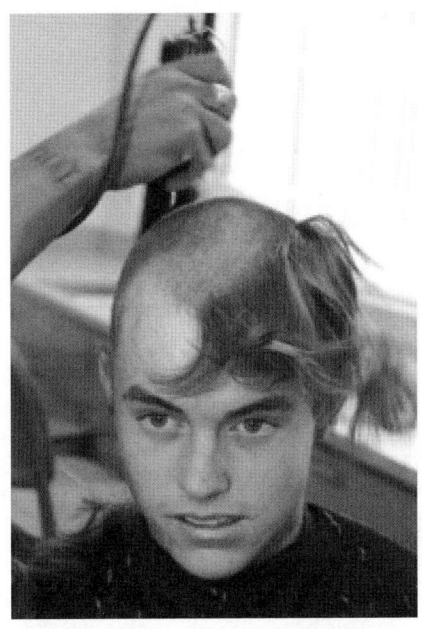

If you think being a cadet will be glamorous, think again.   *Courtesy USAFA*

About the only thing left to build up the ego is to have the high school band playing when the student leaves town to go to the Academy. Rumor has it this has really happened in some communities.

Then what? BCT and screaming upperclassmen telling you how inadequate you are and the inevitable question: WHY AM I HERE? Just how in the world did I get into this?

Nobody wants to admit that they are at the Academy for glamour and recognition. Yet those motives end up trapping young people without them ever realizing it. They usually escape, of course, by quitting or failing. They end up much wiser for the experience, but their ego usually takes a beating.

I WANT TO BE A PILOT.

This is an excellent reason to go the Academy. If you are pilot qualified (PQ) and can do well in the flight screening process at the Academy, you are almost certain to receive an assignment to Undergraduate Pilot Training (UPT) after graduation. (There are no guarantees because the needs of the Air Force change from year to year.) However, you do not have to go to the Air Force Academy to become a pilot in the Air Force. There are alternate routes to pilot training and you should know what they are because one of them might be better for you.

One is to go to a college that has Air Force ROTC. Depending on the needs of the Air Force, ROTC graduates can compete for pilot training slots, but there is no guarantee that many will be available in the future.

There are some advantages of ROTC over going to the Academy. You have much more personal freedom at a civilian college because you do not have to meet heavy demands from military training and athletics which are mandatory for everyone at the Academy. Currently there are from 1500 to 2000 ROTC scholarships available each year. And if you cannot win one of them, you can work or use student loans and still enroll in an ROTC program. Working and going to college might seem difficult, but no more demanding on your time than life at the Academy.

About half of graduates attend pilot training.

You have one more alternative. Go to an accredited college and do well. If you can demonstrate that you are the kind of person who has officer potential, you MIGHT be admitted to the Air Force Officer Training School (OTS). After three months of military training you can get an officer's commission and then go to flight training—IF THE AIR FORCE NEEDS PILOTS.

The quota of college graduates who are admitted to OTS varies with the needs of the Air Force. At times when many officers are needed, the requirements such as the GPA will be lowered. At times when there is a surplus of officers, the GPA could be raised. It is simply the supply and demand curve in action.

Still, the Academy does offer the best odds of becoming an Air Force pilot. In recent years, slightly more than half of each class will attend pilot training, and the number of slots available has been right about equal to the number of cadets who want one.

However, realize that it is possible to go through all four years at the Academy and find that you are not eligible for pilot training. You can lose your PQ in the years while you are there. This happens occasionally. Usually the eyes are the problem. They were okay when the cadet was 18. But in three years the eyeballs grew and changed and they are no longer PQ when the cadet is 21. Other medical conditions that seem relatively minor can disqualify you from flying.

If you lose your PQ while at the Academy, what will that do to your motivation? Decide now so your mind will be prepared.

I WANT TO BE AN AIR FORCE OFFICER.

This is the best reason of all, IF you know WHY you want to be an Air Force Officer. The complete four year Academy program is valued at nearly $350,000. Those taxpayer dollars are intended to be an investment in a career officer.

Try answering the following questions. If you say "yes" to most of them, you are mentally prepared with the best reasons for going to the Academy.

- Do you want to serve your country and defend its freedoms? Are you prepared to go wherever the nation needs you, even into combat?
- Do you enjoy the challenges of leadership?
- Do you want heavy responsibility at a much younger age than you could expect in a civilian job?
- Do you want to take the officer training at the Academy so you will become a better person?
- Do you want to be an Air Force Officer so you can become a pilot?
- Do you look forward to the challenge of a new assignment every three or four years instead of just one lifelong job?
- Do you want more job security than you would have in most civilian jobs?
- Do you want to be able to retire at an age young enough to start another career?

In summary, there are GOOD REASONS and BAD REASONS for going to the Air Force Academy. The first step in getting your mind prepared for the Academy is to know that you are going for the GOOD REASONS.

If you are going for the BAD REASONS, consider doing yourself a favor by stopping right now. If you do not, be mentally prepared for the alternative of saying goodbye to your fellow cadets and figuring out a new plan for college and your future.

KNOW WHAT TO EXPECT

The second thing you should do in preparing your mind for the Academy is to know what to expect when you get there.

Pilots going on a mission meticulously educate themselves about every potential threat—threats such as surface-to-air missile sites, possible concentrations of groundfire, places where enemy fighters may be lurking—not to mention a myriad of emergency procedures they may need to implement automatically and in split seconds. Their rule of survival is to anticipate everything. You should do the same.

Reading this book is a good first step. But there are several other things you can do.

Meet your Admissions Liaison Officer, or ALO. Every high school in the nation has an ALO (details in Chapter 9). If your counselor does not know how to contact your ALO, contact the Academy Admissions Office.

Search for other Air Force officers who will talk with you. They are almost always eager to advise students, especially the retired officers who have extra time. Tell the officer on your first contact that you are thinking about applying to the Academy and you are wondering what being an officer is really like. At the interview ask the hard questions, such as, What are the worst things about being an Air Force officer? What happens when an officer does not get promoted? If Air Force officers make a mistake, what happens to them?

If possible, try to visit the Academy before you apply.

Another thing you should do is discuss the Academy with one or more cadets while they are home on vacation. If you do not know of any, just contact your ALO, and he or she will arrange one or more interviews for you.

The BEST thing for you to do is VISIT THE AIR FORCE ACADEMY. When you get there, you will see what Academy life is like, talk to cadets and staff, and try to picture yourself in the various roles of a cadet.

The Academy offers a number of ways to visit and gain more than just a tourist's perspective.

- Compete to attend Summer Seminar. The week-long Summer Seminar is offered competitively to several hundred rising seniors each summer. It offers a chance to interact with cadets and faculty, live in the dorms, and get exposure to cadet life. (See www.academyadmissions.com for more details.)

- Attend a sports camp. The Athletic Department offers three and five day sports camps for athletes 8-18 in 21 sports from diving to lacrosse. Participants can either commute or live in the dorm. While the focus of sports camps is not learning about cadet life, you will still be able to interact with cadets and become more familiar with the Academy. (See www.goairforcefalcons.com.)
- Arrange a visit with the Admissions Office. On Mondays, Thursdays, and Fridays during the academic year, you can get a full day tour with a cadet, including briefings and classroom visits. The admissions web site has details. You will have to make a reservation ahead of time. If you can only visit during the summer, you will not be able to get a cadet-guided tour but you will be able to get a briefing.

All of these options will cost you money, but the cadets who had visited the Academy before going there all said that it helped them because they knew what to expect. A visit also shows your ALO and congressional interview panel that you have done your homework.

DETERMINATION

Mental preparation for the Academy must include one more task. That task is to convince yourself that you are going to succeed when you get there. You cannot be a quitter.

Some students nurture the idea that, "Oh, I'm going to go give it a try and see how I like it. It might be okay and if it isn't, I can always come home."

True, sort of. You will be better off if you drive such thoughts out of your mind and do not let them creep back in. If you go to the Air Force Academy with your mind just halfway committed, you are almost sure to end up quitting before the year is over. As one graduate commented, "Don't give yourself a back door, a plan B in your hip pocket. Be determined or you will regret it."

If you go to the Academy, you should be 100 percent committed to doing your absolute best for at least the FIRST YEAR. That is a fair trial. The "How To Survive" section of this book will give you some tips, and many people at the Academy are there solely to help you succeed. But in the end, it is *your* attitude that will determine your success.

If you make it successfully through that first year and do not want to go on, fine. You have not incurred any obligation. You know that you did your best and left on your own terms.

Also, you have earned a year of college credit that is transferable anywhere. You know that you survived the most challenging year of your life. You know that you are a winner and not a loser, or a quitter, or a failure. You can leave the Academy knowing that you do, in fact, have the right stuff. In short, if you stick it out for at least one year, you can feel good about yourself.

The same cannot be said if you quit before that. If you do, there is a good chance that you will spend many years doubting yourself and wondering if you really could have made it. And you are not alone. Friends, relatives, teachers—all the people who care about you will wonder what happened.

Many who quit very early spend a great deal of time "recovering" from the emotional impact of that decision. They grieve, doubt themselves, or become indecisive or directionless. Please do not put yourself in that position. Do not brand yourself as a quitter or a failure. Life is tough enough without putting more weight into your pack.

Nearly every cadet and graduate we interviewed said that they had thought of quitting at some point. They found the determination to stick it out, and not a one said, "I wish I had quit after all." They all were glad they didn't.

FIVE
Why You Should Expect Academic Shock

Many cadets face a rough blow to their ego when they begin their academic classes at the Air Force Academy. Those interviewed for this book described it in various ways. Some called it a shock. Others said it was depressing, humiliating, or demoralizing. You may have read some of the graduates' stories of academic shock in Chapter 3.

Why should cadets who have scored high on ACT and SAT tests, and graduated near the top of their high school classes, encounter so much trouble with course work at the Academy?

Understanding the reasons will help you prepare to succeed academically in this challenging environment.

◆ PROBLEM ONE: COMPETITION

Most of the cadets who come to the Academy have been the top students in their high schools. Recent classes have entered with average GPAs of 3.88, and SAT scores over 1300. And they became top students through a competitive process that enabled them to rise above others in their school who were less gifted or motivated.

But how much competition did they really have? Most took classes in which there were students with all ranges of abilities and motivation. Many cadets who were interviewed said that they were able to get good grades without much effort. Several admitted that they got their good grades just by listening in class and relying on their natural learning ability. A few confessed to getting good grades without *ever* doing homework.

Now try to imagine what happens when all of these "good" students get into classes together at the Academy. Suddenly the competitive situation is drastically different. The competition is now fierce and a large number of former "good" students end up on the bottom half of the grade curve. Students who were use to seeing easy grades of "A" are suddenly looking at "D's" or worse.

◆ PROBLEM TWO: OVERLOAD

Most high school students, even the overachievers who receive appointments to service academies, do not experience much stress getting their school work done. Even with extracurricular activities, sports, or a part-time job, finding enough hours to do all you need to has not been a real challenge. At the Air Force Academy, that will change.

Besides taking 18-20 semester hours of challenging courses (compared to perhaps 15 hours their civilian counterparts must take), a cadet has mandatory athletic and military training for several hours every day. During the fourthclass year, many cadets try unsuccessfully to apply the same approaches to managing their homework they used in high school.

They may procrastinate, as they did in high school, until the night before a big assignment or paper is due. Then they realize they have other things that have to get done, or the assignment takes longer than they expected. The result is a poorly-done assignment completed at 2 a.m., and a very sleepy cadet in class the next day.

Or they resolve to do every assignment for the next day to the best of their ability, read every word on every page, and even spend extra time on material that is giving them trouble. Using that approach in high school meant they got top grades in their classes. But by midnight their brain is begging for sleep, and they still have two of their four assignments left to do.

One cadet reported that he did more work in a week at the Academy than he did his entire senior year of high school—and still felt behind. Those who do not figure out very quickly that they must plan ahead and prioritize how every minute of their study time is used will not succeed.

◆ PROBLEM THREE: LETTER HUNTERS

If you are now a student, look around during one of your classes, then ask yourself this question: What do these students, myself included, really want out of this class? If you are objective, you will probably come up with this answer: an "A."

Are you a letter hunter? Or are you really trying to <u>learn</u> the material? In chemistry class do you really want to understand the significance of Avogadro's Number? In history class do you really want to know how the Missouri Compromise affected the next one hundred years of life in America? In advanced algebra class do you really want to know how quadratic equations can help you solve a whole new class of problems?

Or are you memorizing all those things just long enough to get the letters that you want? Many "good" students are letter hunters. They do whatever is necessary to get the first letter or two in the alphabet. Then they go on to the next letter-hunting challenge. Often they don't even realize what they are doing.

So what awaits a "good" student when professors at the Academy expect a cadet to have high school-level knowledge of algebra or history or chemistry? Just having good grades from high school will not cut it. The professors at the Academy are not interested in your high school grades. They ARE interested in building on knowledge that you were *supposed* to have gained during your high school years. That is why, even if you did great in AP Calculus or Chemistry, when you get to the

Academy you will have to prove you have the knowledge before you get course credit.

So be warned. Those who go to an Academy class with just an impressive transcript to wave in their hand, but not the knowledge that should have come with it, had better expect some hard times.

◆ PROBLEM FOUR: ESCAPE ARTISTS

Many "good" high school students have a bag of tricks they can use to escape detection when they come to class unprepared. Some look at their desks and remain silent if volunteers are asked to answer questions. This works especially well in large classes. It is easy to vanish in the crowd.

Another trick is leave the textbook open and scan the lesson rapidly before the teacher begins asking questions. This is a favorite of those who are good readers.

One of the best tricks, when the teacher is not alert, is to listen carefully to what the teacher has said and then volunteer when one of the questions has an obvious answer. That gets the student off the hook, usually for the whole class period. After dodging one bullet, a student is not likely to get shot at again, especially in a big class.

Academy professors believe strongly in accountability.

If you happen to be a "good" student, you can probably add your own favorite techniques to this list. Students have probably been creating them forever. But realize that you might as well leave your bag of tricks at home if you go to the Air Force Academy.

Why? Because the classes are small and every professor will know your name and something about you within a day or two after you start a class. Moreover, your professors believe strongly in ACCOUNTABILITY.

This means that they will hold you responsible for whatever reading or homework they assigned. More important, unlike your high school teachers who were burdened with large student loads, they will do some kind of accounting that will let them know how well you did your assignment.

That might be a quiz. It might be a barrage of questions that you cannot escape. It might even be a trip to the front of the class or to the board so your knowledge, or lack of it, can be displayed for the whole class.

Escape artists do not do well at the Academy. In small classes with determined professors there is no way to dodge the bullets. And if you try, you are sure to get wounded.

◆ PROBLEM FIVE: COPIERS

Some "good" students are able to get the letters they want in high school by cheating. But they present little problem at the Academy because persons with that kind of character rarely survive.

The "copiers" who do have problems at the Academy are not necessarily cheaters, at least not intentionally. On the contrary, they are often very conscientious students.

Are you a "copier?" Here is how to tell. What do you do if your teacher gives a reading assignment and also asks that you write out the answers to certain questions that are at the end of the chapter?

Do you read the assignment two or three times, or whatever it takes to understand it thoroughly? Then do you write out the answers to the questions in your own words, thinking as you write, and taking pride in the care with which you use good grammar, punctuation and spelling?

If so, pat yourself on the back and consider yourself unique among students. Here is how the copier proceeds. With the music turned up, the copier skims the reading assignment, then turns to the questions. As the first question is read, the copier is thinking, "Where did I see something about that?"

Cadets are expected to synthesize and understand what they have read.

Next, the copier leafs back through the pages of the assignment until something looks familiar. Then the sentence that looks like it comes closest to being the answer is copied. However, if the student is a conscientious letter hunter, then an extra sentence or two will be copied, "just to be safe."

There are other places to see copiers at work. One the best places is at the computer where one observes the student laboriously cutting and pasting passages, even entire paragraphs, from various web sites. Serious letter hunters might make an attempt to paraphrase the copied material, and to make sure they get a good grade, will use more sources than the assignment required.

The problem with copiers is that they have not learned how to organize their thoughts or how to write them in a logical, systematic manner. This is a serious handicap at the Academy because there is a heavy emphasis on developing just that skill.

A very important part of an officer's job is writing reports. So writing is required in most classes—not just in English classes—and a student who has been a copier is in immediate trouble with such assignments. Cadets are expected to synthesize and understand what they have read, not just copy it. Even more seriously, if a copier at the Air Force Academy fails to acknowledge his or her sources properly, it constitutes cheating, an Honor Code violation which can result in dismissal.

Writing cannot be learned without practice. The copier has to get that practice at the worst possible time—when all the other pressures on the first-year cadet are at their maximum.

◆ PROBLEM SIX: SENIORITIS

Teachers who love teaching, who would never want to do anything else, who think it is the greatest job in the world, often dislike teaching seniors during their final semester in high school.

The reason: senioritis, a behavior pattern where seniors coast through the last weeks of school with the least effort possible.

Many excuses are used to justify such behavior:
- I'm burned out on school.
- I have worked long enough; now I want to play.
- I already got accepted to the college I want to go to.
- I have taken all the hard classes I need.

Have you heard any of those excuses? You will if you are not yet a senior. But just remember, if you are planning on going to the Air Force Academy, senioritis is a serious affliction.

During the senior year, high school students have the opportunity to take the kinds of classes that will help them the most at the Academy. This is the year when high-level math, science or English courses can be taken. This is the year when creative writing is most likely to be an elective. This is the year when Advanced Placement college courses are available. Most important, this is the time when one's learning curve and study habits should be PEAKING, not declining.

Students who hit the Academy running and in peak form suffer less stress than those who are out of shape mentally or physically. If you are lazy your senior year in high school, beware. The Academy is likely to be harder on you than those who managed to escape the problem.

◆ PROBLEM SIX: SPOONFEEDING

This is the worst problem of all and probably the hardest to cure because it is not the student's fault. But understanding the problem is a first step.

Spoonfed students are the product of a type of teaching common in high schools. The damage caused by this kind of teaching is perhaps best understood by comparing the methods of two teachers.

Start with the teacher who produces spoonfed students, whom we shall call Mr. Gerber. It is the end of a period in Mr. Gerber's class and he has given an assignment for the next day. That assignment is to read

Academy professors will expect you to come to class prepared. *Courtesy USAFA*

pages 110 to 115 in the textbook and write the answers to the questions at the end of the chapter. So that evening you read the pages quickly and do the questions, which means that you follow the "copier" procedure described above.

The next day in Mr. Gerber's class, those who did the questions place them on his desk; then the whole class listens while Mr. Gerber spends the period "explaining" the lesson. The students' minds are anywhere but on the light reactions of photosynthesis, the problems Cardinal Richelieu created in France, or whatever he might be explaining. So from time to time, Mr. Gerber will throw out questions, which a few alert students might answer. But he is more likely to keep talking, having learned that it is embarrassing when even simple questions cannot be answered. Mr. Gerber is doing an excellent job of explaining the assignment for all the letter hunters.

The day before a test, Mr. Gerber spends the entire period asking the kinds of questions that will be on the test. Some students will be able to answer the questions, of course. But many cannot, so he spends much of the review period reexplaining the things he believes are most poorly understood.

The next day the test is taken and there are lots of "A's" and "B's", many students demonstrating that they had memorized and could repeat back what Mr. Gerber had explained to them. Those who used the exact words in the textbook to answer the questions got the best scores. Of course, the letter hunters did the best.

Let us now observe another teacher at work, Mrs. Independence, who is teaching the same subject in the room next door. At the end of class, she gives the same assignment.

The next day, she begins class by saying, "Please take out a sheet of paper; I am going to give you a quiz over your assignment." A very motivated letter hunter complains: "Wait, you can't give us a quiz on that stuff we studied last night; I didn't understand it and I talked to some others before class and they didn't either."

Mrs. Independence smiles patiently. "Yes, I agree. That was difficult material. But this quiz will show how well you did with the assignment; then I will explain everything that you did not understand." The student, still angry, takes the quiz, doing poorly just as she expected.

Then Mrs. Independence says, "All right now, everyone who had trouble understanding that assignment, listen carefully." She pauses, looks around the class, then asks, "Who thinks they answered the first question correctly?"

Several hands go up. Mrs. Independence nods. "Robert, you think you know? Fine. Go ahead, and the rest of you listen and be ready to correct him."

Compare the two teachers and their teaching goals.

What are Mr. Gerber's goals? Clearly, one of them is for the students to understand the subject that he is teaching. Is there anything else? Not really.

What are Mrs. Independence's goals? She wants the students to engage with and understand the subject she is teaching, and also think about it, and be able to explain the material in their own words. She is even MORE concerned that students become independent learners who are not dependent on their teachers to spoonfeed them every answer.

What about results? Mr. Gerber's students learn what he wants them to learn? Most of them, but temporarily. But then they forget most of it. Within a few years they probably will have forgotten almost everything.

What about Mrs. Independence's students? They will learn the subject matter, probably much better than those in Mr. Gerber's class. What about the other things that were learned in Mrs. Independence's class—study skills, responsibility and an independent approach to learning? Those skills will last a lifetime.

Most cadets will come to the Academy having had teachers like the first one. They have been spoonfed for years by conscientious teachers who believed that they were doing what was best for their students. Those students never had the opportunity to learn HOW TO LEARN on their own.

And what do they find at the Academy?

Major Independence, of course. The faculty is loaded with them. Those professors are going to give assignments and hold cadets accountable for knowing AND understanding the material the minute they arrive in class.

Why? Because they have to do it to train the kinds of officers needed by the Air Force.

Air Force officers are in a constant race trying to keep their airplanes, communications systems, and tactics progressing with advancing technology in an ever-changing world. So the Air Force officer's education has to stand the test of time and must include skills as well as knowledge. An officer must have the ability to learn independently, think critically, and adapt to change and uncertainty. To keep up with the changes that will occur in the two or three decades of an Air Force career, officers cannot expect to sit before a teacher whenever there is a need to learn something new.

Air Force officers have to be able to learn on their own, under pressure—whether it is a new avionics system in their aircraft, or a new culture in a country where they will be deployed. In addition, they must be independent minded enough to take pride in that ability. That is why Major Independences at the Academy teach the way they do.

You should now have a better understanding of why many cadets experience shock or embarrassment when they start their academic courses at the Air Force Academy. But what can be done about it? How should a student prepare for the academic challenges of the Academy?

A NEW ATTITUDE TOWARD LEARNING

If you still have a year or more left of your high school career, the best advice is to CHANGE YOUR ATTITUDE.

Change your attitude about competition. If there is little competition in your classes, pretend that you are in a class with students who are all as capable as yourself. Get in the habit of always doing more than you are assigned. Do not worry if your friends think you have lost your mind! Learn to take pride in giving 150 percent effort in the classroom.

You are probably an athlete of some kind. Bring your competitive attitude from the playing field into the classroom. Take pride in never letting up. Treat your course work like an opponent. Master it, not just halfway, but completely.

Also, you should change your attitude about what you want to get out of your classes. Despite what has been said about letter hunting, there is nothing wrong with getting good grades. In fact, you have to have them just to be accepted at the Academy. But letter hunting should not be your MAIN goal. Your main goal should be learning the material in your courses.

If you will do that, and you do it well, and you really try to remember what you have learned, the good letters will come. You do not sacrifice anything by going after knowledge rather than letters. Instead, you get a bonus: you get the knowledge AND the good grades.

Are you a skilled escape artist? If so, quit thinking about the Air Force Academy or quit being an escape artist. If you are the type of person who continually wants to slide by without doing assigned work, your tricks might get you into the Academy, but you will not last. The Air Force does not want officers who are escape artists. If you are that type of person, the upperclassmen and professors will find you out. They will make sure you do not survive long enough to create problems as an Air Force officer.

Do you even need to be told that you should quit copying your reports and answers to questions out of books? Copying something word-for-word from a book or a web site is boring work, and you learn absolutely nothing because your mind is usually elsewhere. In addition, at the Academy it is called plagiarism and is an honor violation that can result in dismissal.

So bite the bullet. Start writing material out of your head instead of out of a book. The effort might be painful at first. But your brain is like your muscles. Use it and it will perform better. Let it remain idle and it will waste away.

Will you catch senioritis? This is a problem you can avoid if you are determined. How? By deliberately taking the hardest courses you can during your senior year and developing a special attitude about those courses. Pretend that they are more important than anything else you have taken in high school. Then go after them with determination. If you have run out of challenging classes to take at your high school, investigate the possibility of taking some college level courses.

> *Your brain is like a muscle. Use it and it will perform better.*

Learn everything that there is to learn in those courses, and more. Once you have committed yourself to this kind of effort, you will not have time to catch senioritis. And when you get to the Academy, you will be up to speed and have one less problem to worry about.

You do have a problem if you are spoonfed. Your main one, if you are still in high school, is that you cannot control the methods your teachers use. And you may not find many Mrs. Independences in your high school. If you do, they probably have a reputation for being tough, but try to take their classes. Otherwise, you are not helpless. Be as prepared as you can possibly be. Even make it a game to try to know more about the subject than the teacher knows, or keep track of everything the teacher says that you didn't already know.

HOW TO PREPARE ACADEMICALLY

Besides developing the proper attitude about learning, what else should you do to prepare for the Academy?

You should take all of the math courses that are available in your high school. Take four years of English and four years of a foreign language if that is possible. Take chemistry and physics—advanced courses if you can.

Many candidates for the Academy take Advanced Placement, or AP, classes. Most cadets and instructors will tell you those AP classes will help you validate core courses or have an easier time in the first semester or two. One word of caveat: Make sure you actually *learn* what the AP classes teach, and remember the material in the classes leading up to the AP class. Take AP Calculus as an example. You must come to the Academy with a good, working comprehension of the algebra and trigonometry you took in high school. You will not get automatic Calculus 1 course credit for having taken AP Calculus; you will have to demonstrate that you know the material, because when you go on to Calculus 2, you must retain, understand, and *be able to apply* all you were supposed to have learned. All the warnings at the beginning of this chapter apply.

> *If you take AP classes, make sure you really learn what the classes teach.*

Speech is an excellent course if you have room in your schedule for an elective. The practice of speaking before a group builds confidence. And it gives you practice thinking on your feet. You will appreciate that experience if you go to the Academy because you will have to stand up and speak in front of your peers, both in the classroom and in other settings.

If you are a slow reader, a reading class that teaches speed, comprehension, and recall will be a great investment. Plowing through several hundred pages a night is not unusual. Being an efficient reader will help you get through all your assignments and still get a reasonable night's sleep.

A final bit of advice has to do with study techniques. Each night, before you start studying, look over all the assignments. Quickly turn through the pages of your textbooks and try to estimate how long it should take you to do each assignment. Then give yourself a time allotment for each one. Leave time, also, for breaks and texting or phone calls. Later, when you finish studying, give yourself a grade on how closely your study time matched your estimates.

Try the above for a few weeks, then start pushing yourself. Estimate the time needed for your assignments and for your breaks. Then try to shorten the study time by pretending that you have other things to do. But do not eliminate the breaks. Short breaks are essential.

Get in the habit of planning your entire week, looking ahead at upcoming papers, projects, tests, and quizzes. Schedule time for each one, and try to stick to the schedule.

This is realistic study practice, because at the Academy your assignments will be long and the time to do them will be limited. You will rarely have enough time to study as much as you would like. You will have to prioritize and make compromises. By learning to do that in high school, you will have one less thing to learn in the high-pressure environment of the Academy.

SIX
What The Professors Say About Academic Shock

After you have survived the challenges of Basic Cadet Training, you may think the academic year will be a welcome relief. After all, you have always been a good student, and the professors are not going to yell at you or make you do pushups, right? But many fourthclass cadets soon find themselves missing the (comparatively) carefree life of the basic cadet. Why?

Most first-year students at the Air Force Academy experience some degree of academic shock. The worst usually comes after the first major test, which is called a "graded review." A "D" is very frequently the first grade that cadets receive. This is not only a shock, say the cadets, but it is also humiliating and often the cause of the lowest moods cadets experience during their entire four years at the Academy.

The previous chapter analyzed some of the causes of academic shock, using information gleaned from interviews with cadets and graduates. This chapter adds another perspective from the experts: the instructors who witness firsthand how cadets struggle with academics. Numerous Air Force Academy professors were interviewed and asked to explain why many first-year cadets, who are the "cream-of-the-crop" from U.S. high schools, experience academic problems. They offer practical advice that will help you minimize the effects of academic shock.

START PREPARING IN HIGH SCHOOL

Taking tough classes in high school is not just for making your transcript competitive. The more solid your academic background, the easier your Academy classes will be. The professors recommend you take the hard classes, including the AP classes, as much as you can. But remember, you have to learn and retain the information taught in those classes, or you are just wasting time.

A chemistry professor who is a graduate of the Academy made these comments: "I see a lack of background as a problem. Many have had a year of chemistry but the quality of the courses many take cannot be very good. In addition, if they took chemistry their junior year, they have had a year to forget it. And worse, there are some who tell us that their counselors recommended that they take chemistry during their sophomore year. That is a terrible mistake! My advice to a candidate would be to wait until the senior year and then take both chemistry and physics; that way they would have the material fresh in mind when they come here.

"My argument is that they should take as heavy a course load and as hard of courses as they can during their senior year. Not only will they come in here with better backgrounds in math, English, chemistry and physics [if they take those courses], but the heavy load will force them to develop good study habits. And if they are reading this and have already taken a chemistry course, I suggest they take another one at a local college if they can. Go after the hard academic challenges; that's the way to prepare yourself for this place."

A math professor echoed the need to arrive with a good working knowledge of the *basics:* "What types of things don't they know? Just the basics of algebra and trigonometry—things like the algebraic analysis of polynomials, polynomial reduction and the addition of polynomials. In trig, it's the lack of facility with the angle functions. Also, they lack skill with inverse trig functions and this creates problems when we get into integrals."

Said another professor who felt quite strongly about the lack of basic skills that he sees: "I would blame the high schools for some of their problems. I think there are too many trying to teach two semesters of calculus just so they can *say* that their students know calculus. We have a lot who show up here who think they know how to integrate, and some of them can do polynomials. The problem, however, is that they can follow the mechanical formula for polynomials, but they don't understand the concept of the integral. Unfortunately, the students know the mechanics—imperfectly—but not the underlying principles. This attitude results in them not working diligently to polish their mechanical skills and even causes resistance to taking the time to understand the concept.

Many cadets lack a working knowledge of the basics of algebra and trigonometry.

"I think the high schools worry about how well the kids score on the calculus advanced placement-type tests. But they're turning out kids with very weak algebra skills. That doesn't make sense and I'd rather see their students show up here with very strong algebra and trig skills. I don't care how good they are at calculus because we're going to teach them calculus."

Another suggested that you spend some time with a math teacher reviewing basic algebra skills that you may have forgotten. You can go to the math department's web site and get some additional preparation advice, and review the algebra/trigonometry placement test you will take when you arrive. Visit www.usafa.edu/df/dfms and click on Placement Exam Preparation.

While math and science are critical skill sets at the Academy, reading, critical thinking, and communications skills will be important in every class you take. Advised one English professor, "Read the harder stuff. Spiderman and Shakespeare aren't the same. Try to figure out, 'What did it mean.' Journal about what you read."

Another English professor emphasized the importance of communicating through writing. "They have to be able to express themselves in more than a Tweet." She recommended, "Find that person to help you. It is not always easy, but you have to seek them out."

The lesson: Do not take advanced courses in high school at the expense of a solid foundation in the fundamentals.

ATTITUDE AND EFFORT

We already mentioned the phenomenon called academic shock. You need to get past the shock quickly and focus on what you need to do to succeed. In academics, as in all areas of the Academy, hard work and a determined attitude generally lead to success.

According to some of the professors, an attitude problem is often apparent in the cadets who have a good math background, especially those who score well on the math placement exam and are enrolled in the honors calculus class—the highest of the three levels that are taught.

A professor who teaches the honors class commented: "About ten percent of the students in our honors calculus class get a "D" or "F" grade on their first graded review. The problem with them is that they come into class and think, because they recognize what we are doing, 'Oh, I can coast in this class because I've had this stuff.'

What worked for you in high school probably will not work at the Academy.

"The problem is that they get a false impression; they think they can get by just sitting there with their book closed, listening in class. They think they don't have to do their homework; then later, when they are faced with problems on the test, they can't remember exactly how to do them and they do poorly. Many exams the freshman year don't necessarily focus on the tougher concepts, but rather test the students' speed and skill in some of the basic mechanics of computations.

"I remember in particular one example of this poor attitude. It was a cadet who came in here with a 1600 SAT score. That first semester he barely avoided getting a "D" and moved back into the lower-level class. He could sit in class and answer all my questions. But he didn't do the homework and when it came to the tests, he couldn't do the problems."

Another math professor, a graduate of the Academy who was also valedictorian of his high school, commented about the poor study habits he observed. He said, "Most of the students who come to us have gotten good grades and never had to study—I was like that—I never studied much in high school. As long as I did better than everyone else, that was all I had to worry about. But here, students run into tough competition. Here, everyone is intelligent and highly motivated. So a bunch of them get "C's" and "D's" and they go into shock.

"The problem is that they try to get by doing what they did in high school. There they studied ten minutes for each lesson and they think they should be able to do that here. Fortunately, most of them are good individuals and after the initial shock, their performance improves."

This comment came up again and again. What worked for you in high school probably will not work at the Academy. The sooner you realize this, the sooner you will start to succeed.

Most professors assign homework for practice. Some will grade the homework, some will require cadets to demonstrate proficiency by working problems at the board, and some will not check the homework at all—the cadets are expected to ask for help if they had trouble. In any case, many professors reiterated the importance of doing the homework.

A chemistry professor likes to use a sports analogy to make this point: "I have a pole vaulter in the class. I say, 'How many times do you do vaults. Do you do 100 of them the day before a track meet? When do you do all of your practice?' The pole vaulter says, 'No, I practice the month before, two months before, the week before.' So using a sports analogy, they can actually see [the need to practice]."

Time and again, professors talked about the poor work habits that many cadets bring to the Academy. They emphasized that practice, spending time repeating the same skills, is not part of most high school students' habit patterns. But this kind of effort is critical to academic success at the Academy. The bottom line: "Do the homework. Do the homework. Do the homework." Put in the effort, and you will get results.

Another attitude change required of many cadets is a sense of responsibility for their own learning. They make a conscious effort to have their role be helping students learn, not teaching them. The difference is that the student is the one responsible for his or her education and understanding, and they will do all they can to help.

Putting in the expected level of effort and showing up with a positive attitude will make a big impression on your professors. A history professor sees that positive attitude as part of the military training at the Academy: "The kids also don't realize how important military professionalism affects their academic achievement. For example, in a civilian institution if a paper is two days late, that might not be a major problem—good excuses would probably be accepted. Not here. Our responsibility is to teach history AND professionalism. So we have severe penalties for late papers. If a paper is two days late, we take off one-quarter of the points; if it is three days late, they lose credit for the whole thing. They put their work off and don't realize what big hits they are going to take. We often see kids flunking as much for tardiness and late papers as for not knowing world history."

TIME MANAGEMENT

Late papers are usually a symptom of poor time management. Many professors emphasized the importance of good time management and not allowing yourself to get behind—*ever.* Said a math professor: "Those who get the "D's" and "F's" are the ones who get bogged down with poor study habits right at the beginning. They are smart; they test well. But they get behind the power curve and try to study the night before the graded review and math cannot be learned that way. For some, the problem is so bad they have to drop out—in fact, every single drop-out I've seen, I can attribute to that problem.

"The root of the problem isn't so much a lack of motivation as a problem of setting priorities. In the squadron they get direct feedback every day—if they don't know their knowledge or their uniforms aren't right, they get hammered immediately. Here, on the academic side, the feedback doesn't come for three or four weeks, so they put off their studies because the feedback is delayed. The feedback is immediate in the squadrons.

"Another aspect of the problem has to do with the nature of the subject. Math is a cumulative subject; everything builds on everything else, and everything has to be learned in sequence. Because of that, cramming before an exam is ineffective for two reasons. First, it's very difficult to learn a lot of math in a short time—you need time for some of it to sink in and be absorbed. Second, cramming results in short-term retention; it may be okay for one test but the math you need for the next test is gone; it has to be relearned. Learning math is a day-by-day process. That's the only way you can get long-term retention; that's really the only way you can succeed in math.

"My advice to a candidate coming here is to try and keep up lesson by lesson. Spread the study time uniformly throughout the whole course so that the things you need to know have time to sink in. Then, as you go along, if there's anything you don't understand, get Extra Instruction immediately so you don't get behind. You can't wait and do like some we see who come in for help the day before an exam. There's no way you can help that type of person.

A chemistry professor made the same point: "The only way to

succeed in chemistry is to do the homework and pay attention in class. Many have poor study habits because they never had to study in high school. Then, when they do decide to buckle down and put in the time on their studies, they go about it the wrong way. They stay up late; then they are too tired to stay awake in class.

"Of course, we don't let them actually sleep in class. Most walk around and fight to stay awake. But others sit there and sleep with their eyes open, off in another world.

"We try to tell them—everybody does: Don't stay up late; go to bed by eleven o'clock and get up feeling fresh so you can stay awake in class. When they miss what goes on in class, they have to try and figure everything out for themselves back in the squadron, so they multiply their problems. It's a vicious circle, and they get into it without knowing how to get out."

Time management is equally critical in other courses, such as computer science. Many first-year cadets complain about computer science, not because it is so difficult, but because it is so time consuming and so exacting.

Said one computer science professor, "The biggest problems are time management and getting them to understand the exacting nature of programming. Let me explain.

"Programming is unlike other sciences. In another course if you make a slight error, you can compensate in some way. But if you make a slight error in a computer program, it isn't going to work. It requires perfection. The students find it frustrating because the only way they can achieve this kind of perfection is to put a lot of time in on the program.

> *When you get behind, you're dead.*

"Now, I am not knocking the kids. In general I enjoy the students; they are very motivated and active in class. But because of all the demands on them, they come to class tired and run down—not really alert. And that compounds their problem because to get the concepts, they have to be very alert. This problem carries over into their homework. They put off their assignments until late at night; then because they're tired, they make mistakes—so they have to take more time and they lose more sleep.

"It is a vicious circle. And it is sad to see them get caught up that way. What they need is not only time management but sleep management. From my personal perspective the most successful students are those who get a good night's sleep every night. Those who come in here rested are ready to participate and they get the most out of the lesson and the lecture.

A final bit of time management advice from a math professor: "It would help if candidates would come here with a different attitude about their weekends. In high school they are used to laying back on weekends. When they get here, they expect to do the same thing. I should know; I had that same attitude when I first started here as a cadet. Now, when I tell my students that they should plan on using some of their weekend time to catch up and keep from getting behind, they look at me funny. But that's just how it is. If you want to stay here, you have to give up something. Why not work on the weekends? Fourthclassmen can't do much else on weekends anyway."

You may have noticed the term "vicious circle" being repeated by the professors. Like being caught in a whirlpool or a rip tide, "behind" is a dangerous place at the Academy. Effective time management will keep you in calmer waters.

LEARN FOR THE LONG TERM

As mentioned several times already, the learning techniques that got you through high school may not serve you at the Air Force Academy. Many high school students succeed by learning just enough to regurgitate it on a test, then forgetting it as soon as the semester is over. At the Academy that approach will lead to trouble. First of all, you will be held accountable for what you learn in one class in all your future classes. Because all cadets are required to take the same extensive core curriculum, your professors know what classes you have taken and what material you should have learned.

Second, the courses at the Academy serve a second purpose beyond preparing you to get an accredited bachelor's degree in the major of your choice. The curriculum is also intended to provide you with many of the skills you will need as an Air Force officer. For these reasons, getting off to a good start the very first semester will be a good investment for the entire four years, as well as after graduation.

A math professor recommends, "Bear down the hardest during the first two weeks; they are the most critical. This is when fundamentals are reviewed. This is the time, even though the squadron may be putting pressure on you, for you to work the hardest. Mathematics builds upon itself and the foundation for all of it is the fundamentals. It is very tempting during those first two weeks to go back to the squadron and during study time say, 'This math, I've seen this stuff before; it won't hurt to slough off on it for awhile; I'd better work on the things that are causing the pressure.' That kind of thinking will lead you into a trap. Work especially hard those first two weeks even though you think you are familiar with what you see in class. Get that solid foundation of fundamentals so you don't have to backtrack when the pressure is even worse."

Make sure you really understand the concepts being taught, because you will be expected to apply them in other courses.   *Courtesy USAFA*

    Chemistry was mentioned by many cadets as one of the hardest courses they take during the first year. Professors who teach the course comment on difficulties their students experience.

    Said one of them, "A lot of their problems relate to math skills. Yes, many of them do come with pretty decent math backgrounds; they can work problems like they find in their math textbooks. Where they have a problem is applying math skills to real live data such as they produce in our labs. When we ask them to take their data and give a slope and equation of a line, they have difficulty. When we have them plot one over temperature in degrees Kelvin or plot the natural log of an equilibrium constant and get the slope and y-intercept, they have a hard time conceptualizing what they are doing. It is very simple math, but it is difficult for them to apply it.

    "The other problem, which is very common, is for them to get behind. And when you get behind, you're dead. Everything in chemistry builds on something that you have had before. If you don't learn stoichiometry, you cannot do redox or acid-base equilibria. Each chapter builds on the next one, and once they get behind, they are dead meat."

    This building-block approach extends beyond math and science. The freshman English composition course is also foundational. Said one English professor, "The focus of the course is on the writing process itself. The four course papers build from relatively simple exercises in basic expression to the rigor of writing a full-length research paper.

Along the way, cadets learn the essential of sound rhetorical strategy, ordered thought, transition of ideas, and, perhaps as vital as any other part of the process, the necessity of proper documentation.

"We emphasize the necessity of evidence to buttress one's argument—that it isn't enough to have a point of view, but that one should be able to support that point of view with substance. That's where the importance of documentation—use and proper citation of sources—comes into the picture. Knowing how to research support for one's argument, properly frame a given reference, and give credit to others' ideas is what the course has as one of its most important lessons."

Said a history professor: "We also heavily stress writing in our course; we work closely with the English Department. We require three papers during the course and all of our major exams have essay questions. Those who have difficulty with composition in English will also have trouble in our course."

An English professor explained the importance of writing ability for Air Force officers: "The emphasis on seeing the world more objectively and rationally defending one's point of view does not in any way discount the value we place on correct as well as well-argued expression. We insist on virtually error-free writing—especially in the final core course—and we see that the foundation for good writing must come early and have constant reinforcement. We use peer editing as part of this process to cultivate good form with good substance.

> **We want future officers who know how to write well.**

The Air Force does not tolerate substandard writing, so we want to make sure that those who will serve as its future officers—some as its future generals—know how to write well."

Another English professor repeated this idea: "The course in freshman composition is only the beginning. The sophomore course in literature and the junior/senior-level course in advanced composition and public speaking complete the minimum experience necessary for a career of service—development of critical thinking skills and ease in both oral and written expression. Entering cadets often wonder, especially with the goal of flying fighter aircraft, why English is so important. Before deciding on his academic major, one freshman cadet asked his father—the Wing Commander of an operational unit and an English major in his undergraduate years—if he ever used his undergraduate major. Said the colonel—reflecting on the amount of correspondence that he wrote, the amount of staff reports for which he was ultimately responsible, the policies and directives that had to be absolutely clear—'I use my English major every day.'"

Retaining what you learn in one course and applying it in another may be a big change from how you approached your classes in high school. Another big change is the level of understanding expected of cadets.

A law professor explained, "One of the reasons it is difficult for some students here is because they are so smart and they can get by in high school on memorization. There are some courses, and I think law is one of them, where just memorization isn't going to get you very far. There are two sides to every story. So I think that sometimes we find that the younger students struggle with that."

Said one math professor, "There is a fundamental difference between college level work and high school level work in that we expect our students to synthesize information, to apply concepts to slightly different settings. For students who have gotten by on memorization, this is a big shocker.

"Our [calculus] courses use a fair amount of technology. We use laptop computers, we have students do group projects, we have students do writing assignments. This is not an experience most students have had in high school. We make them write about mathematics. We focus a lot on their communication skills, on their ability to synthesize."

Virtually every course at the Academy provides information that is either essential or helpful in another class. By approaching the material with that in mind, you can build on what you learn, rather than digging yourself a hole that will be harder and harder to climb out of.

HELP IS THERE FOR THE ASKING

If you do find yourself struggling, for whatever reason, professors at the Air Force Academy pride themselves on being available to help any cadet who asks.

Explained a math professor, "[Cadets] have a lot of things going their way for them. They have an unbelievably accessible faculty.

"We give our home phone numbers. They can e-mail us any time. They don't have to see just their particular instructor; they can see any instructor from the course, which is sometimes a good thing to do because it gives you a different perspective on the material."

A chemistry professor said, "Instructors love to have their students come in. Don't think it's a burden on the instructor. Maybe they're afraid to let their instructor know that they don't know anything. But we're all here to help them out, and we would much rather them come see us than trying to clean up the mess later on, after a GR [graded review] or final.

"Chemistry has an EI [Extra Instruction] room so there is always an instructor available. That will rotate as part of our duties here to work in that EI room. But I have had cadets just wander in, 'I can't find my instructor,' and they just pop into my office. They can get one-on-one attention."

Said a math professor, "It is the policy in the math department that when you are assigned to one of the large core courses, then you are helping all of the instructors to act as a team. We help out, we give EI to each others' students as needed."

A chemistry professor cautioned, "The problem is they would rather go to a classmate who got an "A" on the GR. That's a mistake, I think. It's much better for one of us to help them."

If you can manage your time well and get homework done early, you can improve your grade. Explained a chemistry professor, "Most instructors will review papers, will review lab reports, and they will give feedback. [The students] are guaranteed to get a better grade."

This section of the book is about "How to Prepare" for the Academy. So why such detailed advice about how to succeed academically once you are there?

The hope is that you will understand how much more challenging the academic course work will be compared to high school, and to some extent compared to other colleges. If you realize what is ahead of you now, you can do everything in your power to better prepare yourself before the shock hits you with full force.

SEVEN
How To Prepare Physically

He was big and he looked strong. But he was only two-thirds of the way up the rope and he could go no farther. He tried desperately. With his teeth clenched and his face beet-red in the heat, he pulled with everything that he had left. But every effort failed. He could go no higher.

"Try again; don't give up," shouted his fellow basics and the upperclassmen supervising the event. "You can do it; give it just one more try."

The young man had more than his share of guts. Digging for everything that was left, he tried again. His arms went taut, and he pulled and strained. But he could go no higher and his arms began to quiver.

But there was not one more time left in the young man. He was finished. With his face covered with sweat, and perhaps tears, he slid down the rope and stood on rubbery legs while another cadet took it and climbed effortlessly to the top.

Expect to be pushed to the limit physically. *Courtesy USAFA*

There is a moral to this little episode, witnessed during BCT: if you go to the Air Force Academy, do not get yourself in the position of the man on the rope. Nearly every cadet will tell you that being physically fit during BCT will help you deal with the culture shock and mental stress. BE PREPARED PHYSICALLY.

PHYSICAL FITNESS IS CRITICAL TO SUCCESS

The above warning was repeated time after time by cadets. "Get this in your book. It is the most important thing. Come prepared physically."

Another one spoke of the consequences. "If you're out of shape, you get intimidated by your lack of stamina. Then everything piles up. Your morale goes down and you begin to doubt yourself. Then the other pressures get to you and you don't feel like studying. It's a vicious circle, and you can really get down on yourself."

Many cadets recited sad tales of friends and roommates who went downhill physically, then succumbed to all the other pressures, and finally dropped out. About one out of every four cadets will leave the Academy before graduation. The majority of those quit during their first year, and most of those depart during BCT or in the fall term.

You probably know what happens to your attitude and your mind when you become very, very tired. If not, please believe that you will not feel like enduring a lot of "training" pressure from upperclassmen. Please believe that when you are physically exhausted is not a good time to try to do five hours of homework in a three-hour study period. And most certainly it is not a good time to create an original essay or write a new computer program.

Cadets can be involuntarily disenrolled for poor physical performance. They must maintain at least a 2.0 Physical Education Average, or PEA, which comprises physical fitness test scores and PE class grades. (Your PEA also affects your overall class ranking, which in turn affects your post-graduation assignment and other opportunities.) Only a few cadets are disenrolled each year for an unsatisfactory PEA, because as soon as they start having difficulties, they are given additional opportunities to meet standards, including mandatory reconditioning training in the afternoons.

These reconditioning sessions are run by upperclass cadets, and include training in technique, strength, endurance, and nutrition. The success rate for these sessions is very good, but they are *not fun*, and they take time that could be otherwise spent on military and academic assignments. Also, being on athletic probation will not help you gain respect in the eyes of fellow cadets.

Those few who do fail physically are almost always those who give up and stop trying. They give up because the physical demands, academic demands, and military demands pile up and overwhelm them. So try to remember what the cadets themselves say and use your own common sense. Do all you can ahead of time to help take the stress out of the physical demands at the Academy.

HOW TO TRAIN

Of special significance is the fact that the Academy is 7258 feet above sea level. The heat index can be very high on hot summer days during BCT. In those conditions, they like to say, "the air is rare."

The cadets cheer about this problem when they watch sea-level football teams come to their stadium and start dragging on a hot afternoon, and the altitude is painted in huge numbers above the Olympic pool, so their opponents will think about the disadvantage. But it is nothing to cheer about if you are out of shape when you show up for BCT. And from the upperclassmen, you are more likely to hear jeers for your efforts than cheers.

The first official measure of your fitness in the application process is the Candidate Fitness Assessment. This evaluation includes a basketball throw, situps, pull-ups, pushups, shuttle run, and mile run. Once you become a candidate, you will receive *Instructions to Candidates*, a document that explain the requirements of this test in detail. You are advised to practice for this test before you take it, using the exact requirements listed in the pamphlet.

This pamphlet also contains a very detailed 8-10 week workout plan to help you prepare for BCT. Make sure you do the workouts, with special emphasis on the running.

"You should be able to click off seven-minute miles without any strain," said a basic cadet who, unlike many around him, was enjoying the physical challenges of BCT. "But practice wind sprints from time to time," he added. "Wind sprints mixed with distance running build endurance faster than distance running alone." Try to practice running on hills, because most

You will take the Physical Fitness Test during BCT and twice every semester.   *Courtesy USAFA*

running routes the upperclassmen lead you through involve climbing the Academy's steep hills.

During BCT and then every semester, you will be required to take two physical fitness evaluations. The PFT, or physical fitness test, includes pullups, pushups, situps, long jump, and a 600 yard run. The AFT, or Aerobic Fitness Test, requires running 1.5 miles within a given time, plus pushups and situps. You want to be able to do more than just achieve a minimum passing score—a good score on these tests boosts squadron standings in the annual wing competition, and therefore *your* reputation within your squadron. A high enough score can even exempt you from future fitness tests. Review the specifics in *Instructions to Candidates* so you will know exactly what to expect.

One cadet advised, "Don't wait for your acceptance letter to get in shape. You don't need a gym—do dips, do pushups, and run harder than you think you should because of the altitude." If you work on fitness the entire year before you go to the Academy, BCT will be that much easier. Many who are in excellent condition actually enjoy the physical training aspects of BCT. Because they have the chance to do something they are good at, they can relax mentally, at least for a little while.

You may be thinking, "I'm a varsity athlete. I have nothing to worry about." According to a graduate who now runs the fitness evaluation program, most athletes are successful with the physical demands of the Academy because "they have the self-discipline, motivation, and willingness to work through the pain. But don't have the attitude that it's no sweat. Even athletes need to prepare, and some slack off during the off season. True athletes understand what's required of them."

Be ready to run, run, then run some more. *Courtesy USAFA*

So you have been running hard for the past year, doing the recommended workouts for BCT, and you hit the end of your senior year in the best shape of your life. Then, in the last weeks before high school graduation and the weeks of June before entering the Academy, something happens that sets you back.

Several basic cadets lamented the fact that they succumbed to pressures from their peers and used that time to party, or lay back and take it easy. "Tell them, 'don't do it!'" one overstressed young man said, wiping sweat from his face. "Tell them to resist those temptations, or make sure if they're going to play, that they also keep up on their workouts. I wish I had. Those who are in shape are enjoying BCT [the physical challenges] while dodos like me are struggling."

As the director of fitness evaluations explained, "It's too late to prepare after you show up. You can't be over-prepared for athletics. You can make the physical part come easily. If you are in shape, you will stand out and help motivate others."

One final word. The Air Force's desire is for cadets to learn that pride, confidence, leadership, health, and stress management depend on being in good physical condition. They believe that cadets will develop a favorable attitude toward physical fitness, and form a lifelong habit of maintaining a healthy body and mind so they are ready to perform whatever duties their country requires of them.

EIGHT
Other Types Of Preparation

Some of the important ways you should prepare for the Air Force Academy are not strictly mental, academic or physical. However, some of these "other" ways have a high priority, which means that you are not likely to get into the Academy without having done them. The Academy is looking for well-rounded individuals who can lead, communicate, serve, and juggle multiple demands at the same time. These activities will help you demonstrate you are this type of well-rounded candidate.

Activities that accomplish the goals listed above, plus expose you to military life, are especially valuable. They will help you prepare for the demands and culture change you are about to face, as well as demonstrate your dedication to preparing yourself for military service.

EXTRACURRICULAR ACTIVITIES AND LEADERSHIP

At the top of the high-priority list is extracurricular activities (XCA). High school XCA include athletics, band, drama, clubs, school newspaper, yearbook and student government. Non-school XCA include Boy Scouts, Girl Scouts, church and civic volunteer work and activities in various fraternal organizations.

One of the best of all non-school XCA is membership and participation in the Civil Air Patrol (CAP) Cadet Program or Junior ROTC. In these organizations you will experience military discipline --how to wear a uniform, how to march, and other customs --as well as military history and traditions. If you are involved in CAP, you will be with people who love flying and who will do everything they can to prepare you to be a pilot.

Also highly recommended is the Eagle Scout program. "Eagle Scouts do well here," was a comment heard over and over from officers at the Academy. Eagle Scouting emphasizes character, achievement and leadership—all of which coincide with the goals of the Academy.

Why are XCA so important? One reason is that your participation in them proves that you have had some experience in time management. If you also have a good academic record, it means that you have successfully juggled a limited amount of time between class attendance, study time and time in the XCA.

More important than just participation is demonstrated leadership. Being a captain of your football team says several things about you. One, you are a respected team player. Two, your leadership qualities have been recognized by your peers. Three, you are willing to accept responsibility. All three of those traits are essential for Air Force officers.

Civil Air Patrol is one way to gain experience in a military environment.
Courtesy Jan Rosko

Therefore, those who will evaluate your high school XCA will give a team captain more points that one who has just been a participant—likewise for the editor of the school paper versus a reporter or the president of the French Club versus a member.

Participation in an XCA indicates some ability in time management and perhaps leadership ability. It also tells Air Force Academy officials one more thing about you. It says that you are not selfish with your time; that you are willing to go beyond what is required–which in high school is simply to take the minimum number of classes and disappear. The attitude of the Academy can be inferred from a statement Air Force Major General Pete Todd, a graduate of the first class of cadets, made to a class of basics. He said:

> *I've learned lots of lessons in the nearly quarter of a century since I stood where you are, but one of the most elevating of all has been this: give me 10 dedicated professionals with a selfless willingness to service and I can accomplish more than with scores of 'job holders.' We'll never outnumber our adversaries, so we have to outthink and outperform them. We simply have no room for the 'summer soldier or the sunshine patriot'—in peace or wartime.*

Work experiences also can be important when your record is evaluated, particularly if you also have participated in XCA. This says that you are an even better juggler of time—that you know how to keep four balls in the air (classes—study—XCA—work) instead of just three.

What about the student who works to help support his family and cannot participate in XCA? Do not worry about that if you are one of those students. If you can successfully juggle classes, study time, and work, and if those who evaluate your record KNOW your handicap, you will not be penalized. In fact, you might be given extra credit because you have demonstrated dedication, self-sacrifice, and responsibility beyond what many high school students have experienced.

LEARN ABOUT MILITARY LIFE

Every cadet you may talk to will have his or her own pet list of optional things you might do to prepare for the Academy. But the MOTIVE of the cadets who might give them to you is always the same. They want to make your first year at the Academy easier than they had it themselves.

CAP and ROTC have advantages beyond those already discussed. Not only do they show your commitment to the military and give you a chance to see if military life is for you, they also make the culture you will be transitioning into less foreign. Even a little bit of practice in shining your shoes, saluting, or marching in formation will help.

The mothers of many teenagers will smile at this next recommendation: develop a habit of neatness. With this recommendation the most important word for you to think about is "habit." If something is a habit, you do it automatically, without thinking, and you become proficient at it. A teenager who is not used to making the bed, folding clothes neatly or buttoning shirts or blouses on hangars, suddenly becomes stressed about these things at the Academy. And they are demanded; every morning the doolies' rooms must be ready for inspection, and it is not easy to satisfy the upperclass inspectors checking for dust or out-of-place items. If this seems stressful or difficult, begin practicing for it now.

Upperclassmen deliberately create stress on doolies by requiring them to recite "fourth-class knowledge." They call it training. Training requires you to recite various kinds of general knowledge about the government, the military, military history, and current events, as well as facts and statements that must be repeated verbatim from memory.

One example is current events. Doolies usually rise at 5:30 A.M. (officially they must be up by 6:00) and in the event-crowded moments before dawn they must read a newspaper and familiarize themselves with all of the significant events of the day.

If you are not used to reading and discussing current events, it may be hard to put what you read into some meaningful perspective. Get in

As a doolie, you will spend every spare moment memorizing knowledge. Courtesy USAFA

the habit of reading a newspaper or news web site before you go to the Academy. This way you will already know what is happening on the national and international scene and you can fit most daily events into a meaningful picture.

Many of the trivial things you have to memorize can wait until you are at the Academy. However, there are certain time-consuming things you can memorize ahead of time to make your life easier during the first few weeks. An example is the rank and insignia of all officers and enlisted personnel of the Air Force, Army, Navy and Marines. Another is to name, recognize and know the mission and manufacturer of all the aircraft and missiles in the Air Force inventory. Still another is to recognize the common U.S. military decorations—the ribbons that are worn on the left breast of the uniform. This information can easily be found on line.

Air Force history is a subject that you might also study ahead of time. Especially important are the wartime events, the planes that fought and the key leaders. Much of this knowledge, along with most of the other fourth-class knowledge can be found in *Contrails*, which is an Academy publication given to all new cadets. This "doolie bible" cannot be purchased, but if you have a friend who is an upperclassman or recent graduate, try to borrow a copy.

You would also benefit from learning about Air Force history by reading books about past generals and conflicts. Anything you do to make the military culture less foreign will make it easier for you to adapt.

DID WE MENTION TIME MANAGEMENT?

One final recommendation needs repeating even though it was discussed earlier, and will be mentioned again by cadets, graduates, and professors, because it is so critical.

Start disciplining yourself during study time. A good way to start is to play games with the clock. Look over an assignment and estimate how long it should take you to do it if you work efficiently. Then set your alarm and see if you can meet the objective. Take a break after that—go to the refrigerator, watch a few minutes of TV or call a friend. Then go back to your desk and repeat the exercise. You will become more efficient if you practice this for awhile.

More important, you will be better able to manage the time crunch that overwhelms so many of the new cadets.

Develop a system for keeping track of every responsibility you have—from extracurricular activities to homework to chores and social engagements. You do not want to have to figure out how to track and prioritize your responsibilities in the high-stress environment of the Academy.

If it sounds like you will have to become a whole different person from the bright, successful high school student you are today…you will. When you first see your parents after BCT, or your high school friends and relatives at Thanksgiving, they will remark that you have changed completely. This process is unavoidable as well as stressful.

All the preparation advice in this section will not be able to make your first year at the Academy completely painless, but if you do what you can to get ahead, you will be very glad you did.

HOW TO GET IN

NINE
The First Step: Applying To The Academy

Getting into the Air Force Academy is not an easy process. You will have letters to write, forms to complete, a medical examination, a physical fitness test, letters of recommendation to solicit and perhaps several interviews. You will have to track many different deadlines and appointments.

If you are serious about going to the Academy, you should be happy that the process is so involved. Why? Because the complexity of the process helps eliminate some of your competition.

When faced with all the forms and letters, many students give up immediately. Others start the process but are careless, either with the forms, the deadlines, or the appointments they make. They eliminate themselves. Every competitor who is eliminated helps your chances—if you are determined to do the process correctly.

And you must realize there is a *lot* of competition. Each year, around 30,000 request applications; of these, about 12,000 continue the application process. Out of the initial applicants there may be nearly 2,500 who complete the process, secure a nomination, and are found fully qualified. Yet there are only about 1,165 openings each year! The struggling economy and tightening military budget mean that more students are applying and fewer appointments are available.

Many students give up before completing the application process.

In ski racing, the difference between the winner of a race and those who finish second, third, and fourth may be just tenths or even hundredths of a second. Much the same concept applies to competition among fully qualified Academy candidates.

Fractions of one point often separate those who get in and those who do not. But you should not be discouraged by this. You should look at it as good news because you can gain points in the admissions process, IF you know what to do and what NOT to do.

So here is some advice on the first steps of the admissions process—advice from a variety of sources, including Academy officials, congressional staff members, Admissions Liaison Officers, high school counselors and cadets who retain vivid memories of their own experiences.

GETTING STARTED: BECOMING AN OFFICIAL CANDIDATE

The first step is to determine if you are eligible for the Academy or will be eligible at some future date. Here are the requirements:

- Be at least 17 years old.
- Not yet have passed your 23rd birthday on July 1st of the year you enter the Academy
- Be a U.S. citizen by the time you enter the Academy (international students authorized admission are exempt from the U.S. citizenship requirement)
- Be of high moral character
- Meet high leadership, academic, physical, and medical standards
- Be unmarried, with no dependents (including parents)

Your next step, if you think you meet the above requirements, is to visit the Admissions web site, www.academyadmissions.com The web site contains the most up-to-date information on the admissions process, along with some helpful tips, as well as general information on life as a cadet.

Note that you must complete the Pre-candidate Questionnaire as a first step. Beginning in the spring semester of your junior year, around the beginning of March, the Registrar's office will post the Pre-candidate Questionnaire, or PCQ, on the admissions web site. You will complete the questionnaire on line. Many interested students will go no further than this step, either because they do not have the qualifications, or they lose interest.

If you are not qualified based on the PCQ, you will receive a letter that includes a name and phone number for an admissions counselor so you can call and find out where you are falling short. If you have started early enough, you may have time to improve.

If your Pre-candidate Questionnaire indicates you are qualified, you will officially become a candidate. At this point you will receive a document called *Instructions to Candidates*. Read it. Read it carefully, and then read it again. It will give you information on every step of the process, including the medical and fitness requirements.

Make sure you have some system for keeping track of all you have to complete and the deadlines for each step. *Instructions to Candidates* includes a checklist. Also, the admissions web site has a smart phone app you can download to help you track all the application requirements.

All those who are involved in the admissions procedure recommend that you START EARLY. For example, during your sophomore year you should ask your counselor for the dates when the Preliminary

> **You should complete the Pre-candidate Questionnaire in the spring of your junior year.**

Scholastic Aptitude Test (PSAT) and Preliminary American College Test (PACT) can be taken.

Take one of them and, if you can afford it, take both—and take them as many times as you can. Experience with these tests will almost surely help you later when the regular tests are taken.

During your junior year take the regular SAT or ACT tests as soon as you can and repeat them if you can afford it. The Air Force Academy will accept your BEST scores. The LATEST you should take either the SAT or ACT for the first time is June at the end of your junior year. If you think you could do better on the next attempt, you can and should still press ahead with the application process anyway, and the Academy will fill in the better scores later.

Additionally, if you take the SAT or ACT later, you will probably not have the scores back in time for the deadlines imposed by your nomination sources. Most congressional offices require all applications to be complete in October or November of the year you are applying.

Work closely with your school counselor during all phases of the application process. Experienced counselors have usually been through the admissions process several times with other students. Some have visited the Academy on special orientation programs sponsored by the Air Force.

ADMISSIONS LIAISON OFFICERS

Also, you should work closely with your Admissions Liaison Officer, called the ALO. There are about 1,500 ALOs in the U.S. who are trained by the Academy to serve as Air Force Academy representatives. Most are Air Force Reserve officers, although some are still on active duty and some are parents of cadets or graduates. Many are Air Force Academy graduates themselves.

The ALO's job is to identify and counsel prospective Academy candidates. ALOs will tell you that the sooner you can get together, the more they can do to help you prepare.

ALOs also participate in the selection process. They evaluate each candidate in their district, usually after one or more interviews and after reviewing the candidate's written statements. Their evaluation is very important because it can make up to twenty percent of the candidate's overall evaluation.

How do you find your ALO? Your school counselor or JROTC instructor may know who he or she is. If not, the admissions web site has a place to enter your high school name and find out who your ALO is. Or you can call the Academy at 1-800-443-9266 to find out.

Then what? Telephone or write your ALO as soon as you consider going to the Academy. Often the ALO will try to arrange a get-acquainted meeting with you. He or she will answer your questions, discuss what an Air Force officer's life is like or, if you are more seriously interested, counsel you about preparation or admissions. Do not hesitate to contact your ALO even if you are still in junior high school. ALOs like to counsel students who still have plenty of time to prepare for the Academy.

ALOs are volunteers who assist the Air Force in addition to their regular jobs. Many are airline pilots, teachers and managers. Because they are busy with their own jobs, it may take some time to establish your first contact. So be patient and keep trying. However, if weeks or months go by with no response, call the Academy admissions office.

Before your first meeting with your ALO, study the admissions web site and learn as much as you can about the Academy. That way you can ask specific questions, which demonstrates that you are interested enough to have spent time investigating. That will impress the ALO. Many students want the ALO to do all the work—to spoonfeed them everything they need to know. Everyone in the admissions process expects you to do what you need to do with minimal help. As we already mentioned, that will weed out those who are not sufficiently motivated.

Realize that if your parents contact your ALO for you, the ALO will wonder who really wants you to go to the Academy—you or your parents. Better to call the ALO yourself. Be aware that the first impression you make on the ALO will matter. He or she will be interviewing you later, and the ALO's recommendation will be part of your final package. And common sense will tell you that impressing your ALO can only help motivate the ALO to do everything possible to help you succeed.

In all your meetings with the ALO, including one or more formal interviews, he or she will be assessing certain of your qualities. How confident and mature are you? Do you communicate well? Do you display leadership qualities? Is there evidence of your ability to work with others? How interested are you in an Air Force career? How much effort have you made on your own to learn about the Academy? These are the kinds of questions the ALO must ultimately answer when he or she writes an evaluation for you.

Your ALO will be very helpful in counseling you about the next step in the admissions process, which is to apply for a nomination. ALL CANDIDATES FOR THE ACADEMY MUST HAVE A NOMINATION BEFORE THEY CAN BE OFFERED AN APPOINTMENT. Obtaining a nomination is the subject of the next chapter.

ARE YOU QUALIFIED?

How does the Academy decide who is qualified and who is not? Your ALO will explain the whole process, and the web site has some of the details. But here is a brief summary.

Are you medically qualified? You must meet Air Force and Department of Defense requirements for serving anywhere in the world, under spare or adverse conditions. A medical condition that you feel has little to no impact on your life may in fact be grounds for disqualification. You will have to have a physical exam to determine if you are eligible. Many medical conditions require a waiver, and the waiver process can be lengthy. Furthermore, the Academy has no influence on who gets a waiver. So if you have any doubt at all, this is another reason to start the application process early.

Are you physically qualified? As mentioned in Chapter 7, all candidates are required to take a Candidate Fitness Assessment. Any PE teacher, ALO, or JROTC instructor may administer the test, so you have a lot of flexibility in scheduling the exam. The *Instructions to Candidates* booklet tells you exactly how to perform each step of the CFA, and what average scores are. That should tell you that you can practice, work on your weak areas, and be sure you have a good CFA score.

Do you have the potential to succeed academically? This is determined by the candidate's grades, rank in class, college courses completed (if applicable), and SAT or ACT scores.

The minimum SAT scores are 580 Verbal Aptitude and 560 Math Aptitude. Minimum scores, however, may not be enough to get an appointment. In the most recent class, incoming cadets were in the top 3% of their high school class, on average. Their average GPA was a 3.88, and the average SAT score was over 1300, and ACT scores averaged 30 in each section.

The minimum ACT scores are English-24, Reading-24, Mathematics-25, and Science Reasoning-25. The average scores in a recent entering class were English-29, Reading 30, Mathematics-30, and Science Reasoning-29.

At the Academy all of the academic criteria—grades, rank in class, test scores and college classes completed—are lumped together into one numerical score called the Academic Composite. Over the years, the Academy has found a strong correlation between Academic Composite and academic success. So the Academic Composite makes up 60 percent of the candidate's overall score.

Are you a leader? Another 20 percent of the candidate's overall score is based upon the candidate's extracurricular composite. These include school activities such as athletics, clubs and student government. They include community activities such as scouting, Civil Air Patrol and church activities. They also include summer and academic-year work experiences. More points are awarded for leadership roles than for membership.

Entering cadets have an average GPA of 3.88 and SAT scores over 1300.

The final 20 percent of the candidate's score is the Admission Panel's rating. This includes the ALO's evaluation and your Candidate Fitness Assessment. You will also be required to submit an essay answering two of three questions. This essay will demonstrate your thoughtfulness about the decision to attend the Academy, your character when faced with ethical dilemmas, and your ability to communicate in writing.

AVOID COMMON MISTAKES

Many candidates make costly mistakes in the admissions process—mistakes that hurt their chances of getting into the Academy. Most of these are easily avoided. Here is how.

1. START EARLY, FINISH EARLY

As already mentioned, everyone with expertise in Academy admissions has the same #1 rule for success: **Be early**.

Your senior year of high school will be busy. If you are a service academy candidate, you have a lot to juggle with clubs, sports, academics, and perhaps a job. Spring of your junior year and the summer before your senior year are great times to get ahead of the application process.

Spring of your junior year is a great time to start.

Complete your Pre-candidate Questionnaire in March. Start on the application as soon as you become a candidate. Schedule your physical and fitness assessment. Research the nomination deadlines for all your potential nomination sources, and create a checklist for them.

Being early will help in several ways:
- You are less likely to miss a deadline
- You convey how serious you are about receiving an appointment
- You have time to correct deficiencies, get waivers, and resolve issues
- You could get an appointment earlier, allowing you to relax and stop worrying
- And best of all, being early can give you an edge in getting a nomination. How? If you have completed your Precandidate Questionnaire and at least three of the major steps of the application, AND show outstanding potential, you could get a "Letter of Assurance" telling you that as long as you are medically qualified and get a nomination, you *will* get an appointment. Your congressmen and senators will get a copy of this letter, telling them, this is a candidate you should strongly consider nominating!

What if you are reading this book during October of your senior year, maybe because you just got interested in the Academy, and you have not even started yet? Is it too late? Maybe not, but you will have to *hurry*. Get the Pre-candidate Questionnaire filled out *today*, and contact your nominating sources immediately. If you have not missed their deadlines, and you work hard to catch up, you may still be able to get everything done in time.

2. BE THOROUGH WITH ALL THINGS

"My pet peeve," said a congressional staffer, "is the candidate who leaves empty blanks in a form. Then, when I ask the person why, I get a dumb answer like, 'Oh, my coach is going to write a letter telling you all that stuff.'"

The above incident is one example of how candidates hurt themselves by not being thorough. Another is when the candidate says to his ALO after all his paperwork has been submitted: "Oh, I forgot to put down the summer job I had at Burger King between my sophomore and junior years." How do you think such carelessness might affect the ALO's rating of that candidate?

Be thorough. Complete every form. List every extracurricular activity. Double check every procedure to make sure you have not omitted something. Be as thorough as you would if you were going through the pre-takeoff checklist of a 40-million dollar F-15 fighter. After all, your potential for performing that kind of task thoroughly is partly what your evaluation is all about.

3. BE NEAT

"Can you believe that I get letters and forms in here that are dirty or have coffee stains on them?" sighed a congressional staffer. That was one of many complaints heard from those who must deal with candidate forms and letters. Every year, more steps of the admissions process are electronic. So the few pieces of paper you do submit will stand out that much more.

Neatness is a habit that WILL be learned if the candidate ever gets into the Academy. But those who deal with candidates generally look more highly at those who already demonstrate such habits. Give yourself every chance to be one of those who are thought of in that way.

Be neat. Be neat with your paperwork. And be neat with your appearance—neat hair, shoes, and clothes make an impression on everyone, especially those with a military background.

4. CHECK ALL GRAMMAR, PUNCTUATION, AND SPELLING

It is easy to make mistakes when filling out forms or writing letters. The important thing is to CATCH those mistakes before they go out and tell the world that you use poor grammar, cannot punctuate, or cannot spell.

There is no reason for a candidate to submit forms or letters with mistakes. To prevent this from happening, do two things.

First, write out the answers on a separate sheet of paper and proofread them slowly and carefully. Second, ask your counselor, English teacher, or some other qualified person to read your forms and letters to make sure there are no mistakes in grammar, punctuation, or spelling. Just checking them yourself is not enough.

When you are filling out forms on line, it is very easy to hit "submit" before you have thoroughly reviewed all your responses. But there is too much at stake for you to take a chance. Review every entry for accuracy. And there is nothing wrong with asking for help. After all, professional writers do the same thing. They submit their work to editors who check what they have written before it ends up in print and possibly embarrasses the author.

5. ALWAYS REMEMBER, YOU, AND NOT YOUR PARENTS, ARE APPLYING TO THE ACADEMY

What do you think goes through the mind of an ALO who gets this kind of telephone call?

"Major Smith?"

"Yes."

"I'm Mrs. Helicopter, you know, Johnny Helicopter's mother. As you know Johnny is applying to go to the Air Force Academy, but he's been getting home late from football practice for the last two weeks and hasn't had time to fill out the forms that you sent him. He was wondering if you could give him a few more days to get those papers in."

Many things might run through an ALO's mind upon hearing something like that. But none of them are good for the candidate. Does Johnny want his mother to fill out his forms and write his letters, too? Will Johnny want his mother to make excuses if he is late to an interview? And, if he gets to the Academy, who is going to make Johnny's excuses then? Or maybe Johnny's mother, not Johnny, is the one who thinks he should go to the Academy.

The Academy Admissions Office's Chief of Selections echoed this concern. You are expected and welcome to contact your admissions counselor, he explained, to see if there are suggestions for improving your package or ask questions about the admissions process. The counselor will make a note in your file, including how polite you are, how determined, etc.

Remember you, not your parents, are applying to the Academy.

Imagine what the remarks will say if your parents are repeatedly the ones who make that phone call? Everyone will wonder whose idea attending the Academy really is.

Parents can provide a wonderful kind of support for candidates during the admissions process, and later, too, if the candidate becomes a cadet. But there is a big difference between support and ACTIVE INVOLVEMENT.

Everyone participating in the admissions process is deeply wary of parents who appear to hover like a helicopter over their son's or daughter's candidacy. The tragedies of cadets who were pushed into the Academy by overzealous parents are well known. Every person who evaluates a candidate will be looking for that kind of parent involvement and trying to scrutinize closely or SCREEN OUT that kind of candidate.

So, take charge of your own admissions requirements. Do not rely on your parents to do the work for you or let the process get out of your control. Make all calls YOURSELF. Look upon each call you must make, not as a chore, but as an opportunity to sell yourself. If your parents insist on helping, ask them to read Chapter 25. It is written just for them.

TEN
The Second Step: Getting The Nomination

The spring of your junior year is also a good time to begin your quest for a nomination.

The procedure is much more involved than the application process. In seeking a nomination, you should probably make separate applications to at least four different nomination sources. Your four primary sources are the two U.S. senators from your state, the U.S. representative from your congressional district and the U.S. Vice President. In this book, U.S. senators and U.S. representatives will be called "congressmen" and their nominations will be called "congressional nominations."

You may also be eligible for a number of other nominations if you fit one of these categories:

- Children of active duty or retired military
- Children of deceased or disabled veterans
- Children of Medal of Honor recipients
- Active duty, guard and reserve enlisted personnel
- ROTC and JROTC cadets

The best way to find out if you are eligible for one of these additional nominations is to talk to your ALO.

The simplest of all the applications is the one to the Vice President. This nomination is also the hardest to get since there are only one or two are available each year for the whole United States. A sample letter is available on the Academy admissions web site, and more information is available by clicking the Military Academy Appointments link on www.whitehouse.gov/vicepresident.

Getting a congressional nomination can be a lot more complicated because of the paperwork required. Also, many congressmen require that candidates go before a panel to be interviewed and evaluated.

Many states now hold annual Service Academy Information Days, where staffers from the congressional offices, ALOs, parents clubs, cadets, and graduates make themselves available in one location to talk to prospective candidates. They will answer questions, and give you resources and advice on the admissions process. Your school counselor, ALO, or congressional staffer can tell you if these opportunities exist in your state.

But what about politics? Do your parents have to have political "pull" in order for you to obtain a congressional nomination? Some people believe that your parents have to belong to the same political party as the congressman. Others believe that your parents or relatives have to have helped in the congressman's campaign or contributed money to it.

Thirty to fifty years ago some of those beliefs may have been true—service academy nominations were sometimes awarded as political favors. However, according to hundreds who have been interviewed for the books in this candidate series, the role of politics is relatively unimportant now. Congressmen do not want to waste their constituents' tax dollars paying for the wrong candidate to attend the Academy. They want to make sure the candidates with the best records and the best chance for success receive nominations.

NOMINATION MATH

There are a total of 535 congressmen—435 representatives and 100 senators. Each has a quota of five cadets who can be at each service academy at any given time. Thus, each year there is usually at least one upcoming vacancy because at least one of the five will probably be graduating. For each vacancy, the congressman can make ten nominations.

Do not let all those numbers confuse you. Just remember that for each vacancy, the congressman is entitled to submit a list of ten nominees from his state or district.

There are three ways the congressman can list those ten nominees when he or she submits the list.

By far the most common method is to make what is called a competitive list. By this method the congressman gives all the names on the list equal ranking. By doing it this way the congressman is telling the Admissions Office, "I have screened the candidates in my state/district and here are the ten who I think are the best. Now it is up to you to decide which candidates should be offered an appointment."

The second method is the principal/alternate method. By this method the congressman picks one nominee to get a principal nomination. This principal nominee, if fully qualified, must be offered an appointment to the Academy first, before any of the alternates on the list can be appointed. And if any of the alternates, which are ranked in sequence—first alternate, second alternate, third alternate, etc.—are appointed, they must be appointed according to their ranking if they are fully qualified.

Congressmen want to make sure candidates with the best chance for success get nominations.

The third method, which is the principal/competitive method, is a combination of the previous two. The congressman makes one nominee the principal nominee, but the nine alternates are competitive. The Academy can then decide who, if any, should be appointed from the list of alternates.

Admissions officials will pick one nominee from the congressman's list, either the principal nominee or the most qualified nominee if it is a competitive list. That nominee will be offered an appointment. If he or she accepts the appointment, that person is the one who will count against the congressman's quota of five who can be at the Academy at any one time.

However, the Academy sometimes offers appointments to others who are on the congressman's list of ten. Those who accept are not charged against the congressman's quota. So, even though each congressman has a theoretical quota of five who can be at the Academy at any one time, it is not unusual for one congressman to actually have more than 10 and sometimes as high as 20 or more at a service academy at any one time.

And for you, the candidate, that is good news. It means that even though your three congressmen might only have three vacancies the year you apply, your chances of getting an appointment are greatly increased because of all the alternates who are also offered appointments. Three congressmen with a combined quota of three vacancies could easily end up with 10-15 of their nominees being offered appointments.

The requirements for each congressman's nomination package may be different.

Much depends upon the qualifications of the alternates. For example, on Congressman A's list of ten nominees there might be only one who is highly qualified and in that case only the one might be offered an appointment.

But on Congressman B's list there might be five who are much more highly qualified than the nine who were left on the list of Congressman A. Therefore, Congressman B might have five of his nominees offered appointments.

Now let us turn to politics again. Suppose a senator or congressman did pay back a political favor and give some young person a nomination. In most cases the list is competitive, hence one name on the list would be there because of politics whereas the other nine are there on the basis of their own merits. Since the list is competitive, which nominees are going to be offered appointments?

Answer: The nominees the Academy believes to be the best qualified. Therefore, if you manage to get yourself on such a list, you do not have to worry about competition from another nominee *unless that nominee is better qualified than you.* And if the person is better qualified than you, that person would have gotten a nomination without the political favor.

So, if you or your parents are worried about politics being a part of the nomination process, you are better off to forget it. You will be much better off to concentrate on what you must do to earn your place on one of those three lists of nominees.

GETTING STARTED ON CONGRESSIONAL NOMINATIONS

The first thing you must do is contact the three congressional offices—the offices of your two U.S. senators and your U.S. representative. If your ALO has not already armed you with this information, go to www.house.gov and www.senate.gov. If you do not know the names of your congressmen, just click on your state and the site will lead you to the correct contact information.

Then call each one of the offices—use the one closest to where you live—and ask for the name of the "staffer" who handles the service academy nomination process. Most of the time the staffer who does that is in a regional office.

When you get the staffer on the phone, tell that person you want to apply for a nomination to a service academy—you do not have to specify which one. The staffer will ask you some basic questions such as your age, address, year of graduation, etc.

In addition, there is a good chance you will be asked to write a letter requesting that you be considered as a candidate for a nomination—or a letter explaining why you want to go to a service academy. Why would a staffer ask for such a letter? Why not just send out the congressman's packet of application forms and instructions? There are at least two reasons why a letter may be requested.

First, there is a common problem of young people calling up saying they want to apply for a nomination just on a whim. Typically such a young person is thinking, "Hey, going to the Air Force Academy sounds like a neat idea. Why not go for it?" Senators in heavily populated states will get well over a thousand young people who are serious about getting a nomination. Requiring a letter is one way of eliminating all the paperwork involved with those who are not really serious.

The second reason why staffers may want a letter requires a little more explanation. Staffers know there are parents out there who, for economic reasons or to enhance their own prestige, want their sons and daughters to go to a service academy. Some push their sons and daughters openly—often it is a plea get a free education and save money.

But more often the pressure is subtle—so subtle in fact, that the young people are not really aware that they are being pressured. They are manipulated in such a way that they have begun to think that going to a service academy is their own idea.

In either case, it is the sons and daughters who are going to suffer because the record of those types surviving at any service academy is absolutely disastrous. The academies are very tough—tough academically, tough physically and tough mentally. Those who have very strong self-motivation are the ones who survive. Young people who have been manipulated into going to an academy by their parents normally do not. So, just as ALOs do, congressional staffs try to use the admissions process to eliminate those who are not really motivated.

Is it possible to get more than one congressional nomination? Maybe. Some of the staffs will coordinate with one another to avoid duplicate nominations, so that the maximum number of candidates receive a nomination. Some do not, and if you have an outstanding record you may end up receiving multiple congressional nominations.

One final note on nominations: If you receive a presidential nomination, do not throw your paperwork for the congressional nominations in the trash. The Academy is limited on how many appointments they can offer presidential nominees, so better to have a congressional nomination as well.

DO IT YOURSELF

Staffers say they get many calls from parents wanting to know what a son or daughter has to do to get a nomination. And from the staffers' comments about such calls, the parent might as well be waving a red warning flag in front of the staffer's face. When a parent calls, the immediate question in the mind of the staffer is, "I wonder if this is a parent who is pushing a kid into applying for an academy?"

So, many staffers do what they can to flush out overzealous parents—and to protect young people from the psychological trauma of eventual failure. When a parent calls about a nomination, some staffers will politely ask the parent to have the son or daughter call, saying—to be diplomatic—that there are a number of questions he or she would like to ask the candidate before sending out the congressman's information packet.

Of course, another way to make an end run around an overzealous parent is to require a letter from the candidate. If the candidate is poorly motivated, he or she can procrastinate writing a letter and in this way thwart the parental pressure. At least that is what the staffer is hoping.[1]

Staffers see another warning flag when parents do the calling for you. Succeeding at the Air Force Academy requires maturity, initiative, commitment, and self-motivation. If you need your parents

---

1. *A field representative told the author that he always makes it a point to tell candidates, "Hey, if this is something you really don't want to do but you don't want to hurt your parents, just leave something out of the application that you send to the academy. The academy probably won't call or write you about it and you won't hurt your parents because they will never know that you sabotaged the application."*

to get you through the application process, you probably do not have the traits required to succeed in the high-stress environment of the Air Force Academy.

Remember that you are being evaluated every time you interact with someone involved with the nomination or admissions process, not just when the application is read or the formal interview is taking place. Take advantage of every opportunity to make yourself known and present yourself well.

ATTENTION TO DETAIL STARTS NOW

After you have called the staffers and perhaps sent in letters that were required, you will receive three separate application packets—one from each congressman.

It is very important that you follow the instructions in each packet exactly, because each congressman has his or her own philosophy and his or her own way of awarding nominations. Almost nothing makes a staffer so angry as when a candidate takes the information from another congressman's packet and duplicates it. Do not give the staffer the impression that you are not serious enough to pay attention to the smallest details.

So take each packet and keep your materials for each congressman in three separate files. Also, make copies of everything that you submit, marking on each one of them the submission date, and keep those copies in the three separate files. That way you have a record of everything. You will know what has been sent to whom, and when it was sent. If you would consider going to West Point, the Naval Academy, or the Merchant Marine Academy, be sure to mention that. Give your order of preference; you may receive nominations to more than one academy.

You are being evaluated every time you interact with someone involved in admissions.

Some congressmen will require more input than others, such as essays. Remember that some of your competition may decide to skip this congressman and just apply to the ones who have easier application packages. Use this to your advantage and complete the more complicated package!

Almost every congressman (and also the Admissions Office) will require that you solicit letters of recommendation. Here are some do's and don'ts that will help you get the best possible recommendations.

Do not just walk up to a person from whom you would like to have a letter and ask, "Mr. ___, I'm applying for; will you write a letter of recommendation for me?"

Instead, tell the person you want the letter from that you are thinking of applying to the Air Force Academy and you are wondering what that person thinks about the idea. This way you get a chance to feel out the person to see if he or she thinks it is a good idea. Perhaps that person will hedge a bit and wonder if you have the "right stuff" for such a challenge. Or, that person might have a strong anti-military bias and feel that you would be wasting your ability going to a service academy. However, another person might be very enthusiastic and think your idea is wonderful.

Which person do you want writing a letter of recommendation for you—the person who is hedging or the person who is enthusiastic about you? The latter, of course. That is the reason for feeling out each person first. Find out if the person is solidly behind you, *then* ask for the letter of recommendation. The competition is tough enough already. You certainly do not want any half-hearted letters of recommendation in your file.

When a person has agreed to write a letter for you, you should give that person three things:

(1) If the letter is required in hard copy, give them an addressed, stamped envelope for each letter that has to be submitted. Typically, each person will be writing letters to all three congressman and perhaps the Admission Office, too.

(2) A written deadline that is at least *two weeks* before the actual deadline. Why? Because the person you ask may be very busy and might forget the deadline or forget to write the letter. Then there are those who are procrastinators—they keep putting it off. (According to congressional staffers high school principals are the worst procrastinators of all.) By giving an early deadline you can check to see if the letters have arrived and if they have not, you will have time to prod the letter-writers and still make the real deadline.

(3) A paper that lists all of your school and out-of-school activities, awards, elected offices, test scores, community work, part time jobs—and anything else a person writing a letter needs to know about you. Why? Because that person wants to write the best letter possible (you hope) and to do that he or she needs to know all the facts about you. It would be the rare teacher, counselor or principal who knows all of your achievements even though you may have been in the same school together for four years. So do not take any chances. Give them plenty of ammunition so they can fire their best shots.

Then what?

There is much more advice that could be given, but it will perhaps mean more to you if it is given in the words of some of the 40-odd staffers who were interviewed. Their comments are the subject of the next chapter.

ELEVEN
Tips From Congressional Staffers

The role of the congressional staffer varies considerably from office to office.

At one extreme are the staffers who, by themselves, review all applications, interview all candidates and then make up the lists of nominees that they present to their congressmen, who usually rubber-stamp the list. Staffers like this are very powerful. They know it—and they will probably let you know it.

At the other extreme are the staffers who only handle the paperwork while an outside panel or the congressman reviews the applications and makes up the lists of nominees. Staffers like this are strictly paper-shufflers and have no input whatsoever regarding who receives a nomination.

Most staffers have a role somewhere in between those two extremes. Many screen the applications and use their own judgment—often supported by objective criteria specified by the congressman—on who should be nominated. Also they may sit on panels and help interview candidates, or they may take the ratings of panelists and use them to make lists of nominees for the congressman.

And while most of the latter types will try to pass themselves off to candidates and parents as mere paper-shufflers, *do not believe it.* It is reasonably safe to say that *most staffers have at least some power to decide who does and who does not get a nomination.* Most of them have been in this role for years; they have seen it all, and will not hesitate to decide whether you are Academy material or not. So be careful. When you are dealing with a staffer, assume that this is the person who is going to decide whether or not you get a nomination.

Now let us hear from the staffers themselves. Dozens of them were interviewed. Many told of one or more visits to the academies. Most expressed strong feelings about the country's need for high-quality military officers. And most indicated that they were doing everything they could to recruit and nominate the best candidates from their district or state.

SHOW YOUR COMMITMENT

Staffers have some frustrating problems with their candidates. One of these problems is the way some candidates procrastinate.

Said a staffer from Arkansas: "They [the candidates] put things off till the last minute and don't realize that I have responsibilities other than handling academy nominations. We have deadlines to meet, too. When a kid pushes me because he has procrastinated, it is going to affect his overall rating."

And a staffer from Washington State: "Some call you up the night before the deadline and say, 'I don't have my pictures yet,' or 'I can't take my SAT until next week.' Or they bring in their letters, transcript and etc. the day of the review and want me to put the file together. That doesn't reflect good organizational ability. That doesn't show dedication. We are going to be skeptical about such candidates. Will they follow through if they get to an academy? They didn't follow through with us when they were told in September what we would need by the first of December. How are kids like this ever going to make it at one of the academies?"

And a staffer from Iowa: "They should be more timely because I won't even consider anybody who doesn't get their paperwork in on time. How could they be successful cadets at an academy if they can't do that?"

Another frustrating problem for staffers is candidates who do not follow up and check on their files. They point out that numerous things can be missing from a file. For example, SAT scores could be missing because they went to Winslow, AR instead of Winslow, AZ—mistakes like that occur all the time.

Another common problem is that high schools, including those with excellent reputations, often leave essential information like class standing off transcripts that they send out.

"The problem [with not following up]," said a staffer from Arkansas, "is that few of these kids really understand how important it is to stay in contact with us. Often there is something missing from their files and before the cut-off date we used to write or call and tell them about it. Now, because of the volume of applications, we just can't do that. Now we just use what is here and some kids will get hurt simply because they don't follow up to see if anything is missing. Of course, in our instructions we tell them to do that. So if they fail to do it they are not following instructions and in my book the ability to follow instructions has to be at the top of the list when it comes to considering candidates for an academy."

And a staffer from Texas: "What bothers me is that these youngsters put their trust in the people they ask for letters [of recommendation], then they fail in not double-checking with me...and I'm not perfect—something could get lost here or in the mail. But to be quite honest,

"I won't even consider someone who doesn't get their paperwork in on time."

they are supposed to be mature enough to handle four tough years at an academy...we can't coddle them. I've seen what happens at those academies. I know what these kids are fixing to get into. If they can't get their act together for a few pieces of paper, what are they going to do when they get up there and report to the academies for basic training—how are they going to handle that?"

Candidates who do follow up with staffers almost always leave a good impression.

Said a staffer from Iowa: "We do everything in our Washington, D.C. office, and since I never see any of the kids, it is the contact through the telephone and their letters that we use to help judge them. And one thing we know is that these kids hate to write letters. Therefore, it is really impressive when we get a nice letter or two from a kid checking on his file. Of course, we like them to call, too, but when a kid goes to all the trouble to write a letter, you feel that that kid is really motivated and wants to go [to an academy]."

And a staffer from California: "The bottom line is how much do they really want this thing? If they come to me for an application and for the interview and if that is all, they don't want it. I want them to bug me, to bother me. If they touch base with me, that shows that they want this thing. I remember one young man from a Catholic boys' school where 99 percent of the graduates go to college. Three kids from that

> *Candidates who follow up always leave a good impression.*

school had applied, but only one came in to see me on a regular basis. West Point, his first choice, was not interested in him, but one day he mentioned that he was also interested in Navy. Right away I got on the phone and called them. I asked if there was any chance for him to get a Naval Academy Foundation scholarship. Now, this year, he is a firstie [senior] and has a nomination to go on to graduate school and get his master's. The point is, he came in and I worked for him. Sometimes the academies call me and say, 'What do you think about this guy or that guy?' I'll tell them, 'This guy, yes, because he comes in and follows up—that other guy hasn't shown up so I don't know."

The previous quote shows one way a staffer who is on your side can help you. But there are other ways. Said a staffer from Iowa:

"We had a kid this year who badly wanted to go to the Naval Academy, but his grades were not high enough to make it. He came in for an interview—just to see what other options might be available. The kid looked like an outstanding candidate so later I just picked up the phone and called them and said, 'If you can't take this kid directly into the Academy, will you please consider him for the prep school?' He ended up there and I know that it will help him."

MORE IS NOT BETTER

Some staffers are bothered by things that other staffers do not seem to mind. An example is when a candidate disobeys instructions and submits more letters of recommendation than were requested. Here are some typical comments:

A staffer from Ohio: "It is really dumb when they submit a whole pile of letters—one had sixteen sent, another had twenty and I was about to kill him! I have to write and acknowledge all of them! We ask for just three and we specify that they should be from persons who know them, who have been in contact with them, know their abilities, know their leadership potential, truly know them as a person. It is not going to impress me that honorable Joe Schmo who knew the kid's parents in the forties writes a letter—I'm not even going to put those kinds of letters in the file—I have to make four sets [for the panel who will interview the candidates] and I'm not going to duplicate all of those. Then there are those from the neighbor and Aunt Tillie that tell what a fine person the boy is. I won't put those letters in. Our panel who reviews them doesn't care if your Aunt Tillie says you are a sweetheart and you mow her lawn. They are looking for leaders, not sweethearts."

Don't submit more letters of recommendation than requested.

And said an Arizona staffer: "You know what I do when the applicant doesn't follow instructions and has a whole batch of letters sent? When I get to the Xerox machine to duplicate the letters for the committee, I take the first three letters, no matter who they are from, and I duplicate them. Those are the only letters that the committee sees and the candidate might be hurt if those aren't the best letters. I'm sorry, but that's the way it is. If the candidates can't follow the simple instructions that we give them, how can they expect to get by [at an academy].

Some staffers also complained about candidates who try to puff their applications with extraneous material.

Said another Ohio staffer: "We are not impressed with attendance awards or a twenty-page essay on why you will make a good cadet. We don't request that and we don't want it. We had one kid who put a whole book together—that and fifty cents would get him a cup of coffee."

PARENTS: KEEP OUT

Parents who want to help their sons and daughters with the

nomination process are also a problem—not for staffers—their ability to handle all kinds of people diplomatically is a mandatory skill for their job. Unfortunately, overzealous parents are a problem for those whom they most want to help: their own son or daughter.

Said a staffer from Arkansas: "I've been at this business for 14 years and if there is one thing I have learned, it is to be leery when parents get involved. When mama and daddy are involved, we immediately get worried. We learned the hard way that those kids [who go because their parents want it] don't last at the academies. It is the ones who do it on their own who survive and graduate. My advice to candidates is to not let their parents run the show—we want to know what the applicant wants or desires—we don't want mama and daddy wanting to put their kids in the academy."

> *"When mama and daddy are involved, we immediately get worried."*

Said a staffer from Nevada: "Leadership is what it is all about and they should be able to demonstrate leadership from the moment they start the application. I am not impressed by the child if his parents call me and say, 'What else does Johnny need for his files?' I always wonder what Johnny can do."

Said another staffer from Ohio: "We get a lot of calls from parents, and I'm not saying that is wrong. But, if young people are serious about going to an academy, they should make the calls themselves. They should learn how to do this on their own and they should call again if they have questions. This shows maturity and I will remember a kid like that."

Still another staffer from Ohio was more adamant: "I get these calls all the time. 'My Freddie is interested in going to the Air Force Academy, etc.' and I say, 'That is fine but let us hear from Freddie.' I guess the initial call is fine, but from then on it should be the kid who calls. And to the kid I would say, 'If you don't have the wherewithal to do things for yourself, you don't belong in an academy.'"

It is not always possible for a candidate to keep his or her parents out of the process. But give it your best effort.

When telephone calls need to be made, you make them.

If you need to visit the congressman's regional office, let a parent drive you if necessary, but go inside by yourself.

And by all means, when you go for an interview, do not let your parents accompany you past the door. An Arizona staffer told of one mother who became angry and created a scene because she could not accompany her son into an interview. "Can you believe that?" said the staffer. "How could we dare send a kid like that to an academy when mom is not going to be there to hold his hand?"

THE DO LIST

Most of the staffers' comments you have read have been negative in tone. But they were selected for that purpose because you should know the kinds of things that staffers do not like.

You should also know what kinds of things impress staffers, so it is appropriate to conclude this chapter with a list of these things—some of which have already been mentioned or implied.

Staffers are impressed with candidates who:

- Call them early—say, during the spring of their junior year. They might not be ready to take any of your paperwork yet, but they will know your name and your determination.
- Are polite and use good manners when speaking over the telephone or when they present themselves in person.
- Are dressed neatly and are well groomed.
- Have done their homework—who know what is on the admissions web site, have talked with cadets and graduates, and have either visited the Academy or read about it.
- Get their paperwork in early.
- Follow up to see if anything is missing from their applications.

Perhaps most of all, they are impressed by candidates who write them letters. So, if you really want a staffer to remember you, write when you apply for your application. Write follow up letters to let the staffer know what letters of recommendation to expect and, later, to make sure all of them arrived. Then write again before the deadline to make sure everything is complete in your file. Also, as a courtesy, if the staffer has done some favor for you or if you get a nomination, write a thank-you letter.

The staffers will appreciate the letters because they know how much you hated to write them. (Most of the staffers probably hate to write letters, too.) So, they will get the unwritten message in your letters which says: "Please pay special attention to me. I am not just one of your average candidates. I am much more serious and much more determined than the others—that is why I didn't just pick up the phone and call you like the others will do. I wrote those letters because I want you to know how much I want to go to the Air Force Academy."

The nomination process is difficult and complicated, but it offers you one more chance to show what kind of candidate you really are. Said a staffer from Colorado, "I love this part of my job. I get to work with some really great kids." Be one of those really great kids.

TWELVE
Interviews: Advice From Those Who Conduct Them

Applying to the Air Force Academy will almost certainly involve multiple interviews. These interviews will not change your academic composite or your fitness score. But these interviews can hurt you if you are not prepared, and they can be critical tie-breakers in a very competitive process.

You will be interviewed by your ALO, a representative of the Academy.

Occasionally this interview is conducted in your home so the ALO can also evaluate your parents' attitude. The representative wants to know how strongly your parents are supporting your application. Cadets do better at the Academy when they have strong parental support. The representative also will be looking for warning signs that your parents have *pushed you* into applying for the Air Force Academy. Do not expect a high recommendation unless you can convince the representative that going to the Academy is *your* idea.

The ALO's evaluation of your aptitude and attitude bears considerable weight in the overall admissions package. Ideally, you have interacted with your ALO many times over the past year or more. You know each other fairly well. Do not let this familiarity fool you—your ALO is evaluating you every step of the way. The interview is simply the most formal part of that process.

In addition to the interview with the ALO, you also may be interviewed by staffers or panelists appointed by one or more of the three congressmen to which you will apply for a nomination. (It is rare for congressmen themselves to interview candidates.)

In the case of the congressional interviews it is important that you go into them well prepared.

Your first concern should be with the kinds of questions that will be asked. Surprisingly, after interviewing more than 80 staffers and panelists, it appears that most candidates are asked about the same questions. Also, there was a great deal of agreement among those queried on the kinds of answers that are rated good and bad by the panelists.

THE QUESTIONS

Your interview may be as short as 15 minutes or as long as an hour. As one staffer put it, "The purpose of the interview is to evaluate the candidate's preparation and motivation. We're trying to decide whether they are ready for that kind of commitment." Remember, your record must stand on its own—your grades and test scores and extracurricular activities must be competitive. That is not what the interviewers are trying to evaluate. They are trying to assess whether you have the right attitude to succeed at a service academy. Following is a list of the questions that you are most likely to be asked. After each question are comments about good and bad answers.

➤ WHY DO YOU WANT TO GO TO A SERVICE ACADEMY?

This question is almost certain to be asked. And many panelists said that even though the question is anticipated by most candidates, many of them still find it difficult to answer.

What panelists want to hear is how you personally feel about going to an academy. They want you to talk about your background, your interests and your goals. They want you to explain how the Air Force Academy will fit in with the goals that you have set for yourself. "Personalize your answer," was a statement heard over and over from panelists.

Said an attorney from Pennsylvania: "Part of the problem is that their answers are so predictable. They'll say, 'It is something I have wanted since I was a child.' That doesn't tell me why—it just says that I want it. Or they will say, 'I have read about it somewhere and I've always wanted to do that.' That isn't any more helpful.

"Another predictable but useless reply is, 'I think it would be a challenge.' That doesn't tell me anything, either. "I think they have to dig deeper for the answer to this question. They should relate their answer to their own personality—they should personalize it a little more—they have to talk about their goals and ambitions. They have to express their feelings to the extent that they are telling something about themselves. It is these personal kinds of answers that are impressive."

Said another attorney from Pennsylvania: "I like to hear things that indicate a strong motivation and commitment. I like to hear them talk about the Academy and tell what they like about it—what they observed if they went there for a visit...things that show a depth of knowledge, things that show they have made an effort to learn about it.

"I am also impressed when I hear things like, 'It has always been my dream to have a military career because …,' or 'I know myself well enough to know that I like a disciplined environment,' or 'One of my favorite things to do is to read about battles and wars,' or 'I have grown up hearing my father, a retired officer, and my uncle who spent 30 years in the Marine Corps, telling about their experiences. I liked those stories and I would like the opportunity to experience some of the kinds of things they experienced'—those are the statements that show motivation on the part of the kid; they show that the kid knows what he is getting into. They are personal and you know that they aren't rote, pat answers—that the kid is not just giving a canned response to the question."

Panelists do not want to hear such comments as: "I want to go because it is a place to get a great education." Great educations are available at lots of colleges and universities.

Nor do they want to hear: "I want to go because my parents cannot afford to send me to college and this is the way for me to get a free education." The panelists who object strongly to this kind of answer point out that the Air Force Academy really is not free; a great amount of work is required to get through four years and, in addition, the graduate has to pay the government back by serving at least five years on active duty.

What panelists are really trying to determine is whether or not you really want to serve in the Air Force. That is the sole purpose of the Academy's existence; it is there to prepare a select group of Air Force officers to serve their nation in peace and war.

Does that mean that you have to convince the panel that you intend to remain in the Air Force and make it a 20 or 30-year career?

Some panelists would, indeed, like to hear that kind of declaration. But a majority said they were skeptical of 17- and 18-year olds making such statements. Typical was a university professor from Pennsylvania: "He can say, 'I'm thinking about a military career, but I don't know for sure that is what I'll be doing [in the future].' That's okay, but anybody who tells me at eighteen that he knows he's going to be a professional soldier, that's malarkey. He has to be a lot more mature than the kids at the university where I'm teaching because they're never that sure about their future."

Be prepared to say which academies you want to attend, in what order, and why.

Be prepared to say which academies you want to attend, your order of preference, and why. The author served on a panel for a senator, and found that many candidates struggled with this question. The nomination package had a place to check your academy preferences. If you put Air Force first, Naval Academy second, and did not include West Point or the Merchant Marine Academy, that is fine. Any preference is acceptable, but you must be able to explain your choice logically. One candidate ranked all the academies ahead of Air Force, and when asked why, said because he really wanted to fly and had heard the Air Force was no longer training pilots! This answer showed he had either done insufficient homework or was very confused.

Be prepared to explain why you want to go to the Academy.
Courtesy Senator Al Franken's office

> **WHAT ARE YOU GOING TO DO IF YOU DON'T GET IN?**

The real wording of this questions should be: "How serious are you about wanting an Air Force career?"

If you are, indeed, serious, the panel would expect that you have also applied for an ROTC scholarship. Or that you plan on attending a college with an ROTC unit so you can get the military experience and a year's college which will help you *when you apply again next year.*

If you do not have a contingency plan that involves the military, the panel is likely to think that you have only a shallow desire to go to the Academy. Consequently, do not expect high marks with an answer like, "Oh, I think I'll just go to Ponderosa College and study engineering."

One doolie said this question helped him overcome a not-so-competitive GPA (he had good SAT scores, sports, and extracurricular activities): "I told them that if they didn't give me a nomination this year, I'd be back every year until I was too old. I think that convinced them how badly I wanted it, and to take a chance on me."

> **SUPPOSE YOU WENT TO THE ACADEMY AND LATER CAUGHT YOUR BEST FRIEND CHEATING. COULD YOU TURN IN YOUR FRIEND?**

Some version of this question is asked to see how well you have researched the subject of the Honor Code. The thinking of the panel is that a highly motivated candidate would know about that Honor Code and would already have thought about some of the consequences of living with it. So this question is just another one aimed to measure your motivation. (For a discussion of the Honor Code see Chapter 23.)

> **WHAT MAKES YOU THINK YOU CAN STAND THE STRESS?**

This question is asked so you will talk about yourself. The panel wants to hear about the difficult, stressful situations you have encountered in your lifetime. Perhaps those were on the football field with a tough coach who yelled at you all the time. If so, describe the coach's actions and how you handled the criticism.

But there are other possibilities you might discuss. For example, if your parents are divorced and you suffered in some way in the aftermath, do not be afraid to describe how you coped with the problem.

Basically the panel wants to see if you have had any experience coping with stress. They do not want to hear answers like, "Oh, I'm pretty tough; I can handle it," or "I just know I can do it."

The key to answering this question successfully is to talk freely about yourself and give specific examples that show you have some experience with stressful situations.

> **HOW DO YOU THINK THE UNITED STATES SHOULD DEAL WITH NUCLEAR PROLIFERATION IN IRAN?**

Many panels will ask a current events question like the one above. Some panelists believe that academy candidates should be a cut above the average good student and be aware of world events. However, those panelists are probably in the minority.

According to most panelists who were interviewed, current events questions are asked primarily so the panel can see how candidates handle themselves with such a question. In other words, they think that most candidates *will not* know much about the question that was asked. But, will the candidate fluster or try to bluff his way through an answer? Or will the candidate have the poise and confidence to look the panelists in the eye and say, "I'm sorry, but I can't answer that. I have been so busy the past two weeks I haven't even picked up a newspaper or a news magazine."

It might also help if candidates would explain that they are aware that knowledge of current events is required by doolies at the Academy. But then be prepared for this question: "If you are too busy now to keep up with current events, how are you ever going to do it at the Academy when the pressure is much, much greater?"

> **WHAT ARE YOUR STRONGEST AND WEAKEST POINTS?**

This is a common question designed, not so the panel can pick at your weaknesses, but to get you to talk about yourself.

Show confidence when you talk about your strongest points. Many panelists say that young people are often too shy when talking about themselves. Try to remember that one of the things the panel is doing is evaluating your potential ability as an Air Force officer. And a leader cannot be shy. On the contrary such a leader must project a strong image. So do not hesitate with the panel. They asked you to talk about your strengths so this will probably be your best opportunity during the interview to sell yourself.[1]

Be cautious when discussing your weak points. The panel does not want to hear about your sins or mistakes. Mainly they want to know what traits you are working to improve upon. For example, do you procrastinate like most people? If so, admit it, but also explain what you have done recently to try to overcome that weakness. Do you keep a messy room? If so, describe how you are trying to change so you will be ready for the orderliness at the Academy. Do you have a quick temper? This is a more serious weakness, so be ready to explain how you are learning to control it.

> **HOW ARE YOU PREPARING PHYSICALLY?**

The Air Force Academy is a very physical place and most panelists know it. Therefore, you should be prepared to discuss a specific physical conditioning program that you plan to follow.

You are not likely to get good marks for an answer like, "Oh, I played football; I'm in good shape."

> **HOW HAVE YOU HANDLED FAILURE?**

It is very difficult for some young people—particularly high achievers who are good candidates—to handle failure. To be sure, some high achievers have never experienced failure. Many candidates struggle with this question because they have never thought of themselves as failing at anything.

However, if a panelist asks that question, it is probably because he or she knows that failure at the Academy is inevitable. Not major failure, of course, but failure in small things is purposely induced by the upperclassmen.

So think about this question before you go before a panel. You have probably had at least a small setback that taught you something about leadership or about yourself. If you have not experienced failure, you should present an attitude that says, "If I fail and I have done my best, then I can't do anything else about it. But the important thing about me is that if you keep knocking me down I will keep getting up. Temporary failures are not important to me. I am not the kind of person who gives

---

1. *One panelist chided the author about this comment, saying that a candidate came before him boasting of his achievements. He cautioned: "Sell yourself, but use humility. Don't come across as boastful." Remember, they have seen your record.*

up when things are going bad. I am not a quitter."

HOW TO PREPARE

So much for the typical questions. The next thing you should know about the interviews is how to prepare for them.

The most important thing you can do is to arrange a practice interview. This may sound silly to some candidates and, if fact, one cadet said, when the practice interview was mentioned in a discussion, "What kid is going to go out and arrange something like that?"

The fact is, most candidates discover that they do two or three times better in their second interview than they did in their first one. They give better answers to the questions, and they are more poised and confident.

Another fact is that you are reading this book because you want to get an edge on your competition. So try to remember what the cadet said and realize that *he is right.* Most of your competitors will *not* take the trouble to arrange a practice interview. So do what they will not do and get ahead of them!

Some of the best people to conduct a practice interview are military officers from any branch of the service. They can be located in almost any community or neighborhood and most would be very willing to give you a good workout—especially retired officers who have plenty of free time. Your ALO may also work with you. Not only will she be pleased to do it, but it is almost guaranteed that she will be impressed with your determination.

PRACTICE before your interview.

We have been telling you that your parents should be hands off in the application process; however, they may be a big help preparing you for the interview process. The congressional interviews are not so different from many job interviews, so your mom or dad—or a family friend—can give you tips and help you practice, even if they have no military experience. Whom you go to for help matters less than making sure you *practice before your interview.*

As soon as you know when your congressional interviews are to be held, begin making specific plans for them.

For example, plan what you are going to wear well ahead of time so your clothes can be ready. As for what you *should* wear, most panelists were in agreement.

Most panelists believe that men should wear slacks, a dress shirt and tie. Many suggested that a sport coat should also be worn; however, most felt that a candidate should not go out and buy something just for an interview. Several said they would just as soon see a young man in a nice sweater as a coat.

Several panelists mentioned shoes—some with negative comments about old dirty "sneakers" and leather shoes that were scuffed and unshined. The best advice is to wear well shined leather shoes if you have them. If you do not, at least wear the nicest, newest athletic shoes that you have.

Women candidates should come professionally dressed as well, whether in a dress, skirt, or slacks. Most who commented on the matter cautioned female candidates not to come dressed like they were going to a party. Go especially easy on frills, jewelry, makeup, and high heels. Said a woman panelist from Nebraska, "I'll never forget one girl who came in teetering on high heels; the panel was not impressed."

While discussing clothing that candidates should wear, almost every panelist gave examples of bad taste that they could remember, such as color mismatches of ties or socks. So get some help in coordinating colors if you are in doubt about your judgment.

Others mentioned poor grooming—things like dirty fingernails and unwashed or uncombed hair. Several panelists laughed about some candidates who come in jeans, T-shirt, without socks or in a sweat suit. One staffer, laughing and shaking her head, remembered a candidate who came in shorts and sandals.

Come to the interview dressed professionally.

A retired general and graduate of West Point from Washington State perhaps summed up the matter the best. After discussing his belief that young men should appear in a coat and tie if they can, he said: "[These kids] are looking at a very significant event in their lives. That little session [the interview] could change the next thirty-five years of their lives. A lot of the kids come in, first of all, not fully appreciating that, and certainly not showing much deference to the critical juncture where they find themselves."

The candidate should also plan ahead to make sure to be on time. If transportation looks like it might be a problem, plan ahead. Ask for help from your counselor or your ALO. Said one staffer, "Map the route ahead of time. Read the letter informing you of your interview very carefully. We've had candidates lose their letter, come at the wrong time, even come to our office when we were using a different location for the interviews. Read the letter closely!"

And by all means, telephone the congressional staffer should an emergency arise that will cause you to be late for the interview or miss it altogether. Make sure your reason stands up to scrutiny. Said one staffer, "We conduct about 125 interviews each year. When someone calls to reschedule for a dumb reason, it makes us wonder about their commitment." They realize you are involved in many activities—all serious candidates are. But if you cannot rearrange your schedule to make this important interview, it had better be for a very impressive reason. The sports awards banquet, piano recital, or debate competition will have to go on without you.

PRESENT YOUR BEST SELF

Now the planning is over. You are sitting in the congressman's outer office with many other candidates, waiting. And you are nervous. But you look around and see only one or two who look like you feel. But the others ... they look so calm! Seeing these others looking so confident may suddenly cause your self-image to fade. You may even begin doubting whether or not you should be competing in their league. And you may ask yourself: Wouldn't it be better just to ease out of the room and forget about the whole thing?

Not if you really believe you have what it takes to be a leader. You can believe that everyone waiting with you is just as nervous as you are.

Leaders must have the ability to control their fears and make those around them believe that they are full of confidence. And if those who are waiting with you for an interview do, indeed, convince you that they are confident, give them an "A" for leadership potential. They are probably as nervous as you are, only they are controlling it and projecting another image.

So, make up your mind that you, too, are going to take control and project a confident image. That is what the panelists will be looking for. Said a rough-talking, retired colonel from Georgia, "[The interview] is a test. Part of the challenge is to keep from being flustered. You get a guy who goes all to pieces and wets his pants—you don't want him leading a platoon in combat and creating a panic."

What else can you do while you are waiting? Rather than rehearsing possible answers to questions in your mind, you are probably better off trying to keep your mind uncluttered so you can give fresh, thoughtful, original answers to the questions when you get before the panel. Several panelists mentioned candidates who appeared to have all their answers memorized, then gave them with robot-like speeches.

Many panelists also complained about candidates who give brief answers to questions. "To get anything out of some of them, you almost have to drag it out," was a typical comment. While you are waiting, try to remember that the panel is waiting to hear what you are going to say. They want to do very little of the talking. So convince yourself that when they start asking questions you are not just going to give an answer—you are going to *discuss* the question with them.

Also program your mind so you are ready to discuss *yourself.* Every question they ask will be of a personal nature to some degree. *Project your personality into that discussion.*

One further thing you can do while waiting is to ask the receptionist or staffer for a list of the names of the panel. You might not be able to memorize all of them, but you should at least know the name of the chairman. Later, it will be impressive if you can reply to Mr. Williams or Mrs. Johnson when you only heard their names once during the introduction.

Now the time has finally come; it is your turn to go in and meet the panel. Usually the staffer will come out to the waiting area and escort you into the room with the panel. Then you will be introduced, typically to the chairman first; then to the other panelists.

Who will sit on the panel? It varies widely from congressman to congressman. They may be ex-military officers, community leaders, or parents. There may be only two or half a dozen. They all bring their own experiences and values to the interview, as well as guidance from the congressman as to what he or she is looking for in a service academy candidate.

If it seems appropriate and natural, shake hands with the chairman and, perhaps, with the others as well. And if you do that, shake hands with a *firm grip.* Many men (and perhaps women, too) harbor very negative feelings about any person who gives them a limp handshake.

You will be given a chair in front of the panel and it is important that you sit erect. Of course, you will not be expected to sit as erect as you would a year later should you make it into the Academy. But panelists often criticized the posture of candidates, especially those who slumped badly.

Panelists were also critical of those who cannot control their hands. Excessive wringing of the hands was mentioned several times, as was nervous movement. Probably the best advice is to put your hands in your lap or the arms of the chair and use them only for your natural gestures.

Another thing that bothered panelists was the use of current high school slang, and the excessive use of "you knows," "umms" and "uhs." Candidates who expressed themselves well and who used good grammar were commended. Panelists also commented favorably about candidates who exhibited good manners and who used respectful terms like "sir" and "ma'am."

Some panelists believe that candidates should maintain eye contact throughout the interview. The strongest statement came from a panelist in Arizona who served on a panel one of us observed. She said, "That's the single, most important thing that you can tell a kid who is going before a panel. Have him make eye contact and keep it. Now I don't mean that he is to look at my hairline or at my chin or at my nose. I want the candidate looking at my eyes! I watch for this with each candidate. The ones who are insecure and lack confidence don't do it—at least that is my impression. Those who have poise and confidence in themselves do. And which do I want to send to a service academy? No way am I going to vote for a kid who doesn't have confidence in himself, because he'll never make it."

You can also demonstrate confidence by hesitating after one of the panelists asks you a question. The natural reaction, if you are tense, is to blurt out answers as fast as possible. Fight that tendency. Pause and think for a few seconds before you reply. Of course, that requires poise on your part. But outward poise is one of the best indicators of inner confidence.

Panelists also have complained that candidates often either do not listen to the questions that are asked or that they ignore them. "Either way, he makes a bad mistake," said a panel chairman. "The candidates who consistently get the highest ratings are those who answer the questions precisely."

How do you give an answer that is not too brief or too rambling? One ALO gives the following tip for formulating your answers: "I like the STAR method—it stands for Situation or Task, Action, and Result." This simple technique keeps the candidate from giving short yes or no answers that do not fully answer the question. For example, if you are asked about your weaknesses or your ability to handle failure, you could describe the *Situation* or *Task* you had trouble with, then what *Action* you took to improve yourself, and the *Result* of that action. When you do your practice interview, get comfortable with this or a similar technique for answering.

Avoid giving a simple yes or no answer.

At the end of the interview the candidate is usually asked if he or she has any questions of the panel. Typically, say the panelists, the candidates are surprised and often they think they should ask something. Typically, they ask, "When am I going to know something?" which is a question that is better asked of the staffer before or after the interview.

If you know that one of the panelists is a service academy graduate or veteran, you could ask a question about their service, such as what they liked best about serving in the military. If you do not have a specific question in mind, several panelists suggested that the candidate should use the time offered to say something like: "I really don't have a question, but there are a couple of things you didn't ask me which I think are important for you to consider. Would you mind if I just took a couple of minutes to go over them?"

Remember that panelists are human. In the course of one or two days of interviews they will sometimes forget to ask things that are important. So, during the interview, keep in mind the things you *have not* been asked—especially those things, when brought out, that might make a difference in your evaluation. Then use the time at the end of the interview to point out those things.

Now the interview is over. The chairman will probably stand up, and perhaps the other panelists, too. If it seems natural, shake hands again. But for sure, *thank the panelists* for giving you the opportunity to meet with them. Also, make it a point to *thank the staffer*, too.

PRACTICE, PRACTICE, PRACTICE!

This chapter is nearly over and the author can breathe a sigh of relief, having given you every important bit of advice that came from all the panelists and staffers.

But you, the candidate, cannot relax. You still have the interviews to face. And probably you are trying to juggle all the important do's and don'ts in your mind:

- Do use good English
- Do give complete answers, but …
- Don't ramble
- Don't wring your hands
- Don't slump in the chair
- Don't use high school slang or too many "you knows"
- Do look the panelists in the eye
- Do use good manners
- Etc., etc., etc,.

All of that together is enough to put anybody's mind into overload, especially when you have to go into a room with strangers for the first time.

And what to do about that? Perhaps the advice in the following story might help.

The original author of this book received a telephone call from a candidate in Kentucky whose father is an old friend. The candidate had used the raw manuscript of *The Naval Academy Candidate Book* to guide his own candidacy. He called with the news that he had just received his appointment. That was wonderful news, of course, and, in the discussion that followed, the young man was asked what advice helped him the most.

"There is no doubt about that," the young man replied. "The recommendation you made to do a practice interview is the best advice in that manuscript. Be sure and put that in the book."

The author replied: "Should I say anything more about the practice interview—something that would persuade others to do it?"

"Yes, tell them that it helped tremendously, and I *mean* tremendously!"

That conversation relates directly to the problem of the candidate trying to keep all the do's and don'ts in mind as the first interview is impending. And the best advice for the candidate is: *Do not let the first interview you do be the one that counts.*

Arrange one or more practice interviews. And use them to *practice* the do's and *practice* avoiding the don'ts!

After you have completed the nomination interview, provided you have completed everything required for your application, all you can do is wait to find out if you received a nomination. It may take another month or even longer before you hear. In the meantime, if you have taken another ACT or SAT, finished your Eagle Scout requirements, or won all-state honors in your sport, be sure and let your Academy admissions counselor know so that the information can be added to your package.

Doing a practice interview is the best advice in this book.

Most of all, be realistic about the fact that you might not get a nomination; or you might get a nomination but not an appointment. Keep working on your Plan B.

If going to the Air Force Academy is your one true passion, the next chapter tells you about some alternate routes to get an appointment.

THIRTEEN
Alternate Routes To The Academy

The first time you apply to the Air Force Academy you may not get a nomination. Or, you may get a nomination but not get an appointment. In either case, if you are really determined to go, you should have an alternate plan of action.

The first part of that plan should include an analysis of why you did not make it. But do not rely solely on your own opinion. Get some opinions of those who were involved with your application.

If you did not get a nomination, call one or more of the congressional staffers who have your file. Explain that you have no intention of giving up—that you want to apply again next year. Then ask the staffer if he or she would please look over your file and make recommendations on what you can do to make yourself a better candidate. Realize, of course, that the staffer probably cannot do this immediately while you are on the telephone. So, with your request, also ask when it would be convenient for you to call back. This will give the staffer time to review your case and to think of advice that would be most helpful.

If you received a nomination but not an appointment, there are two people you should contact. One is your ALO. The other is an admissions counselor at the Air Force Academy. Try to convince both of your determination to do whatever you have to do to get accepted for the next class. Then, as with the congressional staffers, give them time to review your application before you call them again. Also, you may receive a letter from the admissions office at several points in the process, providing you feedback on how to become more competitive.

While you are consulting with those who will be discussing your weaknesses or deficiencies, be very careful not to get defensive about yourself. Just listen to what they are telling you, and even if you think they are wrong, thank them for their efforts.

After the consultations, the next step is to evaluate what you have heard. Then you should develop a new plan of action based upon your options.

HOW TO BECOME MORE COMPETITIVE

One of the most common problems of unsuccessful candidates is an academic deficiency—demonstrated by a low grade point average or low test scores (SAT or ACT), or a combination of both. If this is your problem, you must demonstrate as soon as possible that you are capable of academic success at the Air Force Academy.

How?

Get into a college as soon as you can. And take hard courses. Take calculus. Take English. And take chemistry. And work as hard as you can. Do more than you are assigned. Get A's if you can and if you cannot, at least get B's.

Also, take the SAT and ACT as many times as you can—remember, your highest score is what counts.

In addition to your college classes, you should also consider taking a specialized course designed to help you increase your SAT and ACT scores. Ask your high school or college counselor about local programs.

What kind of college should you attend?

A general recommendation would be to go to the best college you can afford and the best college that will admit you. Even better would be a college that has an ROTC (Reserve Officer Training Corps) unit that will accept you.

Ideally you should try to get into an Air Force ROTC program. However, if this is not possible, do not hesitate to get into an Army or Navy unit—you are seeking an opportunity to prove yourself to military officers. The branch of service is of minor importance.

Perhaps your problem is not an academic deficiency. Perhaps you were not involved in many extracurricular activities while in high school. Perhaps those who evaluated your application felt that you were too "bookwormish" to make a good cadet. If so, what can you do?

First, go on to college and do what has already been recommended. But get active in things other than academics. If you are in ROTC, get active and try to become a leader in whatever other clubs the unit sponsors that interests you. As one admissions officer at West Point said, "Get in and get dirty...and prove yourself."

ROTC cadets can compete for a special category of nomination. But even more important, being successful in ROTC will demonstrate your commitment to becoming an officer, and your ability to handle military *and* academic challenges at the same time.

Get involved in student government, the school newspaper, dramatics, intramural sports, clubs, or whatever else interests you. And strive for leadership positions.

Do not worry that you cannot be elected president of a club as a freshman. Do what you can. Volunteer for committees and take as much responsibility as the organization will give you. There are always opportunities. For example, few organizations will deny an eager freshman the opportunity to lead a clean-up committee.

And remember what you are seeking. You are seeking leadership experience. Also you are seeking leadership *credentials* that you can cite on your next application.

Remember that if you decide to apply again, you will have to juggle adapting to college life at your new school with the nomination and application process. However, by the end of your first semester of college, you will have demonstrated your ability to succeed in college level classes while juggling work or extra-curricular activities. And you will show just how determined you are.

JOIN THE FORCE

What if you cannot afford college? You can enlist in the Air Force—the active force, the Air National Guard, or the Air Force Reserve—with the goal of earning one of 165 appointments given to airmen each year.

You should realize that this option is much more risky than the college option. With the college option you can go on and get your degree, then perhaps get an officer's commission. But if you enlist in the Air Force, you might never get to be an officer. You might join for three or four years, not be admitted to the Air Force Academy, and end your enlistment without any college credit.

If you do decide to join the Air Force, here is some advice that has been handed down from others who have entered the Academy from that route.

First, you must excel at everything you do in order to earn good recommendations from your supervising officers. In basic training, try to be the outstanding basic. In whatever technical training program you enter after that, strive to be at the top of your class both in academics and in military qualities. Later, when you are given your active-duty assignment, try to be the best airman you know how to be.

In addition, make sure you have a copy of the Air Force Instruction that explains the academy application procedure. Cadets who went this route explained that it is not uncommon for squadron personnel to know very little about the procedure. So do not depend upon someone else to tell you how to apply.

Cadets who came from the Air Force also recommended that you should let your supervising non-commissioned officers (NCOs) and officers know that your goal is to attend the Air Force Academy. Those supervisors may give you responsibilities that will allow you to prove that you have leadership potential.

A word of caution: Some of your peers or immediate supervisors may not understand why you want to go to the Academy. They may even try to talk you out of pursuing an appointment. Why? They may feel you are betraying the enlisted force by seeking an officer's commission. Or they may resent you for taking a valuable asset (a hard-working, well-trained airman) away from the unit. You will have to resolve to stay committed to your goals, and look past this kind of short-sightedness to pursue them.

While you work through the process, remember that you still have opportunities to improve your academic ability. Enlisted personnel can subscribe to a number of college-level correspondence courses. Also, most bases have off-duty college classes available that you may be able to take.

Few airmen go directly from the Air Force into the Academy. Most spend a year at the U.S. Air Force Academy Preparatory School, which is located on the Air Force Academy, a few miles south of the cadet area. The purpose of USAFA Prep School is to bring potential cadets "up to speed" in math, English and the physical sciences. Military and athletic training is also included, but it is not as rigorous as at the Academy itself.

PREP SCHOOLS

Prep schools are designed for promising candidates who are not quite ready to enter an academy. Often these are candidates who have promising leadership potential, but who are slightly deficient academically. Many are recruited athletes or enlisted personnel.

Such promising candidates are offered an opportunity to attend either USAFA Prep School or one of several private preparatory schools that have a cooperative arrangement with the Air Force Academy.[1] USAFA Prep School is the best offer because the candidate enjoys free tuition as well as free room and meals and a small salary. There is no process for "applying" to USAFA Prep School—the slots are awarded to appropriate candidates who have applied for an Academy appointment.

Unless the candidate can demonstrate financial hardship, the expenses at the private prep schools must be paid by the candidate or the parents. One exception: the Falcon Foundation provides partial scholarships to private prep schools for a small number of candidates. Like USAFA Prep School, you cannot apply directly for a Falcon Foundation scholarship. Instead, the Admissions Office forward names of promising candidates to them.

In either case, at USAFA Prep School or at a private school, if the candidate does well he or she is likely to receive an appointment to an Air Force Academy class the following year.

Candidates typically react in one of two ways when they are offered the prep school option. One candidate says, "Wow, that's a great opportunity. Where do I sign?"

---

1. *These include Valley Forge Military Academy in Wayne, PA; Kent School in Kent, Connecticut; Greystone Prep at Schreiner University in Kerrville, TX; Randolph-Macon Academy in Front Royal, VA; Marion Military Institute in Marion, AL; Wentworth Military Academy in Lexington, MO; New Mexico Military Institute in Roswell, NM; and Northwestern Prep School in Crestline, CA.*

The other candidate says, "What! You expect me to waste a year of my life in a prep school? You have to be kidding. I would rather forget about the whole thing and just go on to a college and join ROTC."

Before you react either way, you should think about some of the advantages of the prep school option. First, it will give you a chance to strengthen your background in the subjects that are most difficult for first-year cadets.

Second, and perhaps more important, the instructors will see to it that you learn how to study. Not knowing *how* to study is the biggest problem of first-year cadets who enter an academy right out of high school.

Third, you will have one more year of maturity before you start the rigorous schedule of a doolie. That year of maturity will help you adapt to the many stresses of that first year. You will also be over the pain of homesickness, a malaise that creates problems for many who leave home for the first time.

Fourth, you will learn a great deal about military training. You will know how to shine your shoes and put your room in inspection order, and you will learn some of the military knowledge and culture that most doolies first see in BCT. This knowledge will give you more time to focus on your studies, and the opportunity to establish yourself as a leader among your Academy classmates.

Most prep school graduates receive appointments to the Academy.   *Courtesy USAFA*

A bonus of a year at a USAFA Prep School is that you will already have about 200 friends when you start as a doolie. Those will be some of your fellow cadets at the Academy. Friends are valuable in any kind of stress situation. They are especially valuable when you are undergoing the pressure that the upperclassmen place upon the doolies.

The author interviewed many cadets and graduates who had spent a year at the Prep School. They all agreed that it was the best thing they ever did—that they came into the Academy much better prepared academically and militarily than those who came there right out of high school. Many graduates who attended prep school recall the mental pressures of BCT being not such a big deal. Other cadets and graduates can recall leaning on a prep school graduate for help shining shoes and folding socks or emotional support.

San Antonio Spurs Coach Gregg Popovich, who coached basketball at USAFA Prep School for several years, offered this opinion: "It's the greatest deal going. What an opportunity to spend a year maturing physically and intellectually. You'll be better prepared, and better understand the purpose of the Academy."

The following are two profiles that are typical. They are models for many students who are either poorly prepared academically, or feel that they are not ready for ANY college after graduating from high school.

THIRDCLASS CADET, 21 YEARS OLD, PRESIDENT OF HIS CLASS AS A FOURTHCLASSMAN. I wasn't a good student in high school. I didn't work at it—I didn't see any reason why I should. Then I woke up my senior year and decided that I had to do something with my life, and I got interested in the Air Force Academy. I applied but there was no chance. So I enlisted in the Air Force. I worked hard and won Outstanding Airman awards. Eventually I applied and was accepted into the Prep School. I had lots of support from my officers. That got me in. Then, at the Prep School I worked hard, especially on the math. I did well, and the military part was easy because of my experience. I was offered an appointment the next year and I took it.

For me the doolie year wasn't all that bad. Mostly that was because I was older and more mature. I knew what I wanted while lots of the younger doolies were questioning themselves. My worst problem was as the class president, I couldn't get away with anything. The upper classmen were always saying, "Hey, you're supposed to be a leader; you're supposed to be setting an example." That got old. Also, I think some of the upperclassmen resented me because I was older. I know it bothered them when they tried to give me a hard time. I looked at it as a game, a challenge that was fun. Some thought I was cocky. Actually, I was just trying to keep from laughing a lot of the time. My advice to kids who were like me in high school? Don't give up. Nobody respects a quitter. Everybody respects hard work and determination. Go for it. If I made it, you can make it.

FIRSTCLASSMAN, ONE WEEK BEFORE GRADUATION, 24 (ALMOST 25), PARACHUTING INSTRUCTOR. I had a 3.5 GPA in high school but I got out at 17 and had no desire to go to college. I enlisted in the Air Force just to kill some time. When I got in, I began to admire the officers I saw and thought that I would like to be one. I started applying for the Academy after I was in six months, but I didn't get accepted until I had served for three and a half years.

But they were good years. They sent me to the language school in Monterey, California. I spent a year learning Korean. Then they sent me to Korea where I had a good job and got the opportunity to master the language. I had a good time. I saw a lot of country. Bought some good stereo gear. Saved lots of money, too. They sent me to the Prep School first, which was good because I came into classes at the Academy really prepared.

"The Academy was a lot easier for me than for my younger classmates."

And I did well, although I did have some problems. It was tough taking orders from younger upperclassmen, but I adjusted to that okay. The hardest part was to get into the spirit missions—the pranks my classmates wanted to play—like painting numbers on the mountain. I remember one time I refused to go on a spirit mission and was criticized for it—but I was into running and I was scheduled for a marathon the next morning.

But I never did think about quitting. I got hooked on flying after they gave me a ride in a [Cessna]. And I liked parachuting so much they made me an instructor. I've made over 600 jumps. I'm going to instruct this summer, then I'm heading for the University of Washington where I won a scholarship in Asian Studies. After that I'm going to flight training.

My advice is not to come here right out of high school. Take some time off. Get a job and some real world experience, if you don't want to go into the Air Force and take your chances of getting into the Academy like I did. I definitely think the Academy was a lot easier for me than for my younger classmates.

One final bit of advice. Be realistic about your potential. For example do not expect to get into the Academy with SAT scores in the 400s or a 2.8 high school GPA, no matter how determined you are or how strong your leadership potential. However, do not let anybody discourage you if you truly believe that you have the potential to make it. The author has heard numerous stories of high school counselors, ALOs, and even Academy admissions officials discouraging young people who defied them all and got an appointment and graduated from the Academy.

So do not give up without a fight if the Air Force Academy is what you really want. And even though you might have to struggle to make it, just remember that almost everybody has sympathy for the underdog. Keep trying, for two or three years if you have to, and you might be surprised how many people may end up helping you.

Yes, the Academy wants cadets with academic ability and leadership potential. But they also want cadets with determination and guts.

So if the Air Force Academy is for you, give it all you have—and do not give up until you have become too old to apply.

HOW TO SURVIVE

FOURTEEN
The Rugged Doolie Year

Most candidates have heard about the first, or doolie, year at the Air Force Academy. If you are typical, you know that it is going to be a long, very difficult year.

While most cadets and graduates agree that you can never fully understand what it will be like until you are there, learning a little about what to expect, and how to deal with it, can lessen your stress levels a bit. So what is going to happen?

During BCT they are going to yell in your face. Loudly. You are going to be criticized more harshly than you can even imagine. And it will happen often, always in front of others, and for reasons that will seem trivial, or even nonsensical.[1] Of course, many candidates have heard all this before. Yet, they go there believing that it will not happen to them, that they can avoid the criticism if they perform well and at the best of their ability—that the criticism is for those who screw up, or for those who are not giving it their best effort.

Wrong. Wrong. Wrong. You will not be able to escape the criticism because you will rarely perform as well as the upperclassmen expect—even when you perform at the best of your ability, even when you are performing far better than you ever dreamed possible.

PUSHED TO YOUR LIMIT

They will take away your freedom. All of it: your cell phone, your civilian clothes, your watch, your contact with your friends and family, and your control over your life. You will have to do everything they tell you to do, when they tell you to do it, no matter how stupid or irrelevant or trivial the tasks seem. There will be no questioning their orders, and the only rationale you will receive is what they elect to give you. That will be very little, because they want you to get used to obeying orders that do not make sense.

They will place great physical demands upon you. You will exercise, and you will run, and you will stand in formation, and no matter what kind of athletic background you have, you will get very, very tired—so tired at times that your body will cry out for rest and sleep.

---

1. The former Vice Commandant put it this way, "When doing a book on entering the Academy, you have to be as accurate as you can be. If they are not prepared the first day when they get off the bus for someone in their face, they are going to be surprised and upset. They should be prepared for the in-the-face yelling; the very day they get here on the bus someone will be in their faces yelling at them."

The harsh criticism begins the minute you step off the bus.
Courtesy USAFA

Why? Because you will always be performing at your maximum potential. They will not let you run 6:30 miles if you are capable of doing them in 5:45. You will not stop at ten pullups if you can do twenty. In addition, you are doing all this at over seven thousand feet above sea level. Despite assurances from Academy officials that you will quickly adapt to the altitude, the cadets believe that the high altitude creates much more fatigue than they might experience otherwise.

The upperclassmen will require you to perform a host of tasks with incredible precision and detail. You will spend hours and hours shining shoes and preparing your uniforms. You will spend many more hours cleaning floors and mirrors and sinks and window runners—cleaning them so meticulously that they could pass inspection in the operating room of a hospital—and yet you will discover to your dismay that they still do not met the standards of the inspecting upperclassmen. On many Friday nights you and your roommates will stay up until two, three, or even four o'clock in the morning to get ready for a SAMI (Saturday

Morning Inspection)[2]—and during the inspection you will discover that your efforts were inadequate and the results unacceptable.

They will force you to memorize pages and pages of information. They will continue to pile on the work until your brain screams and your thoughts seem to be drowning. And just when you are on the verge of finally memorizing more than you ever dreamed possible, they will assault you with more information to be memorized.

You will be forced to do things that seem trivial. In the morning and at noon you will have to stand in the hall and be a "minute caller"—you will count down the minutes before formation and shout them with as much power as your lungs are capable so the upperclassmen can pace their routines without looking at the clock. At meals you will shout answers to a myriad of trivia questions dreamed up by upperclassmen at your table. And at various times throughout the week, you will undergo "training" sessions, which is a catch-all expression for a variety of military indoctrination exercises—much of which you, as a doolie, will interpret as meaningless upperclass harassment with lots of pushups.

And while you are undergoing all of this, you will lie on top of your bed at night (few doolies sleep under the covers because they do not want to sacrifice the time to make their beds in the morning) and think about home and your friends and how much fun they are having and how nice it would be to jump in your car and go to McDonalds or out for a pizza.

And then darker thoughts will creep into your mind—thoughts of that athletic scholarship you could have had at State, or of the girlfriend who may be texting a guy you dislike, or of your wild little brother eyeing the keys of your car. The blackness and gloom will descend upon you like a heavy blanket. And then one question will begin to crowd in on your thoughts, and soon it will dominate all others. It will keep coming back; over and over in an incessant voice you will hear yourself ask: Why am I here? Why am I here? Why am I here? Why am I here?

LIFE AS A DOOLIE

Once you have survived the challenges of BCT and started the academic year, you are not simply a college student trying to succeed in your classes, although that is certainly important. You will likely take five courses (15 semester hours) your first semester, and six the second. The classes will be challenging, including physics, calculus, chemistry, and computer science.

In addition to the course load, much more will be asked of you. You will get up around 6:00 a.m., shine your shoes, put your room into

---

2. *The frequency of SAMIs will depend upon the personal philosophy of your commandant. One might want them every Saturday; another might want them infrequently.*

inspection order, and study some of your doolie knowledge. You will likely march to breakfast—after upperclassmen look over your clothes and shoes for the smallest flaw and drill you on your knowledge.

Meals are eaten at attention, meaning your posture must be rigid and your eyes straight ahead. You will not be able to speak unless spoken to, and you will comply with strict rules for every procedure at the table, such as how to ask for the milk or where to put your drinking glass.

After repeating this same stressful situation at lunch, you may have military education. Then you will go to more academic classes, or to practice if you are an intercollegiate athlete. The afternoons are for intramural athletics and more military training. Finally, after dinner, you have study time. Then you collapse into bed and do it all again the next day.

Walking in the middle of the hall is a privilege reserved for upperclassmen.
Courtesy USAFA

Weekends can be a little more relaxed. But just a little. Weekends are labeled either Silver or Blue. During Silver Weekends, Friday night and Saturday are taken up with training, briefings, inspections, parades, and football games. On many Sunday evenings, you will take a knowledge test. If the doolies in your squadron perform poorly, you are all in for a long and difficult week.

Blue weekends, you will be happy to hear, are basically yours to do with as you would like. Can you put on your jeans and go catch a movie downtown? You will have to go out in uniform, if you are allowed to go out. Depending on your squadron's performance and policies, as well as your own accomplishments or difficulties, you will have passes you can use to go off base.

But the cadet who uses the weekend *just* to relax is usually the one struggling during the week. So most find a balance and use at least part of the weekends to get ahead on military training, working out, and studying.

Meanwhile, if you Facebook your friends from high school, you may find out they have their first classes at 10:00 and party all weekend long. They can decide for themselves what they do every minute of every day, what they wear, or if they will ever clean their dorm room. College, they say, is a blast. You just might question your decision to attend the Air Force Academy. You hear those voices again: Why am I here? Why am I here?

SURVIVING THE DARK DAYS

How do you survive the onslaught from those demons? When you hear them—and almost everybody does—you will be sliding downhill into a pit of despair. And you will know that there is a quick fix for your problems. You will know that the Academy has a gate that separates it from the civilian world. You will know that the light is brighter outside that gate—where the Golden Arches and the pizzas and the girlfriend or boyfriend and the car keys wait. You will be tempted by the urge to quit and go home, say the cadets who have gone through these periods of depression.

Is there a way out of the darkness without succumbing to the lure of the outside world?

Yes, say the cadets and graduates who have fought and won this battle. All you have to do is use the right weapons. Here are three of them, and the following chapters offer many more.

- ♦ **Remember Your Goal**

The first is something that you must possess when you arrive at the Academy: you must come with a clear goal. You must know exactly why you wanted to come to the Academy in the first place, and that purpose must mean more to you than anything else. When the voices in your head are saying to you, "Quit and go home and all the suffering will be over," their noise has to be drowned out by thoughts of what you want to achieve by staying: "I want to be an officer!" "I want to graduate!" "I want to serve my country!" "I want the Academy education!"

If you do not possess a clear goal, the cadets say you will lose the fight—you do not even have a chance of winning. Every cadet can tell stories of roommates and friends who lost the fight and went home; the cadets have seen the casualties and most of them wear scars from their own battles.

Remember your goal: to be sworn in as an Air Force officer at the end of four years.
Courtesy USAFA

♦ Reach for Help

The second weapon is something you *must* do. You must not try to survive by yourself. If you try to go it alone, say the cadets, you will lose. You must reach out to your roommates and friends and family. Your mom or dad may have just the right positive words to help you remember why you are there, or remind you that you are a smart, capable person who can succeed. When things are bleak, let those around you—your friends and roommates—help you pick your way through the troubled times.

And you will do the same for them when they are down. It is a mutual dependence that you and all your classmates must develop. That is how the system works. If you do not get discouraged, and if you do not have to lean on your roommates and friends for help, then the system has failed. And that rarely happens.

♦ Keep Your Perspective

The third weapon is special knowledge—knowledge that allows you to know why the system is the way it is, knowledge that enables you to understand why the upperclassmen treat you the way they do.

One of the main goals of the fourthclass system (the name for the system that creates misery for the doolies) is to expose the undesirable traits that many incoming cadets bring with them—traits that have to be eliminated or modified during the first year.

Many cadets who arrive at the Academy are too self-assured, or cocky. And why not? They graduated at the top of their classes, they were good high school leaders, they are intelligent, they are good athletes and great physical specimens, and for the past few years they have heard little else but compliments for all their fine qualities and achievements.

The goal of the fourthclass system is to strip away all the glitter from these high school heroes. The system must expose the doolies to a new environment where they have to start from scratch and prove themselves again. Nothing that the doolie achieved before is of any importance; there must be a new beginning. The doolies start out as nothing and they must earn new respect with determination, hard work, and sheer guts.

Another goal of the system is to build a new kind of self-confidence—one that is based upon solid achievements, and one that will hold up under the kinds of adversities that warfare can bring. Do not ever forget that you are being trained to become a U.S. military officer—a person who must assume the massive responsibility of protecting your fellow citizens against any enemy, and at the risk of your own life.

Think about that for awhile. You are not being trained to lead a sales force selling computers. You are not being trained to lead a company that manufactures bicycles or raises chickens. The Air Force Academy has a deadly serious mission; if you go there you will be trained to hold up in the chaos of war, and that requires a special kind of self-confidence, one that must be far more trustworthy than the confidence you gained in high school leading your football team or your student body.

They also want cadets to develop humility and a knowledge of their own limitations. So they must make sure that the doolies experience repeated failures. Humility seldom comes to those who have not suffered the frustrations of failure. And how can cadets ever know their limitations if they have not stretched their abilities until they have failed?

And why do the cadets need humility and a knowledge of their limitations? Because there is the danger that they might enter the Air Force with an arrogant attitude, and that would be a disaster. At best, such an officer would be an ineffective leader. At worst, that arrogance could cost lives.

You also must realize that the military is a demanding profession. And not just in wartime, either. During peacetime the military spends perhaps 90 percent of its time preparing for war and practicing whatever is necessary to win it. The demands on the individual officer can be very great. The workdays can stretch into seven-day weeks and thirty-day months. Under crushing fatigue and heavy responsibilities the officer must slog ahead to overcome stress and uncertainty, always performing as best he or she knows how.

PUSHED TO BE YOUR BEST

But how do you take young men and women out of high school, where they have seldom experienced any adversity or deprivation, and turn them into the kinds of officers who are ready for the demands of the military profession? The answer is that you put them into such a demanding environment where, if they survive, they will have to have developed the strengths needed for the profession.

So the officers and upperclassmen running the fourthclass system want the doolie year to be tough and demanding. They want you to experience hardships. They want you to know that you can function when you are extremely tired. They want you to experience failure so that you will have to pick yourself up and try again ... and again ... and again. They want you to push yourself further than you ever thought possible, to be better than you ever thought you could be. They want you to know your strengths and weaknesses very well.

When you are going through all of this, you must remember that it is nothing but a series of tests—tests designed to make sure that later, in combat, when everything is going to hell around you, that you stay and fight rather than run, and that you will stubbornly do your duty rather than give up and quit.

In short, they want every cadet to develop the traits of one of the Academy graduates for whom one of the two cadet dormitories was named: Captain Lance Sijan, a Medal of Honor winner who died in North Vietnam after being shot down and captured. His story is chronicled in the book *Into the Mouth of the Cat*, by Malcolm McConnell. The incredible tenacity that Lance Sijan displayed during his ordeal is a shining example of everything the Academy is trying to develop in the doolies. If you will read that book, you should never have any doubts about why they want to make that first year so rough for you.

If you are eager for a big challenge, and really and truly want to be pushed to be the best person you can be, the doolie year will make sense to you.

FIFTEEN
Survival Advice From The Doolies

Now it is time for the doolies to speak. Their comments were made in interviews conducted during Christmas vacations as well as during the school year—while they were still experiencing pain and while they were still practicing the survival techniques that are being passed on to you. Of all the chapters in this book, we recommend that you read and reread this one if you accept an appointment and are actually going to the Air Force Academy.

THE ONE THING YOU CONTROL IS YOUR OWN ATTITUDE

The first comment is from a doolie who did everything he could to prepare himself:

"I thought I was well prepared when I got there; I had visited the Academy, I had talked to a lot of cadets, I read your book, and my ALO told me everything that was going to happen. But it was still a shock when I got there because everything happens at once. I knew I was going to get yelled at and that I was going to be drained physically and that I was going to have to memorize a whole lot of stuff. But it was like I had put each of those things in separate compartments of my mind. What I wasn't prepared for was for all of those things to be happening at the same time. So I suffered under the pressure—not as much as the others, perhaps, but more than I thought I would.

"My advice—go there realizing that everything that they can do to you is going to be piled on all at the same time. That's the system. That's the way they teach you to handle pressure."

The same doolie talked about those around him who gave up and quit: "Once you screw up, everything snowballs. Then you're trying to catch up, and they're on you more, and then you start getting down on yourself. This happens to everyone but it gets to some more than others. I had this one friend who got behind on his knowledge. The upperclassmen saw that and started picking on him—which is the system. He kept trying but he got a mental block against the memorizing. He said he couldn't do it. Then he got down on himself and wanted to quit. We all talked to him and told him to keep trying but he gave up. It was sad. If he had kept trying, he would have made it. They wouldn't have kicked him out; all they wanted to see was a little improvement. In the next edition of your book definitely tell them that no matter how bad it seems, do not give up. Keep trying. Show just a little improvement. It is the attitude they're looking at. If you are really determined, they respect that."

Another doolie talked about the attitude he would advise incoming candidates to have when they arrive: "I would tell them to live just for the moment. You say to yourself, 'Just let me survive until breakfast; just let me make it till lunch; just let me make it through one more hour.'

Resolve to survive from meal to meal. *Courtesy USAFA*

"At the beginning you never look ahead, even one day. If you do, you will scare yourself and get depressed. It's like eating the elephant. Put your head down and take just one small bite at a time. Don't look at the elephant. You'll get discouraged if you look and see how big it is.

"But anybody can take anything for five minutes or ten minutes and that is how you have to think. Later, after a few weeks, you might look ahead an hour or two. Maybe during the first semester you can look ahead for even a day and, later, perhaps a week. But that's dangerous because it is so easy to be overwhelmed by it all." Many cadets echoed this idea: take it one day at a time, meal to meal, expecially during BCT.

Another cadet, whose father is a high school principal, added: "I was complaining in a telephone call to dad about how rough it was and he asked: 'Are they hurting you? Are you suffering any physical pain because of what they are doing?' I said, 'no!' Then he asked, 'What are you complaining about then? If you're not suffering physical pain, you can take anything else, can't you?'

"I had to agree. And, later, as I lay in bed thinking about it, I realized that I had something I could stick into my mind that would help me. And it did. When I thought things were getting bad, I kept saying to myself, 'It's not hurting, is it? You're not suffering any pain, are you?' That worked for me. I don't know if it would work for somebody else."

Your *attitude* as a doolie is what is most important. You have to have confidence in yourself and you have to want to fight back in your own way when they are getting on you. A female cadet tells how she did that:

"Unlike the others, I loved the training sessions where we would all be together with the upperclassmen giving us a hard time. When they asked me for something, I loved yelling it back at them just as loud as I could. It was a way for me to get all that resentment out of my system and to get rid of the frustrations. I made a game out of it; when they thought they were giving me a hard time, I used those times to get back at them—that's how I thought of it when they had me yelling knowledge. Also, when you're all together in group training, you develop a feeling of togetherness—they call it class unity. It is a good feeling. And afterward, we would talk about how ridiculous the upperclassmen looked when they were yelling at us. We would talk about anything like that that made us feel better.

"But even with the best of attitudes, you will find that there are some hard times. Before recognition [usually right before spring break] they have a tendency to gang up on you. They separate you out away from your friends and pile it on. But I knew that they were just trying to make me cry. My advice when that happens? Believe in yourself and don't let them destroy your self confidence. That's what they're trying to do. Just don't let them succeed."

COPING WITH CONSTANT CRITICISM

Taking criticism was what bothered most doolies. And even though they had visited the Academy and seen upperclassmen yelling at doolies, it was a whole different experience when it actually happened to them. And it will happen to you! No matter how hard you try, you cannot escape the criticism. How does one handle it? Here is what the doolies say.

Said one: "You can't take it personally, no matter what they say or do. This dude will come up to you and yell that you're a dirtbag, or that you don't belong in the Cadet Wing, or—this is the one that got to some of the girls—'you shouldn't have come here because you're never going to make it.' All the time they're yelling at you, you just have to look straight ahead and pretend that it isn't a person saying that, it is the system. You have to realize that they are just trying to test you, to see if you fluster, to see if you can control yourself. They have to do that. Would they want to turn a pilot lose with a 50-million dollar airplane and a load of nuclear weapons who flusters or loses his cool? It has to be that way."

An older cadet added, "Yeah, it was tough when this little runt of a woman three or four years younger than me starts yelling up at me saying that I am a poor example of a cadet, that I'm too cocky. Sure you're bothered for a few seconds but just look straight ahead and think how nice it's going to be sitting in the cockpit of that F-16. You do that and you almost forget about what she's saying."

Another cadet commented on taking criticism: "I got a lot of criticism. I smile a lot because that's my nature and they kept telling me that I'm too soft, that I'm never going to be tough enough to make it. I think they thought I was going to break down and cry. Maybe that's what they wanted me to do. But I fooled them. I'm here. Some of them still may think I'm not tough enough, but I made it. I survived and I'm going to keep on surviving."

You will get yelled at, probably every day. And you will have to learn how to cope with all that criticism.   *Courtesy USAFA*

Another cadet, whose father was an officer, said, while discussing upperclass treatment of doolies: "It helped me to keep repeating in my mind, 'The real Air Force is not like this; the real Air Force is not like this.' I knew that because I've been around it all my life. I was raised on Air Force bases.

"Some say that the upperclassmen treat you like that because they want to give you a taste of the military. That's not true. You won't find anything in the real Air Force like the treatment you get from upperclassmen. They treat you like grown men and women in the real Air Force. They have to. They need every trained person they've got. Can you imagine what a crew chief would do if a pilot bawled him out like an upperclassman does one of us? No way.

"So why do they do it here? Not to give us a taste of the military so we'll know what we're getting into. This is not the military. This is a test, period. It's a test to see if you're a quitter, if you give up easy, if you fluster easy, if you're the type who's going to give in and squeal on the others in a POW camp. I knew all that. I was expecting the things they did and they didn't bother me. In fact, sometimes my biggest problem was just to keep from laughing in their face. Some of them were not very good actors."

Said another cadet: "Yeah, but it is really hard to believe in yourself sometimes, especially after being at the top of everything in high school and then getting here and realizing that you are at the absolute bottom of the totem pole. After awhile they make you believe that you are the lowest thing on the earth. The doubts creep in; you can't help it. Believe me, it's a terrible feeling. You want to get out of it; you get tired of being at the bottom.

"What helped me the most was a saying that I was given before I left home. This guy told me: 'Remember when they are pushing your face into the dirt, keep looking up at the sky where you are going to be in a few years.' That's all he said, but I never forgot it. I want to fly more than anything, and whenever I got down, I always looked up at that blue sky and knew that it would be mine someday.

"I have wanted to go to the Academy since I was in the eighth grade, and I did everything that was recommended in order to prepare. The best thing I did was to go out for cross-country running. Someone recommended that as the best sport. I can't tell you how valuable that was for me. In cross-country running you have to gut it out every day. You run when you don't feel like it. You run when the weather is bad and when you are hurting. But in doing that you develop a mental toughness—a tough attitude—an attitude that causes you to keep going when you're suffering pain and your body is screaming for you to slow down and quit. You get here and no matter how bad it gets, you say to yourself, 'Hey, I've been through this before. I know it hurts, but you have run through the pain before and you can do it again.' I definitely recommend cross-country running to anyone thinking of coming here. If you can survive that sport in high school, you'll come here equipped with what it takes to survive here."

Another cadet added, "I was in super shape and the physical things didn't bother me. But there are things that happen that you just can't prepare for. Like not being able to call home for three weeks. That was the hardest thing for me, not talking to my parents and not talking to my girlfriend.

"The mental part was also tough. I'm not good at memorizing and in the pressure situations it got to me—I just couldn't perform the way they wanted. They began to get on me—you could see that they thought I was going to be a weak one. The pressure made it worse and then I got really scared. In the back of my mind I guess I believed that they wouldn't kick me out, but it is hard to believe that when they start talking to you seriously—they have a way of making things sound bigger than they really are. But I kept at it, and after the acceptance parade [after BCT when the doolies are accepted into the Cadet Wing] I realized that there wasn't a chance that they would have held me back.

"But no matter how well prepared you are, when they tell you you're going to fail, you're going to believe them after awhile—they have the ability to put you in such a state of mind."

One doolie advises, "Don't sweat the small stuff. It's not the end of the world if there's a scratch on your boot. Remember that feeling you had when you got accepted. When you're running the strips [doolies have to run everywhere they go, and stay on the marble strips that outline the central terrazzo area], just remember how much you wanted to be here."

Said another, "Don't get flustered. It isn't personal. They're gonna yell."

ATTENTION TO DETAIL

Many cadets learn to adapt to the criticism and the memorizing, but the hours and hours they have to spend on seemingly trivial chores in the squadron and in their rooms drags down their morale.

Said one cadet:

"The details are mind boggling. You start preparing for a SAMI Friday night by cleaning the squadron area. Then you go to your room and maybe by eleven or twelve you'll have the beds ready—I mean that's difficult, starching and ironing the corners so they are perfect, and ironing the cuffs of the sheets that fold over the blanket. But then you've got everything else. Everything in the closet has to be by reg [regulation], every button buttoned, every zipper zipped, the bottom of the closets dusted, shoes tied with bows just right with the ends of the laces inside the shoes, boots laced up all the way—of course, before that all the uniforms had to be ironed and the shoes and boots polished perfectly. Then it goes on and on. In the medicine cabinet all labels have to be facing outward, storage boxes have to be organized in descending order of size, the laundry bags have to be stuffed into two compartments just right, and empty laundry bags have to be on each valet with the U.S. symbol facing outward—and you have to iron that to make it look nice. And then there are the window runners; you dust them and five minutes later they are dusty again—so you keep after them as you go along.

"But then no matter how well you do, even by staying up till three or four o'clock in the morning, they can come in and always find something wrong. And they use those inspections to get on somebody who has been screwing up. There was this one guy in the squadron who had stolen some food and had done some other things that the upperclassmen knew about. During a SAMI they tore his room up three times—first the bed, then the closet, and, after each time, they told him he had an hour to get it in SAMI order. Of course all of us ran in there and fixed it up, but then they tore it up again and give him another hour to fix it. There were twenty-seven of us at that time and we were all trying to help him at first, but then some of the others gave up and they [the upperclassmen] got mad about that because we weren't showing class unity. Eventually they [the upperclassmen] got so mad they left him alone.

"After that I was beat, I was tired, I was sleepy, and I was behind in my classwork and needed to spend the weekend studying. That is when it begins to get to you and you start asking yourself why you are putting up with all of this, and do you really want to go through a whole year of this kind of crap. I was really down that day, but then a classmate came by and settled me down. We talked and we laughed about the way the upperclassmen had acted and I got over it. But you have to realize that these things are going to happen. In this particular case, the guy they were on kept getting into trouble and was brought up on an honor violation. He was found not guilty but was moved to another squadron and we all think he'll eventually punch out—he doesn't belong here. But because of him all of our lives were made miserable. Yet, that is what you have to expect if you come here. You have to put up with everything even if it isn't fair."

Another cadet commented on handling attention to detail: "That was the hardest thing when I came here—paying as much attention to detail as they wanted. In a way it was like trying to drink out of a fire hose—there was so much thrown at us at once. But I handled all the yelling and the physical part and the memorizing—what was hardest for me to accept was that the mirrors had to be perfect and the little corner on the bed had to be just so. What helped was the examples they gave us to show why we needed to pay attention to details. The one that stuck with me was the story of the jet pilot in North Vietnam who made a bomb run and as he was climbing out of the delivery pattern his fuel light came on. He checked his instruments and, believing he was out of fuel, punched out. Then, on his way down he remembered that he had forgotten to

The upperclassmen will ensure you pay close attention to the smallest details.
Courtesy USAFA

throw the auxiliary tank fuel switch—and he spent four or five years as a POW because of that. Some of the squadrons use examples like that to try and convince the doolies that little details are important—I know that one helped me."

IT'S HOW YOU PLAY THE GAME

Several of the cadets admitted, after questioning, that handling all the little details would have been easier if they would have accepted at the beginning that they would have to conform—if they had admitted that there was no way to escape doing things exactly the way the upperclassmen wanted them done. So the best advice for the candidate is to be ready at the very beginning to spend hours and hours in your room, learning to do things exactly as they are supposed to be done.

That early effort can pay off. Said one of the cadets: "When you get into the squadron the first time, work as hard as possible during the first weeks. If you give [the upperclassmen] the first impression that you are really good, they will have a tendency to leave you alone. I call it the 'halo effect.' If you bear down that first month and everything is good—you always know the knowledge from *Contrails* [the little book that you memorize from], you keep your uniform sharp—the upperclassmen will stay off your back. They will begin to lay off and this makes life a lot easier."

Many cadets look at the military training system as a game—a game with clear rules and consequences for violating those rules. Their advice is, "Play the game." Advised a doolie football player, "Enjoy your time at home; then when you get here, play the game. It's all about who you want to be, your personal goals." When pressed, they all acknowledge that the "game" has a serious purpose. As one cadet said, "Remember you're being paid to be here. It's a job. Your country deserves your best."

Many doolies advised keeping a low profile. Standing out, either for your abilities or your shortfalls, will get you extra attention, which is rarely a good thing. Said one, "Be a stealth cadet. Never be first; never be last."

DOOLIE SURVIVAL TIPS

But there are bad days, really bad days, say the cadets. How does one get through those?

- **Expect Bad Days**

A cadet comments: "You have to be ready for them. There will be a day when you get a bad grade on a test, and you are hassled at lunch, and you are tired but have to go to your intramural sport. You get back to the squadron, tired, but nobody has any compassion for that. You've got a big test the next day and you don't understand the material, and all you can think about is how much you would like to lie down and sleep.

"But they tell you when you get here that you have to 'suck it up' and that is what you have to do. You just keep going, but you have to be mentally ready for days like that. You have to expect them, and when you do, you'll get through them. If you want to. That's the key. You have to be ready for the bad days; you have to know that they ARE coming; and you have to have the desire to keep going."

And another, "Remember, there is always someone else who has it worse than you. In the end, it goes by quicker than you think."

Still another doolie shared the same thought: "If you keep going, you're going to get to the end, right? You can't think like the rabbit in the story; you have to think like the tortoise. Keep rumbling along. Grind, grind, grind, one hour at a time at first; then one day at a time. Then, after recognition, you look back and can't believe how fast the time went, or that you're here; you're out of it."

- **Remember to Laugh**

"But you can't do that," challenged another cadet, "without a sense of humor. In my opinion those who had the easiest time of it were those who could close the door of their room and laugh at themselves—really laugh.

"I felt sorry for some who took everything to heart, who just kept grinding along with a big long face, never laughing, never seeing anything funny. I think they suffered much more than those who had a sense of humor and who could laugh when they needed to.

Another cadet agreed but added: "Besides using my sense of humor, I did one other thing when things began to get bad. I always looked around to find the gorkiest looking upperclassman I could find. Then I would tell myself, 'Hey, if that one got through all this, I know I can.' Maybe that wasn't a nice thing to do, but it helped me."

One suggested, "Sing in the showers or while you're your cleaning your room. Find your happy place."

- **Lean on Others**

Countless cadets reflected that the strength of the bond they shared with their classmates was the number one factor in getting through the hard times.

One cadet reported thinking about quitting in BCT but ended up staying: "I wrote home and collected my thoughts, then decided to stick it out a little longer. The opportunities here are amazing compared to other schools. My support comes from my friends and my roommates. Going through it together makes you so close."

One of the discussions focused on the Joe Studs who came in with their class and one cadet, after remaining quiet for some time said:

"I was one of those you're talking about. I got good grades without working for them, captain of the football team and all that good stuff. But I also had enough sense to know there was trouble ahead and that I needed help.

"I asked for it and got plenty of it. I spent the whole year just learning how to study and I barely got by. But I made it and I think you should recommend what I did to others. These people here are dying to help you if they see that you have the desire to make it.

"The key to surviving is to admit your problem EARLY. Don't wait until you're going down under the water. Ask for help. Admit that you don't know how to study. The Joe Studs [who quit] were those who had too much pride to admit their faults. That's just my opinion, but I really believe that's why I'm here and they're gone. I wasn't afraid to admit that I needed help."

IT'S NOT *ALL* BAD

Up to now all you have read about are the bad things that happen to the doolies. Of course, surviving those bad things is essential. However, there is more to survival than that. You also have to keep reminding yourself of the positive things about the Academy.

Said one cadet: "You have to remember this and it will help. Keep thinking how nice it is to have all of your needs taken care of. You never have to give any thought about your food or your clothing or anything else that the regular college student has to worry about. You can concentrate 100 percent on just getting by each day, without any worries about the next day or the day after.

You will form strong bonds of friendship.

"And remember that they're paying you for doing this, and you're getting a great education, and all you have to do is bear down and get through one day after another. You have to think how good the system is and not how bad it is. The other stuff isn't important and it won't be if you keep it in perspective."

Many doolies talked about feeling like part of a team, about the strong bonds of friendship that formed very quickly—friends they can joke with and talk to when they are down. When doolies were asked why they came back from Christmas vacation, a common response was, "My best friends are here."

A soft-spoken cadet from Virginia said, "The one thing I would tell a friend is to always remember that no matter how bad it is, things are always going to get better. Each day that you survive just brings you that much closer to the end.

"And if you just keep going, nobody else is going to stop you. Nobody is going to hit you over the head and keep you from going on. So keep plugging away and things will get better, then before you realize it, you are out of it. And then you've got it made. You've got three years of college ahead of you, all paid for, then a guaranteed job when you get out. Besides, you're going to be a better person. I guarantee it."

One doolie remembered stopping by the B-52 bomber on display during Parents Weekend: "A ten-year-old boy saw me in my uniform. He came up to me and asked me to teach him how to salute. It was a real moment of pride. There's nothing more fulfilling than having someone say they want to be in your shoes." Another responded, "We're living the dream."

Many cadets interviewed emphasized that you should not study in your room all weekend or you will become too stressed out. They agreed with the cadet who said, "You have to do something [for fun] or you'll go crazy." Chapter 22 will discuss in more detail all the ways cadets unwind and have fun.

It is perhaps appropriate to close the chapter with an excerpt from a late-night letter written by a doolie to his parents during BCT. His words may predict how you will feel if you get there. He said:

> *Mom and Dad:*
> *I'm glad I expected this place to be worse than*
> *I expected it to be. Please excuse the poor writing.*
> *I'm in bed in the dark. The things expected of us*
> *get harder every second. The harder it gets the more*
> *I hate it, but I also like it more. That doesn't*
> *make any sense but life is a challenge now...*

SIXTEEN
Survival Advice From Upperclassmen

This chapter contains survival advice from people whose comments are especially valuable because they have seen the fourthclass system from two perspectives. First, they struggled through the system themselves when they were fourthclassmen, and, second, they have had one, two, or three years' experience "dishing it out." What advice do upperclassmen have for the doolies?

KEEP YOUR PERSPECTIVE

Said a thirdclassman: "One of the big problems I'm seeing this year is doolies blocking up. By that I mean that when we ask them to recite knowledge, they become so nervous, so overstressed, that their mind goes blank and they can't perform. I had this problem myself so maybe I'm a little more sensitive when I see them having problems. It's strictly a case of the system putting them under so much pressure that they block up.

"What those coming in here need to realize—and I'll admit that it took a long time for it to get through to me—is that we're doing all this for their own good. We have to teach them to perform under stress, and they have to learn it. That's the only way they can be trusted with responsibility when they become an officer, and especially if they go on to pilot training. Peak performance under pressure is the name of the game.

"I had a lot of trouble even though I played football and was used to having coaches yelling at me. But it was different in those halls; when they started yelling at me, my mind just blanked out. Finally I learned two things. First, I learned to ignore much of the yelling; I concentrated on letting the words go in one ear and out the other, keeping only what was useful.

A firstclassman commented: "Of course, the fourthclass year was difficult for me—that's the way it's meant to be—and I will say that it's a lot more enjoyable being at this place when you are an upperclassman.

"The hardest thing was the regimented life—being told what to do and when to do it. I wasn't used to being a conformist; I was used to being a leader in high school, making decisions on my own. Then suddenly, as a fourthclassman, I had to be like a robot—I couldn't make any decisions on my own. They were all made for me. Looking back at that fourthclass year, it was the day-to-day stuff that tended to get to me. But from this perspective [as a firstclassman] I realize that it was just a game that everyone has to play. What you have to realize [as a fourthclassman]—and I know it's hard to believe—is that those people who are yelling in your face are going to be your friends and teammates after graduation. And they will judge you by how well you stood up to the pressure.

"Also, it helps to understand the upperclassman's perspective. For example, if we have a fourthclassman who can't shine his shoes, doesn't know his knowledge, and can't discuss three current events, you worry about him. Do you want him as a maintenance officer on your airplane or as your wingman in combat? It really scares you as an upperclassman when you see incompetence. So you really get serious with cadets like that, and you worry that they are going to get through and get into the system.

"In the Air Force a lot of junior officers have heavy responsibilities—not only in flying, but in maintenance, in intelligence and other support fields. Often first lieutenants and junior captains are making decisions that can greatly affect the organization. If they are not willing or able to perform their jobs, I wouldn't want to be getting into my F-15 when somebody responsible for it is that kind of person. I wouldn't want to trust that person with my life. In the air, some of the procedures are intricate and very demanding—such as a refueling procedure when you have to hold a plane steady in turbulent weather outside a thunderstorm. And what if you had it in your mind that one of those persons [one of the two pilots in the refueling operation] had been at the Academy under you and you knew that person couldn't or wouldn't do their job. How would you feel in that situation? You know that your life would be in danger and that the performance of the whole mission might fail because of that person.

"What we are doing has applications that are deadly serious."

"We use these examples when we talk to fourthclassmen; we try to make them understand that what we are doing has applications that are deadly serious. We try to stress the long-range implications—that we as upperclassmen can get written up for not doing our job and that this would be bad for the squadron. But when we become officers, the repercussions, if we screw up, can be dead men and the inability of the Air Force to perform its mission."

REALIZE THAT YOU CANNOT BE PERFECT

The same firstclassman continued: "The second thing I learned was to admit that I can't be perfect all the time. It was hard but when I admitted that to myself, I started to accept myself. 'Let them yell at me all they want,' I said to myself. 'But I'll just do my best and I can't do anything more.' It all sounds simple the way I'm saying it. But I was like a lot of doolies I see now who have an immense amount of pride, who have always excelled, but are now facing situations where they not only don't perform well, they sometimes can't perform at all!

"My advice is this: Learn to do your best at all times, but realize that you can't do everything perfectly. There are simply too many demands. You have academics, which is more than enough all by itself. But then you have the military indoctrination and all the knowledge you have to memorize. On top of all that I had football and I came back to the squadron beat and tired and definitely in no mood to look forward to the training sessions and uniform grades. All these demands will break you if you persist in being a perfectionist. Don't even try it. As soon as you can, admit that you will give it your best shot but that what you do will never be enough."

Added a thirdclassman: "I see them [doolies] making a lot of the same mistakes I made—little things like not reading things at the right time, not falling in properly, having a bad uniform—and at the meal table not using any common sense, not thinking that we all want to get done with the meal and get out of there. "But the most important thing of all is to have a positive attitude—to really believe that what we're doing to you is all part of a game. Try to believe that we are coming down on you for your own good, that we don't hate you, that we're trying to make you into a better person.

A firstclassman put it this way: "We all know that people coming in here were doing what I was doing in high school—that they were captains of teams, presidents of classes and student bodies and all that. But from the fourthclassmen's perspective, when they are being yelled at and treated as if they know nothing, it's hard to believe that we know how good they are. What they have to realize is that we know they can do better than what they are doing, and that they can do more than they think they can do. And they are not going to find out any of that unless they're pushed to where they have to set new limits.

"Also, I was told by somebody before I went that I might get praise for something someday—something that I did a good job on. But I should always remember not to expect praise again for that same thing because it should then be a new standard for me—something that I should do routinely from then on. This was a good point, because it helped me see that the experiences weren't all bad—that I was going to be forced to grow and become a better person."

Another firstclassman said, "I'm the Wing Honor Chairman this year so I have a different perspective—I see the real problems that these cadets have.

"The problems are unique for the fourthclassmen, and what makes it difficult is that many of them have never been under real pressure before and they don't know what to expect. They don't come in here realizing that the first year is *meant* to be a pressure-cooker experience—that we design it to be that way. So what happens, it all hits them at once, then they start losing perspective on why they came here. They get so involved in the day-to-day and minute-to-minute things that they lose the big picture. There is a 'threat of the day' every day and they have to figure out how to get through the next hour. But while they're in that pressure cooker, they often feel like they are drowning—that they are going to go under. Under this stress they lose perspective and what they came here to accomplish slides into the background. We compound the problem by not giving them a lot of time to step back and think about why they came in the first place.

"If I could pass on any wisdom, it would be for them to make time to step back and take themselves out of the cooker long enough to ask themselves why they are here. If this happens to you, and if you can't answer for the right reasons, you're probably better off leaving because you're not going to be a benefit to the Air Force and the system will catch up with you eventually. In my own case, every time I stepped back to ask those questions, I knew I was going in the right direction."

COPING WITH STRESS

A thirdclassman: "I had a terrible time as a doolie, and even though I had wanted it [the Academy] badly, I was ready to punch out [quit] during BCT. What helped me, and what I recommend to candidates coming here, is to take advantage of your right to go to the chapel in the evening. Nobody can touch you or yell at you—it's like a haven. I remember the first time I went, I saw many classmates on the steps and it seemed gloomy at first. I remember a lot of the girls were crying, and some of the guys, too. But the chaplains were cracking jokes and trying to lighten the mood—they told us we looked like fuzzy tennis balls with our hair cut so short. Now, I can't imagine why anybody would want to go to their room and write letters; we went to the chapel every single night during BCT when we learned how valuable it was for us. Also, it's a great way to meet friends and to get away from the squadron and talk about your problems.

"And I would pass on this bit of advice. You can talk over your problems—that's one thing, but this is no place for whiners. Nobody wants to listen to whining—the kind of comments that say, 'Oh, poor me, they're picking on me and that's not fair.' Your classmates don't want to hear this and definitely the upperclassmen don't want to hear it. They told us when we got here that there is just one thing to do if

When times are hard, rely on your friends. *Courtesy USAFA*

you feel that you are being picked on, and that is to 'suck it up.' In other words, just take whatever comes your way and shut up about it. I will warn any candidate, if you really want to attract the attention of the upperclassmen, just start whining. I guarantee that you will get more attention than you want."

Another firstclassman recommended, "Get a buddy, or two, or three, or four. You'll miss home, and you'll have tough times. So you need to have someone to talk to when things start piling up. You need a release."

One firstclassman suggested, "Know what you like to do, and find opportunities to do it. There's flying, jump [parachuting], horses, falconry, athletic clubs, mock trial, the Drum and Bugle Corps, debate, language immersion—so many opportunities. So find what you love and go for it. Those are the good times that counteract the bad. Focus on the good times. If you focus on the bad, it'll weigh you down and you'll be miserable."

Yet another firstclassman: "I remember before I came here, I talked to as many people as I could—cadets, officers who had graduated, others who had gone for visits, even a couple of instructors. I tried to make a picture in my mind what I was going to have to do. When I got here, I found the picture I had created was different from what was here. They can tell you what it's about until they are blue in the face and it is never going to be like you think it is. There's just no way to explain to somebody what it feels like to get up at five in the morning, to be disoriented without a watch [they take away all watches and cover all clocks during BCT] and have to tell time by the meals. But you find a way to adapt and you discover little things that get you through it.

"What helped me was a daily journal that I kept, and the day-by-day little games I played inside my head. For example, when I got yelled at for having wrinkles in my shirt or for not having a good tuck in my shirt, I would look at the person yelling at me. If his shirt was wrinkled or he hadn't tucked his shirt in right since he was a freshman, I chalked up a point for me—that told me I was doing something right. On the other hand, if he was truly sharp and my uniform wasn't as good as his, I gave him a point. I actually kept track of points like that because by accumulating them I learned that I was better than they were saying I was. That was positive reinforcement for me at a time that I needed it.

"Another thing that helped was keeping in touch with my friends at home. When I started to get down, I found out what they were doing. They were working 37 hours a week at McDonalds; they hated their classes with lecture halls holding five hundred people and never with instructors available to them. Here my largest class ever was 25 and I always had the home phone numbers of my instructors and the privilege of calling them. That's when I realized that my circumstances weren't great but that they were a lot better than many of my friends. At least I haven't had to hold down a job while I've been here. And I've got a guaranteed job and security when I graduate; my friends don't have that.

Live day by day and keep the big picture in mind.

"Sure, I thought about quitting, like most people do at one time or another, but I sat down and weighed the things that were important to me—I wanted to be an officer, I wanted the security, I wanted a job that I could enjoy and that would be challenging. And I truly felt that I could make a difference and do something to change the bureaucracy of the Air Force and that I could contribute in a small way to the defense of the country. All this sounds heavy, I know, but those things were on my mind when I was considering quitting. And I'm glad now I made the decision to stay. Graduation is just ahead and I'm ready to go!"

The comments of another firstclassman, a Cadet Wing Commander [highest ranking cadet at the Academy], conclude the chapter:

"If you don't at least think about quitting, you're crazy because you're not supposed to enjoy it [the first year]. But when I'm counseling four degrees [doolies], I try to get them to focus on two things.

"First, they've got to see the meaning of the system they're in—they have to see the reasoning why they have to be treated the way they are.

Hopefully, when they do that, they will see that the purpose behind it is an honorable one; it is to make them into better cadets and better persons. If they can accept that, even when they don't understand some things, it will make their situation more bearable. Just have faith and believe that it's all worthwhile. As a fourthclassman, believe that you'll be much better for it if you can stick it out.

"The second thing they need is a sense of humor. If they have that, they can take whatever comes at them and turn it into a grain of salt—something they can laugh at later. The sense of humor is like an antidote to those who tend to take the criticism personally. And the key is what you do when you go back to your room. Do you sit on the bed and get down on yourself because you let the criticism get to you? Or do you joke and laugh about it with your roommates. In my opinion you have to do the latter; otherwise it will build up inside and then you'll have problems.

"I'm not ashamed to admit that I got down and depressed when I was a fourthclassman. The evenings were best because you knew that you got through another day. The mornings were the toughest because you had the whole day in front of you, and you knew that no matter how well prepared you were, that something could always happen—like one of your classmates could screw up and then you would end up in the hall getting trained. But you just have to live day-by-day; you have to crawl before you walk. You have to keep the big picture in mind and ask yourself over and over, 'Why am I here and why do I have to do this?' If you are here for the right reasons, you'll get through each day and that is one step closer to getting through it.

"You take it in stages. You get through BCT, then until Thanksgiving, then until Christmas, then spring break, and, looking back from my perspective, it's over quickly. Before you realize it, you're an upperclassman and you are better for it."

SEVENTEEN
Getting Along With Classmates And Roommates

If you are going to survive at the Air Force Academy, you must be a strong person—strong physically and strong mentally. Are you that kind of person?

Pat yourself on the back if you can answer in the affirmative. That, indeed, is good news for your candidacy.

But now you have to accept some bad news. People like you, who are strong physically and mentally, can have some problems at the Air Force Academy. Why? Because people who are strong also have a tendency to be independent, sometimes fiercely so. If you are such a person, you probably take pride in doing things on your own. You see asking for help as a sign of failure. Also, you probably resent those who are always telling you how to do things. Perhaps, too, you have a tendency to be a loner—a person who likes to do things without the company or help of others.

If the above traits describe you, the next question is: Can you modify your thinking and change your attitude?

A person who goes to the Air Force Academy and tries to retain his or her independence will eventually fail. The word "impossible" is a very strong word, but it is probably impossible to survive at the Air Force Academy if you insist on maintaining an independent attitude and behavior.

Here are three reasons why independent behavior is incompatible with the Air Force Academy.

First, the fourthclass system forces each cadet to obey orders promptly and without any questioning. If your independent nature causes you to obey orders reluctantly, or to hesitate, or to obey the orders in a way that attempts to circumvent them, your upperclass supervisors will come down on you with a vengeance. You must do exactly what you are told, when you are told, and to the absolute best of your ability. You will do that from the first day you arrive until the day you are recognized almost ten months later. Period. No exceptions. And later, both as an upperclass cadet and as an officer in the Air Force, you will follow orders, although not in the robot way of the doolie.

Second, every one of your basic freedoms will be taken away from you. This includes your freedom to say what you want, your freedom to go where you want, and, perhaps more significantly, your freedom to live and associate with whom you want. You will have absolutely nothing to say about this total loss of freedom. As the year goes by some of your freedoms will be returned to a limited degree, and they will be called privileges.

Third, the whole philosophy of the fourthclass system is to convert cadets from individuals into team players. So from hour one, day one, you will be judged constantly on how well you bury your individualistic, go-it-alone behavior and sacrifice your own needs and desires to the greater benefit of the teams to which you belong. The first of these teams is the roommate team, which, during your fourthclass year normally consists of three cadets. Other teams include your element, your flight, your squadron, your group, and the cadet wing—plus other groups such as clubs or athletic teams. In all cases you are taught by the fourthclass system that the needs of the team come first, and your individual needs come second—if at all. And woe to any fourthclassman who refuses to conform to that philosophy. To do otherwise, to persist in individualistic "selfish" behavior, is to invite all the wrath that the upperclassmen can bring down upon you.

The Academy will teach that teamwork is essential.   *Courtesy USAFA*

Why is this so important? In the Air Force, everyone depends on one another. The lead of a fighter formation counts on his wingmen to be there, protecting his (or her) flank. He expects the tanker to be there with his fuel. He expects the ground crew—the maintenance team, the fuels crew, the weapons loaders, everyone—to have done their job so his aircraft is safe and mission ready. The wingmen, in return, expect their flight lead to take them safely to and from the target, to keep them from running into a mountain or running out of fuel. If one of them has to eject from a disabled aircraft, another member of the formation will fly overhead to protect them and try to help with the rescue effort—leaving only when their own fuel runs out.

Everyone counts on one another in combat. If one person has trouble or makes a mistake, the entire unit is weaker because of it. So everyone watches out for one another, and everyone is responsible for one another. That is the attitude you are being taught at the Air Force Academy.

GET ALONG WITH YOUR ROOMMATES

Depending on your squadron, you may not have anything to say about who you room with. Since you will be held accountable for each other's mistakes, you *have* to learn to get along. If you work together, you can make life easier for all three of you. If you do not get along and cooperate, you will make a hard year even harder.

Said a thirdclassman: "You have to get along with your roommates, and this requires a certain amount of understanding because people come here from different parts of the country and with a lot of different attitudes and ideas.

"The most important thing in getting along with roommates is to keep a sense of humor. There are times to get serious, but there also times to look back and laugh about the troubles you've had—especially near the end of the semester when you get on edge because of finals and because you're looking forward to going home. That's the time when you're stressed out, and just a little something one of your roommates does may set you off—you're with them all the time and even little things can build up.

"But you can't let little things ruin the relationship. You have to work them out. It helps, of course, if you can develop a friendship with your roommates. But even if that is impossible, you have to get along with your roommate or you cannot survive; there's no way you can get through the freshman year by yourself.

"You have to help each other. When you get up in the morning, the room has to be cleaned. But you have to split up the different tasks—one takes the valet and sink, another picks up the rest of the room. If one guy is good at shining shoes, he shines the shoes of the other guys. If one is good at polishing or ironing, he will do that stuff.

"What's hard to realize at the beginning is that the upperclassmen hold you responsible for your roommates. For example, if two of us leave the room with good uniforms and the third roommate's uniform is not good, who do you think gets into trouble? Not the one with the bad uniform! The two with the good uniforms get into trouble because they have not done a good job looking out for the third roommate.

"And it's that way in all other things, like in room inspections. If a roommate has a bad bed and the others are good, the one with the bad bed is not blamed; the blame is put on the other two. This is how the system works. This is how they teach you to look out for each other. They're preparing you for when you are flying in combat—when looking out for each other makes the difference between life and death.

"Occasionally someone will get a real slob for a roommate—someone who is messy and won't do his share of the work. I saw that this year and I'll admit that it is very difficult on the other roommates. But if this happens to you, you just have to do your best to get along and hope that the upperclassmen see the problem. Most will—they know what's going on. They might stay on you for awhile, just to test you, but if the guy is really bad they'll get on him, too. If the problem looks like it is getting out of hand, the next step is to go to your element leader. If you have tried to do everything right, your element leader should listen to you and try to work with the guy. In the worst case you'll just have to do the best you can until the semester is over and you change roommates—and you can hope that the guy will quit, which is what usually happens with those who won't pull their weight."

Roommates are taught to look out for each other.

Another fourthclassman recommended this approach, "I think it kind of starts with yourself. We all have little things about ourselves that probably other people don't like. Focus on yourself and ask your roommate what you can do better. Along with telling them what you think they should fix, ask what you can fix. By taking responsibility yourself, that is the first way to solve the problem. That is the way it starts."

His classmate added, "Fighting with your roommate is just going to get you more spiteful. Be smart and calm. It's all about finding a middle ground and being reasonable."

As with everything at the Academy, the right attitude is key:

"Most important for a roommate is a good attitude—an attitude where you want to cooperate, where you want to do the best you can, an attitude where you don't care if you have to do more than your roommates. If you're lucky to have roommates with a good attitude, then you work like a team. In the morning the valet has to be cleaned, the mirror polished, the window runners cleaned and the whole room dusted. Normally we divide up the chores and it all gets done rapidly. However, if I have a test [coming up] and need a few minutes of study, the others will do the work and not think anything about it. They know that I'll do something to help them."

"It really helps if you have a roommate you can talk with, but if you don't, there's another solution. You make friends in different squadrons.

You can't go into another squadron, but on my computer I can put a message out over the net that I'm going to the library or that I'm ice skating at four o'clock and anybody who wants to come is welcome. Your friends see that and they'll come. Then you can talk over problems."

Said another fourthclassman: "Advice on getting along with roommates? Don't argue—that's the main thing. Even if you think you're right, don't argue. Forget about the differences and concentrate on what you have to do together to get things done. Give and take. All the time. Even if one of them does something you don't like, tell him once, but don't harp on it."

WORK TOGETHER

You will learn to work with and rely on your roommates, but you will come to identify most closely with your classmates—especially the 25 or so doolies in your own squadron. You will be tested, stressed, evaluated, and granted privileges as a group. The more you work together, the more you will succeed.

Said a thirdclassman: "My advice to fourthclassmen is to stick with your classmates and don't even try to get friendly with the thirdclassmen—I mean, don't try to get on their good side. Everybody sees that [your classmates and the upperclassmen] and you'll get in trouble on both sides. Your classmates will resent you and the thirdclassmen will think you're pimping.

The more you work together, the more you will succeed.

"Pimping is a term we use here for those who try to get ahead by showing up their classmates. If you get to formation before your roommate, for example, you get criticized; we say that you tried to pimp your roommate over—you tried to make yourself look good at his expense.

"I remember when I got accused of that. When we first got here and were in BCT, the upperclassmen came around to the rooms in the morning yelling that we were late. That bothered me and I kept wondering why they didn't wake us up earlier if we were always late—I know now that it's just a strategy to put the basics under pressure. But back then I was bothered, so I decided I was going to wake up early and get into the hall as fast as I could. What a mistake! They really jumped on me! I was pimping my classmates; I was trying to look good at their expense.

"What they want is for you to cooperate at all times. Like when an upperclassman addresses a fourthclassman, that fourthclassman has to stand up. But if you are nearby, you should stand up, too. You do that even if it means that you are going to get trained [yelled at]. You do it to show your classmate that you are with him.

"Here's a story that illustrates what I mean. In BCT there were two in my squadron who were putting on their blues [dress uniform] for an inspection. But they didn't know where to put their name tags, so they put them on their left side [they belong on the right side]. When they got to formation, the upperclassmen started laughing hysterically. Then the two got yelled at, but they were also commended for being identical, which meant that they were working together."

A fourthclassman comments on the problems of dealing with pimping: "It was really hard for me to walk the line between supporting my classmates and pimping them. I know now that if I see any of my classmates in the hall getting trained [yelled at], I should go out there and join them to show my support. That's easy. But what happens when the one standing next to you forgets a line that he is supposed to have memorized? I can prompt him—that is help. But if I go on and recite the rest of the stuff, that would be a pimp.

"Another example: Suppose a guy next to me is asked to name the Chief of Staff of the Air Force and he doesn't know the name. If I just spout it off—'Sir, the answer is...' that's a pimp. But if the thirdclassman asks me if I know the answer, I have to say 'yes.' To say otherwise would be lying and that would be an honor violation."

A fourthclassman describes another type of cooperation: "We did really well on our SAMIs—we were first in the group. But we did it by splitting up the work. There were thirty-three freshmen in the squadron. First, we worked together to clean the common use areas—the television room, restrooms, etc. Then we divided up into specialties. Some who were good at beds went around to all our rooms and made them. Others did valets and mirrors, some shined shoes, and some even specialized on the window runners, which are always dusty—to clean them you have to use cue-tips.

"I remember the first SAMI—we were up till 5:30 in the morning—but we were doing them individually. Later, when we got organized and started dividing up the work, we got to bed by midnight. I don't think any other squadrons were able to do that."

When you learn to cooperate effectively, three things happen. First, the thousands of tasks you have will get easier, take less time, and be done better. Perhaps more importantly, because you are performing well and performing as a team, the upperclassmen will be happy. And when the upperclassmen are happy, your life is much better. And finally, when you are not focused on yourself, you are not focused on your troubles.

As you give up your individualism and independence, you will

The bonds forged through shared experiences will last a lifetime. Courtesy USAFA

discover the rewards of close relationships formed through shared experiences, very challenging experiences. So this chapter concludes on a positive note, with a fourthclassman's thoughts about the value of the friendships forged at the Academy—words that were repeated with slight variations again and again in interviews: "I have thought about leaving a couple of times. The first year is always rough; you're away from home and stuff. What keeps me around is friends. You have your best friends here. That's what makes it a good experience."

EIGHTEEN
Academic Survival

All the preceding chapters on survival have dealt with the problems of surviving the military training at the Academy. There is a good reason for that. The military training is vastly different from anything candidates have experienced before. And it is very difficult—so difficult that cadets, regardless of their ability, are stretched to the limits of their physical and emotional strength.

But there is an important thing for you to keep in mind, and it was best said by a thirdclassman: "They won't kick you out of here if your shoes aren't shined right, but they'll sure kick you out if you screw up the academics."

Academics? Are they going to be a problem for me? Surely not. After all, I scored 1400 on the SAT and had a 3.9 grade point average in high school. And I've had a year of calculus and a course in computer programming and I know I'm pretty smart. Sure, I'll have to study more than in high school. But I'm ready for that. So what's the big deal?

Does this sound like the thoughts in your own mind right now?

If so, you may be in for a shock, as were many of the cadets whose comments you have already read. No matter how good you think you are, you are probably going to have some struggles with academics, and perhaps even end up on academic probation.

But it should be far more convincing for you to read more about what cadets say about the kinds of academic problems you will encounter. They have been over the hurdles and they have suffered the shock—and they have survived. They also have great 20-20 hindsight; they can tell you what they <u>wish</u> they had done from the start, if only they had not been so assured by their own high GPAs and SAT scores.

<u>NOBODY</u> CAN DO IT ALL

The first cadet to speak was one who was an excellent student in a very good high school, very highly motivated (she had a rope in her back yard that she climbed to develop her upper body strength), and probably went into the Academy with as much knowledge as any candidate. When she was interviewed during Christmas vacation of her first year, this is what she said about the academic challenge of the Academy:

"The academics were a lot harder than I thought they would be. I thought I would have more study time. The first couple of months I tried to do everything, and I was getting about four hours sleep at night. That didn't work.

"Yes, I was told by everyone that I couldn't do everything. [And she had read an earlier edition of this book!] I knew it in my mind but I didn't believe it. I still tried to do everything—I tried to have a great uniform, learn all my knowledge, and do well academically. But then everything seemed to cave in on me. I got stressed out and really tired, then I fell asleep during a calculus Graded Review; the night before that my computer ate a paper I had written and I only got forty-five minutes sleep. As a result, I ended up on academic probation.

"That was very humiliating, but it caused me to admit what I should have known all along: you can't burn the candle at both ends; you have to make compromises with what you can and cannot do. You have to prioritize and do the things that are most important at the time, and let the other things go. What you don't get done, you don't get done. And you have to get your sleep. Tell everyone that: get your sleep!"

You have to prioritize and do the things that are most important.

Everyone, no matter how much of a superstar they were in high school, has to learn to prioritize their tasks. One graduate who became a Rhodes Scholar and is now a general put it this way, "No individual class or demand is that hard. It's all of it together that makes the Academy so hard. 'Living the brochure' is really hard to do."

IN CASE YOU MISSED IT: IT'S ALL ABOUT TIME MANAGEMENT

A thirdclassman said, "Time was my biggest problem. You don't have as much as you need and there are so many other things that can suck it up.

"In high school I didn't study much; I went to class, listened and got by with good grades. Don't even think about doing that here. You have to put your time in.

"Here I ended up in the most difficult courses because I tested well. I was in top-level chemistry, calculus and English. I was also playing freshman football, which took a lot of time. I found out that I couldn't keep up with everything and ended up with C's. That really hurt.

"What I learned was to become more efficient. I made a time budget and each night, during study hours, I went down the list and did the things that were most important.

Said a fourthclassman: "I had a really good background. I went to an excellent high school, then the Valley Forge Academy for a year, then a junior college for a year. I thought my study habits were in place when I got here, but I experienced academic shock just like the others.

"Mostly it was because I didn't know how to use my time efficiently.

The Academy knows that is going to be a problem so they spend time with us trying to teach time management—how to make a time budget and follow it.

"I really didn't pay as much attention to them as I should have. I thought, 'Oh, I've been through a lot of [academic] pressure; I know what I'm doing.'

"I had to learn the hard way, and from those experiences here is what I would recommend. First, I would recommend to anybody coming here: do not try to study in your room. I haven't seen many squadrons that are quiet—there are always interruptions, noise in the hall, your roommate wanting to talk, or somebody coming by the room to see me or one of them [roommates]. My advice is to start from the beginning and go to the library, or better, an empty classroom in Fairchild Hall. There you won't get the interruptions. In my opinion the squadron is a terrible place to study.[1]

Time management is not just about how you use your time, but also where. While some cadets preach the advantages of going to the library during your free periods or in the evenings, beware: the library is a place for fourthclassmen to socialize, especially on the main floor, since they are not allowed to visit other squadrons. Advised one doolie, "The higher up you go, the quieter it is." So if you have a limited time to get a lot of work done and you go to the library, do not get sucked into a gripe session with your classmates. Find a place that lets you do some real studying.

If procrastination is one of your main time management issues, you may have trouble at the Academy. "You get a lot of big projects that take a lot of time—there are a lot of papers and computer programs to write. Don't put them off. You can't wait and do them the night before they are due. If you have a paper due, start that sucker early. You really have to get serious about that. That's the biggest shock of all for those who breezed through high school, getting A's and doing papers the night before they were due. It is not the same—trust the people giving you the briefings [those who try to teach time management at the beginning of the year]. What study time you have is so valuable you need to account for every minute of it."

Many cadets and professors spoke of the need to account for adequate sleep in their time budget. They noted that class time is wasted time if you are too sleepy to pay attention, and wasted time is lethal for a cadet. As one firstclassman succinctly stated, "Sleep at night, not in class."

---

1. *Some squadrons crack down on noise and their halls are patrolled to keep them quiet.*

USE YOUR WEEKENDS WISELY

One cadet recalled, "I also did something that I hated at first. I started working on the weekends. That first year it was a bummer—I couldn't go skiing, couldn't go to my sponsor's house as much as I wanted. It was a real drag.

"But it did allow me to catch up. And it gave me time to work on papers and get them done ahead of time. Now that I'm used to it, I don't mind so much—in fact, it's kind of relaxing to know that I'm not going to get behind. This year I work about every other weekend and it's nice to know that I can spend the whole Saturday in the library."

A football player, a fourthclassman, said: "My study habits are drastically different than when I was in high school. I get back from football about seven-fifteen and I work till eleven—I really have to apply myself because I have military study in addition to the academics and because of football practice. I don't have the extra time other people have.

"Now I'm getting used to studying on weekends. I used to think horribly of it at first; I used to think it would take away what little freedom I had. Now it's a necessity and putting in an extra seven hours on the weekend is no big deal any more. I'm getting used to it and it becomes second nature after awhile.

"I use six or seven hours on Saturday, sleep in on Sunday, go to Arnold Hall and watch a football game during the afternoon, then go back and start studying again. Sometimes a lot of Saturday is taken up by training so I have to spend more time on Sunday. But that isn't so bad. It's all a matter of getting used to it."

A doolie agreed: "Be ready to give up some of your weekends. That's hard to accept, I know—it was hard for me. But just think about it this way: you have to sacrifice a lot that first year, so just consider the weekends as a part of that sacrifice. I didn't give up all mine—I still managed to go skiing a few times and to my sponsor's house. But if you're serious, you do what you have to do."

A math professor agreed that weekends are very important: "The temptation for cadets is to treat weekends as their own, not accepting the fact that the time available to study during the week is completely inadequate to master the material. Rather than 'vegging out' the entire time, the smart cadet will take one day to relax—duties permitting—and use the other day to either catch up, or even better, get a little ahead by prereading the next week's material. There is nothing more relaxing than being truly prepared for class.

GOOD STUDY SKILLS ARE ESSENTIAL

Said a thirdclassman: "Academics were a big shock for me because

I came from a small high school. But the Academy looks out for that—they put me in beginning-level math and science, which made it easier because the pace was slower. I was underloaded with five rather than six classes the first year and that really helped.[2] But the disadvantage is that now I'm overloaded with seven classes—and the courses are more difficult this year.

"Basically, I learned to study all over again last year. In our high school the teachers taught the tests—they were verbatim what they had said in class. Here, they expect you to cover the assignment. They may go over part of it in class, but not all.

"Also, here you can't blend into the woodwork. All my classes have been very interactive. You're expected to participate; you're asked for opinions or for answers to questions. With such small classes it is very difficult to go in unprepared without them knowing that.

"The best advice I can give is to take notes intelligently. The teachers are going to foot-stomp on certain things they want to emphasize. You know when they do that, you're going to see it again. So make sure to mark those things in your notes and make sure you understand them when the test comes around.

Here, you are expected to participate in class.

"You have to take good notes if you want to have something to study for the GR's. They'll use a lot of examples when they discuss a concept and you'll have a tendency to listen to them and not take notes. That's a mistake. Jot down a few words of the examples—enough so that you know what they are—because later, on the GR, you'll be asked, 'This is an example of such and such,' and you have to make the choice.

"The hardest thing about taking notes is to pay attention when you're dying for sleep. It's really tough as a freshman because you have all these things you have to do so you stay up all hours and don't get enough sleep. Then, when you get to class, you start nodding off halfway through it, and you don't pay attention. That really hurts you. My advice is to get as much sleep as you can so you can stay awake in class. The professors highly encourage you to stand up and walk around when you're sleepy—they'll tell you that the first day of class. You'll have to do that if you want to stay awake.

"In theory we were supposed to have the time from eight o'clock until eleven o'clock for Academic Call to Quarters—study time [it is

---

2. *Cadets who are identified as academically at risk, based on grades, SAT scores, and other factors, are given a reduced load their first year. Eventually, they have to catch up, either by taking classes over the summer or overloading during later semesters.*

now seven to eleven]. But what happened was that the class reps would use that time to get stuff organized for the freshman. You spend a lot of time on a lot of different stuff—posters for football games, organization of spirit missions, etc. Also, that is the time others can find you for military things. Then there is the noise, which varies from squadron to squadron. I recommend that you go to the library to study—although not so much because of the noise, but because you won't get interrupted like you will in your room. In the squadron you always have friends dropping by, and to be honest, you look for it because talking with them is a pleasant form of relaxation. But it is a trap because you can blow a whole lot of study time.

"This past year I started going to Fairchild Hall [the academic building] to one of the empty classrooms. Sometimes a friend joins me and we start writing things on the board, which is a good way to study with somebody else. If something stumps you, the other one may understand it.

"But when you're in one of those classrooms, it is easy to lose track of time. And there will be times when you are very tired and need to lay your head down and rest. You say to yourself, 'I'm only going to lay my head down for ten minutes.' But that can turn into an hour. An alarm clock on your wrist is helpful because you can easily sleep through the deadline for getting back to your room.

Some very bright cadets have trouble managing their time.

One of the professors (a graduate) who tutors cadets with academic problems and helps them develop good study techniques had some other specific recommendations:

"I believe strongly in outlining, and I actually force all the cadets I work with to do that for assignments in subjects like psychology, chemistry and history. After they do that, they can then go to class and really pay attention to what the professor is saying—without having to work so hard taking notes. Then, when the professor emphasizes something, the student can highlight that material in the outline—or he can write notes along the side. It may be trivial but I want them working in loose-leaf notebooks so they can add material that might not be in the outline.

"By having the outline in class it eliminates the frantic effort to keep up. Also, when students are concentrating so hard on taking notes, they can't take the time to evaluate what the professor is saying—they can't really think about the material and decide what is most important. With the outline in front of them, they have the luxury of time when they are in their classes.

"And if they are worried that outlining is going to take too much time, they have to realize that the time has to be spent one way or another, but that time spent concentrating in class pays off much better than the time spent in the squadron.

"I also insist that they make a time budget using three colored pens: a black pen for blocks of study time that are mandatory; a red pen for blocks of time for more casual study—like required reading; and a green pen for free time. The latter is very important; every hour should be broken up with green time so they have a reward to look forward to and so they can get up and move around and start back more refreshed. Along with this, we require them to set their alarms so they have the clock ticking in front of them. That way they are not as likely to start daydreaming. [Another professor listening to these comments added: "I tell them to clean off their desks and put away their pictures of girlfriend and family so they won't be tempted to daydream."]

"Lastly, I recommend that if they have any trouble studying in their squadron, they should go to the sixth floor of the library where they are least likely to be disturbed. One interruption, when they are concentrating on a subject, can cause them to lose 15 or 20 minutes, which is a time loss they can ill afford."

The Deputy Head of the Math Department added, "I serve on the Freshman Academic Review Committee[3] as well as teach lots of math courses. On the committee, I get a chance to see what our poorest performing cadets are like, because we interview those that, based on their performance, warrant being academically disenrolled. I've seen very bright cadets with solid SAT and ACT scores who never figure out how to manage time or put out consistent effort. Students come to us with fall semester GPA's under 1.00!

"If there were two things I'd tell every cadet candidate, I'd say:

(1) While still in high school and you have the chance, practice being organized and getting every written assignment in a day or two early. Work every homework problem in the book! I don't care what you learned in AP calculus or high school calculus—most people need two serious exposures before it really sinks in. And even if you did these things, don't assume you can coast, because you develop dangerous habits that WILL get you the second semester.[4] (2) Every cadet day is 16

---

3. *The Academic Review Committee reviews the records of academically deficient cadets and recommends whether they be allowed to stay at the Academy.*

4. *The Academy's core curriculum is designed to be cumulative, so professors will hold cadets accountable for material they learned in earlier classes, even from different subjects. For example, engineering professors know what cadets were taught in calculus, and expect them to be able to remember and apply that knowledge.*

hours long and as much as 15 of them are filled with either academics, athletics, or military training. By far, it is academics that cause people to be disenrolled from here. If you get behind, your chances of catching up are small."

Realize that studying at the Academy will be different than studying in high school. It will take longer, and require more thought, practice, and preparation. A quick review of the highlights will not be sufficient. You will have to focus on learning the concepts, rather than just getting the right answer for the homework.

TAKE ADVANTAGE OF THE EXTRA HELP

A firstclassman recommended taking advantage of the study skills classes: "I took the reading class. I used to try to absorb everything I read. I couldn't do it all."

Another firstclassman also credits the study skills program for her

Academy professors will do all they can to help you.   *Courtesy USAFA*

academic survival: "I got counseling from study skills [the Student Academic Services Center]. They helped me learn how to study, how to be efficient. For example, now I stay in Fairchild Hall to study between classes." This saves the time spent walking back to the dorm, and prevents the distractions that are common in the squadrons.

One fourthclassman who plays intercollegiate tennis said, "EI (Extra Instruction) is a major factor. It's how I survived the fall semester. I went to school about three days a week because of traveling with the team. So I got EI if I missed a class. They told me what I missed and what was important."

Several cadets pointed out that the professors will do all they can to help. Many hand out their home phone numbers so you can call them late at night if you get stuck on an assignment, and all are required to be available for Extra Instruction during the day. Most will work with cadets via e-mail as well, answering questions or providing feedback on advanced drafts of papers.

Many cadets resist asking for help. The Dean of Faculty, who was on the track team as a cadet, said "Learning to ask for help when you need it is a different mindset for most cadets. It's seen as a sign of weakness. I was the same way, until someone told me, 'Go get EI.'"

A firstclassman offered that same recommendation: "Everyone said, 'Get EI,' but I never took it seriously until now. Whenever you don't get something, especially at the beginning of the semester, go in for EI. It's not a sign of failure. The teachers are here for you; they want you to learn. Just e-mail your instructor and go in for EI."

Some cadets wait too long to ask for help because they think that next lesson, next week, next chapter, it will all begin to make sense. But the opposite is true. Next chapter may build on the current one, and as soon as you have a gap in your understanding, you start to fall helplessly and hopelessly behind. Asking for help before you get in this type of bind is essential.

You can get academic help from a number of other sources as well. For example, the Quantitative Reasoning Center and Writing Center have professional tutors from all the applicable subjects. These are experts who specialize in getting you over the rough spots.

A doolie suggested you also take advantage of the upperclassmen's knowledge and experience. "The majority are on your side. They're especially willing to help with the subject they're majoring in. And your squadron Academic Officer has a list of people who can help you."

The comments of a firstclassman, who was an outstanding student, summarize this chapter:

"I had a different background; I was prior enlisted so I had an edge because of my maturity. Also, I knew what I wanted and I worked as hard as I could. What I learned might help those coming in here as freshmen.

"When I first got here, I was baffled as to how I could do all the work that they assigned. I always had more than I could handle, so I stayed up till one or two o'clock every night and knocked myself out studying. I got a 3.14 the first semester but the grind was killing me. I knew I had to find an easier way or I wasn't going to last. That is when I decided no matter what I have left to do, I am going to bed at taps—at eleven o'clock. I made up my mind I was never going to stay up after that—it wasn't worth falling asleep in class.

"The second semester I had to prioritize every night. I did that and made decisions like, 'I can only study three [assignments] for tomorrow; I'll have to catch up on the rest this weekend.' That semester I ended up with a 3.6 average—all A's and B's instead of one A. What I found was that by getting the proper amount of sleep I was able to stay more alert in class. So I learned more there and didn't have to spend as much time studying what I could learn in class.

"The weekends were my savior—I used them to catch up on everything I missed during the week. I also used them to work ahead on projects, which set me apart from my classmates—who always wanted to wait until the last night before things were due. To me this is the real key to surviving [academically]. My friends are up until three in the morning trying to do papers, but they're so tired they do a bad job. I get A's on all my papers because I turn in rough drafts as much as a month and a half ahead of time. Once when I did that, a professor said, 'If you will do the final draft of this paper and do this and that, I'll give you a 100 percent score. So, by working ahead, I was able to do excellent work and had no worries, while at the same time my friends were working and worrying right up to the last minute.

> **Use the weekends to get ahead.**

"Besides starting on projects early, I strongly recommend that you learn how to prioritize. They [the professors] know that you are being given the fire hose of education—that a whole lot is being thrown at you in a short time. They know you have to kiss off some assignments. What each student has to learn is what you can blow off and what you can't blow off.

"My final bit of advice is for those who slip out of the squadron and go study in the library or Fairchild Hall. It's okay to do that. In fact, it may be better to do that, depending upon the squadron. But, be aware of the fact that you can get a bad reputation with your classmates or the upperclassmen if there are things going on where your help is needed. My advice is to carry your fair share of the [military] load and don't get the reputation of being a stealth cadet or a blowoff. You might get ahead academically, but you'll pay too high a price."

NINETEEN
Reach Out For Help

"You can't do it alone."
"You can't do it alone."
"You can't do it alone."

The doolies hear that statement over and over, mainly from the upperclassmen whose goal is to encourage teamwork that will get the doolies over the endless hurdles that are put before them during the first year.

The Academy goal is broader than that. It is to develop a team mentality in every cadet—and eliminate lone-wolf tendencies that cadets might have brought from their civilian lives.

But there is another reason to convince yourself that you cannot do it alone. It is so you will reach out and use the helping hands that are a part of the Academy support system, and have the best chance for *success*.

If you have read the preceding chapters, you have seen repeated advice about getting extra help from your instructors if you are having academic difficulties. But whom do you go to for help with everything else, such as getting through a bad week in your squadron, homesickness, or everyday stress? The following are some of the resources available to you.

THE SPONSOR PROGRAM

The sponsor program is one very important part of that support system. It is administered by the Academy and was warmly praised by almost everyone who was interviewed for this book.

The heart and soul of the sponsor program is the network of more than 1,800 families in the Colorado Springs area who volunteer to become sponsors. Such families open up their homes for one or more cadets to use whenever they have free time and can get away from the Academy.

In many cases the sponsor's home becomes a home away from home for the cadet. The husband and wife often become surrogate parents. If there are children in the family, they may become like younger brothers and sisters.

Many times a very close relationship develops between the sponsor and the cadet. For example, it is not unusual for a cadet to carry a house key, have refrigerator privileges, and enjoy the use of the sponsor's car. Most sponsors can't do enough for their cadets. According to the staff member who administers the program, one family that already sponsors

10 cadets called asking for more. They installed a hot tub, just to give their cadets another place to relax.

The close relationship between sponsor and cadet often extends to the cadet's parents. Many parents learn to call the sponsor if they have not heard from the cadet for awhile. Some parents stay with the sponsoring family while they are visiting the cadet.

And many of these relationships are enjoyed for years after the cadet leaves Colorado Springs. Sponsors often attend weddings, cheer when promotions come along, and thrill to birth announcements as enthusiastically as grandparents.

Then there was this story: A handsome lady, known to be an octogenarian, was observed at a recent graduation exercise and was asked, "Are you the sponsor for one of the cadets?" The lady smiled and replied, proudly, "Yes, and I sponsored his father when he was here, too!"

So the advice from practically everyone who has had anything to do with the Air Force Academy is to get a good sponsor as soon as you can during your first year.

The cadet's first experience with a sponsor-type relationship is the doolie dining out visit, which occurs during Basic Cadet Training. Sometime during BCT, basic cadets get most of the day to spend with a family, eat dinner, call home, and relax. However, the family the cadet joins on that weekend may not become the ultimate sponsor because some families take on more doolies for that day than they can ultimately handle on a long-term basis.

A good sponsor can be imensely helpful. *Courtesy Klenk Family*

Shortly after BCT begins, each fourthclassman is assigned a sponsor family. The cadet is computer matched with a family that has filled out a questionnaire listing their priorities, if any, regarding such things as cadet gender, religion, geographic origin, academic specialty, ethnic background, leisure time interests and family background. Also, cadets who have family friends or relatives in the area can request to be matched with them.

All cadets are briefed on sponsor relations, proper manners and protocol that should be used with the sponsor. Specifically, they are reminded of their duties as guests in the sponsor's home. Also they are taught the kinds of courtesies that are often expected by the sponsoring family.

According to sponsor program staff, the biggest problem comes from cadets taking advantage of the sponsor. "They call late at night to borrow a car, or use them as a taxi service." Complaints also come when the cadet does not respond to invitations. And if you finish off the last of the milk or laundry detergent, at least let your sponsor know it is all gone.

Cadets can also have problems with sponsors. It might not be something serious, simply a matter of not "clicking" with your sponsor family. If your relationship turns out to be unsatisfactory, DO SOMETHING ABOUT IT RIGHT AWAY. DO NOT STRUGGLE THROUGH THE FIRST YEAR WITHOUT GETTING A SPONSOR WHO IS GOOD FOR YOU.

There are many ways to get a new sponsor. The officially recommended way is to go to the Arnold Hall office where the program is administered and request a new sponsor. Those in charge of the program know how important it is for each cadet to have a good sponsor, and they will bend over backwards to rematch the cadet in an attempt to establish a more harmonious relationship.

Cadets also have unofficial ways they have found new sponsors.

One that seems to work well is to attend services regularly at any one of the many Colorado Springs churches. In the understated words of one sponsor (who also is an Academy professor), "The environment in the local churches is a lot more compassionate than the dormitory on a Sunday morning."

The mother of a cadet described her son's experience, which is probably typical. "I knew my son was homesick so I suggested that he might enjoy attending a small church in the community—a church like he was used to attending at home. Well, he went and each Sunday some family would invite him home for dinner. Eventually a retired colonel and his wife ended up taking him home regularly and they became almost like grandparents to him. He now goes to their home whenever he's free. He does his laundry there and they take him to the shopping center...they pick him up and take him back to the Academy. He doesn't see his original sponsor much because the colonel and his wonderful lady have been so good to him."

Another unofficial way to find a good sponsor is to tag along with a roommate or friend who has one, then hope that the sponsoring family will adopt you, too. Cadets who found new sponsors this way claim that the extra burden on the sponsor should not be excessive IF the cadet will help out with household chores such as baby sitting so the sponsoring couple can enjoy free time away from home. Most sponsors will make it clear that the "extra" cadet is welcome.

Still other cadets find a sponsor when they "click" with a faculty or staff member they have met—perhaps in a class, sport, club, or other extracurricular activity.

All the sponsor families ask in return is a little courtesy. Clean up after yourself, be on time to meet them, fill the tank if you run their car out of gas, etc...common sense acts that show you appreciate your sponsors.

The bottom line is that *every* cadet needs to have a refuge in the community where they feel comfortable and welcome.

COUNSELING

Another leg of the Academy support system is the Peak Performance Center. This Center is staffed by officers who are nationally certified counselors.

The counselors listen to the problems of cadets and help them work out solutions. They are trained to deal with issues from anger management to eating disorders. Despite their outreach and education efforts, cadets are sometimes reluctant to seek counseling out of fear that they will be stigmatized or there will be career fallout. But the Counseling Center offers confidentiality in almost all cases, and cadets are told ahead of time what is covered by confidentiality. Counselors cannot maintain confidentiality in cases involving drug and alcohol abuse, crimes, and safety issues.

According to the director of the Counseling Center, the most common reasons cadets seek help are relationship issues and stress. "It's normal when you separate from your home and family to have challenges adjusting. It's a very competitive environment, and it's ok to visit the chaplains, the Counseling Center, or faculty members for help." All college students deal with similar issues, but in the competitive environment of the Academy, they may be exacerbated. In addition to one-on-one counseling, the center offers a massage chair, a relaxation room, bio-feedback, and other stress management tools.

According to a professor who works closely with the counselors, "The problem is that those [cadets] who try to do it all by themselves, without help, end up with the stress becoming paramount in their lives. They don't fight the stress; they end up avoiding it, and it builds until it creates real problems.

"If I could give one piece of advice to cadets who are experiencing undue stress it would be this: go to the Counseling Center and let one of the counselors help you work your way out of whatever problem is bothering you. That is what the counselors are there for and I really believe they can give a lot of help."

Chaplains are another set of helping hands on the Academy staff. The Academy chaplains are skilled at handling personal crises. In addition, the cadet is entitled to COMPLETE confidentiality in all communications with any chaplain. That is something to remember if you ever believe yourself to be in real trouble.

The Counseling Center's director offered a word of warning against alcohol use. The Academy treats underage drinking and alcohol abuse very seriously, while you may come from a community with a more lax attitude towards alcohol. "It's presumptive disenrollment for alcohol issues," meaning if you get into trouble that is alcohol-related, you will have an uphill fight to stay in the Academy.

OTHER CADETS

It might seem odd to rely on another cadet, not much older or more experienced than you. But real teamwork requires the members of that team to take care of one another, and cadets try to do that whenever they can.

Cadets who are older than most of their classmates often take on a supporting role. Some who have prior enlisted time, attended the Prep School, or even went to a civilian college before the Academy bring a few more years of wisdom and experience that their classmates come to rely on. One AOC explained, "Two of the older cadets in my squadron are women. They're more mature, they're natural leaders. Remember cadets are 18 to 22 year olds, for the most part. They are going through *life* as well as the Air Force Academy, and they have life issues. These two women have become like big sisters to the other cadets."

Cadets will try to take care of one another.

The Peak Performance Center also trains "PEER Counselors." These are more than 100 cadet volunteers who are trained to identify signs of stress, relationship troubles, possible suicide risks, and other problems. PEER counselors talk to cadets having troubles, and if necessary refer them to professionals.

Roommates, athletic teammates, fellow club members, cadets from your high school, older brothers and sisters who are also cadets ... there *will* be someone to whom you can relate and share your problems and anxieties. Said one firstclassman, "As a four degree [doolie], get a buddy, or two, or three, or four—maybe someone with the same class schedule or a roommate. It's tough when you're on your own. You need to have someone to talk to or things start piling up."

You *can't* do it alone.

WHAT ABOUT MOM AND DAD?

Many cadets have always relied on mom and dad when they get down, stressed out, or unsure of themselves. This pattern continues at the Academy. They call home, unload their troubles, and instantly feel better. Great, right?

There are two main problems with using your parents as counselors. First of all, unless they are Academy grads or at least military veterans, they probably do not really understand what you are going through. Nor will they always have the best advice to offer you, because the Academy is such a unique place.

Second, after the phone call is over and you have moved on to a new day and a brighter outlook, what is happening at home? Your parents may not know that six days out of seven you are perfectly fine, that you are adjusting well and just needed to vent a little. They are left thinking that you are absolutely miserable and worry until the next time they hear from you. Or they pick up the phone and call your AOC, who probably has no idea how serious your complaints are.

No one will tell you not to go to your parents for help. But you are advised to think about what you will say, and what you expect to accomplish, before you make that whining phone call. The Academy may have a better counselor for you.

The Air Force Academy deliberately makes life difficult for cadets, especially the fourthclassmen. But no cadet is left to cope with the stress alone. Classmates and roommates rally around those who are troubled. Squadron leaders and the Air Officer Commanding keep an eagle eye out for stragglers and strugglers who need help.

In addition to all that, there is a support system in place which every cadet can use. Every cadet is advised to reach out and use the helping hands when the burden gets heavy.

Everyone at the Academy—your classmates, the upperclassmen,

your instructors, your AOC, the entire staff—genuinely wants you to succeed. It is very doubtful any civilian university could honestly say the same. In the words of the former Vice Commandant, "We treat [cadets] like they're our own, with one-on-one attention, care, and true concern."

CHAPTER TWENTY
Advice For Intercollegiate Athletes

The intercollegiate athlete at the Academy has a unique experience—compared to athletes at civilian schools, and compared to other cadets at the Academy.

Consider intercollegiate athletes' life at a civilian school. They may take 12 semester hours, or four classes, arranged to accommodate their practice schedule. Some days, say on Tuesdays and Thursdays, they may have only one or maybe even no classes, so they can focus 100 percent on their sport. On weekends when they aren't traveling, they may sleep late or catch up on their studies.

In contrast, an athlete at the Academy will take the same course load as other cadets—six or seven classes most semesters—including classes like computer science, chemistry, and electrical engineering. Some athletes will have a morning practice at 5 a.m. before attending mandatory breakfast and classes. All their classes are scheduled back-to-back in the morning, so afternoons are available for sports. They will march to lunch with their classmates before heading down to the gym for afternoon practice. Physically exhausted, they hike back up to the "hill" and get some dinner, and perhaps attend a training meeting in their squadron. Around 7 p.m., they finally sit down to do homework or military duties such as shining their shoes, memorizing knowledge, and cleaning their room. Exhausted, they drop into bed and get some sleep before starting all over again the next day. For cadet athletes, weekends may include practices or games, along with more military training, or meeting with a tutor or instructor to make up work they missed on a trip.

Compared to their civilian counterparts, cadet athletes are very busy people. Even compared to their classmates at the Air Force Academy, they are very busy people. According to a 2004 independent study, intercollegiate athletes have less than half the free time of other cadets.[1] Half of "not much" is "precious little."

It all sounds incredibly hard. Why do they do it? And how do they do it?

WHY ATHLETES CHOOSE THE AIR FORCE ACADEMY

Many cadet athletes never considered or even heard of the Air Force Academy until their high school coach suggested it, or an Academy

---

1. The Ryan Report reviewed the structure of the Academy's athletic program, compliance with NCAA rules and US laws, and facts and perceptions of recruited athletes.

coach began to recruit them. Then they begin the task of examining the Academy and weighing their options. Most recruited athletes are offered a recruiting visit, where they have a chance to talk to other cadet athletes, attend classes, and get a feel for cadet life. Many of those recruits quickly realize that the Academy offers opportunities they cannot get anywhere else.

All the reasons for attending the Air Force Academy outlined in Chapter 4 apply equally to athletes. Many cadet athletes we interviewed were attracted primarily by the chance to play Division I college sports. Some would not have started or even played on a Division I team at a civilian school. The Academy offered them their only opportunity.

Most cadet athletes are enthusiastic about their athletic experience at the Academy. The coaches are good, their teammates are competitive, and they enjoy traveling and competing against some of the top-tier teams in their sport. Even though sheer athletic ability and amount of practice time available tend to favor teams from civilian schools, Academy teams do surprisingly well. As one tennis player explained, "Our coaches say that we go through so much, we deserve to win as much as anyone. And we do win some matches we shouldn't, just because of our attitude and our competitive spirit." That spirit, determination, and discipline draw crowds of dedicated fans to Air Force Academy sporting events.

For some athletes, the Academy is their only opportunity to play Division I sports.

The quality education is what draws many cadet athletes to the Academy. Even though balancing athletics on top of all the other demands of cadet life is a big challenge, the Academy offers athletes the chance to graduate with the same first-rate education as their classmates.

One cadet athlete selected the Academy because she wanted to be a doctor as well as play college sports. At a civilian school, she felt she would have had to choose between her sport and a pre-med academic program. At the Academy, she is able to pursue both, and hopes to be an Air Force doctor in the future.

This type of long-range view, a view that includes goals beyond college and sports, tends to be common among cadet athletes. They are realistic about the odds of playing professional sports or making a career out of their athletic interests and abilities. They realize that at any time, an injury could end their athletic careers. They know that a good education, the opportunity to reach their potential, and a guaranteed job after college are real assets. A football player explained, "I was looking at other Division I options, but I came on a visit, just so I could see

Colorado. I talked to a two degree (junior-year cadet) about why he came. He told me about the education, the discipline, and the preparation for life you get here." That sold him.

Some cadet athletes choose the Academy with the goal of being

The Academy's athletic facilities are first-class.   *Courtesy USAFA*

a military officer. Others who never really thought about the military before BCT often find they adapt quickly to the military culture. They already understand teamwork, dedication, and hard work. The concept of military service is something they learn and often embrace once they are at the Academy.

Many athletes are offered an appointment to the Prep School if their high school grades or SAT scores are not quite where they need to be. The year spent in Prep School might seem like an inconvenient delay, but it offers many benefits. Prep School students learn many of the military skills and knowledge they will need as doolies, such as shining their shoes, making their beds, and arranging their rooms in inspection order. They make friends with several hundred of their future classmates, grow more mature, and get acculturated to military life. They also spend the year practicing their sport and conditioning, which may make them more competitive once they are on that Division I team. Prep School graduates report entering the Academy much more prepared, both mentally and physically, than they were the year earlier.

A final word of warning: Nearly every cadet athlete interviewed pointed out that if your sport is your sole focus in life, the Air Force Academy is *not* for you. There are too many competing demands, and you will not be able to dedicate the time and energy to athletics that you would like. And you will be required to serve in the Air Force after you graduate.

However, contrary to popular belief, those cadet athletes who really excel in their sport actually do have an opportunity to play professional sports. Some, like former Dallas Cowboy Chad Hennings (interviewed in Chapter 3), may serve their military commitment and then return to their sport. Some participate in a training program as part of their Air Force duties, especially those with promise as Olympic athletes. Others serve a shortened active duty tour, then are released to play sports while serving in the Guard or Reserve. The Air Force understands that graduates who are professional athletes become great ambassadors for the Academy.

Graduates who play professional sports are very rare, however. So if your hopes and dreams are pinned on a future as a professional athlete, a service academy is probably not the best school for you.

HOW CADET ATHLETES MAINTAIN THE BALANCE

For most cadet athletes, BCT does not present a huge challenge. First, because BCT emphasizes physical conditioning, most athletes have an advantage. They normally do not struggle with the running and calisthenics, even despite the altitude. Also, many athletes adjust easily to the mental stress, having faced tough and demanding coaches in high school. Comments such as, "My football coaches yelled at us more than the upperclassmen in BCT did" were common. BCT presents the athletes an opportunity to shine and lead their classmates. Many athletes, especially football players, do lose weight during BCT.

The academic year brings added challenges, however. Throughout this book, you have read about the critical importance of effective time management for all cadets. For the cadet athlete, good time management is even more essential. This includes prioritizing what assignments you will spend time on, looking ahead toward travel schedules, and using every minute as wisely as possible.

For many cadet athletes, the demands of high school sports already taught them to manage every minute of their time wisely, stay focused, work hard, and not allow themselves to fall behind. One graduate who played basketball remembered, "If you're that busy, you *have* to focus your time. It's black and white. I became very efficient."

Some cadet athletes struggle with time management. A senior who plays soccer reported being so overwhelmed by all the tasks before her in that first semester that she had a hard time even knowing where to start. She found herself on academic probation before she learned to manage her time effectively. Then, she realized that she had the course syllabus for each class to use as a road map for the entire semester. A study skills class taught her how to get organized, look ahead, take things step by step, and calm down—and her grades went up.

Cadet athletes have to learn to take advantage of every free moment to do homework—a free period, a half hour between appointments, weekends, whenever those moments appear. They also discover the importance of getting a good night's sleep to stay sharp, both mentally and physically. One doolie said, "I don't stay up past 11:00. I don't want to be tired. I want to focus in class, take good notes, and do all the example problems." Being alert and paying attention in class pays big dividends, making homework assignments and tests that much easier.

As with all cadets, athletes have access to Extra Instruction, or EI, whenever they need it. All they have to do is ask. Instructors understand the challenges athletes face, and appreciate their discipline, positive attitude, and extra efforts to stay caught up and learn the material. Also, tutors travel with athletic teams, so even on the road cadets can take tests or get help with homework and prevent falling further behind.

Many cadets are unused to asking for help. But cadet athletes quickly find out that *if they are willing to work*, so many people will work with them to ensure they succeed—academic instructors, staff officers, coaches, peer counselors, upperclassmen—as one cadet said, "it's almost impossible to fail."

Chapter 17 discussed the importance of working together. Teamwork is a lesson many cadets have to learn, sometimes the hard way, at the Academy. But most athletes have learned teamwork long ago. They find that their team gives them valuable support to get through the challenges and discouraging moments. An athlete who graduated in the 1980s reports, "My teammates are *still* my friends. I love them."

The military class system that exists on the "hill" means that doolies are not allowed to form friendships or social relationships with upperclassmen. That class structure does not apply so strictly to sports teams, so doolie athletes find themselves able to relax, let down their guard, and get to know upperclass athletes on their team. Those upperclassmen often provide them valuable encouragement, advice, and mentorship. A doolie football player appreciated two upperclassmen on the team pulling him aside and saying, "Just call if you need any help."

Cadet athletes also say that their sport gives them a much-appreciated mental break from the other challenges of Academy life. For some, practice is relaxing; it provides a chance to get away from the classroom and the military training environment, and spend a large part of each day doing something they really love to do—and do very well.

THE TERRAZZO GAP

You may have sensed a contradiction between the unique experience of a cadet athlete, and the idea that at a service academy, everyone must blend in and be treated equally. There is tension between these two facts. The cadets and staff call it "the terrazzo gap."

Consider the following scenario:

Cadet Fourthclass Smith is mad at his roommate. The squadron woke the doolies up at 0600 hours for a morning run and training session. Cadet Smith spent 45 minutes being yelled at, doing pushups, and wondering what he was doing at the Air Force Academy instead of State U. He had to scramble to get his room in inspection order, shower, and get to breakfast and class on time.

His roommate, Cadet Fourthclass Jones, was not there to help. He was not there to clean the room or suffer beside his classmates or have his day ruined before the sun came up. Cadet Jones was on a wrestling trip, far from the Academy, joking around with the upperclassmen as if he were a real human being.

Cadet Jones is mad at Cadet Smith, too. He has been practicing extra hard, trying to earn a spot on the varsity roster. After being thrown around for three and a half hours every afternoon, he is almost too exhausted to do his homework at night. While Cadet Smith was home on Thanksgiving leave eating Mom's turkey dinner and catching up with his friends, Cadet Jones was on a bus, on the way to a wrestling trip. This past Friday he missed the review session before the chemistry test because he had another wrestling trip. After the long bus ride back to the Academy on Sunday, instead of hitting the books, he had to listen to his roommate complain. Cadet Smith complained about the training Cadet Jones missed, about having to clean their room for inspection by himself, about the fact that Cadet Jones gets to leave the Academy and take a "break" every time they have an away event.

Some cadets think athletes have too many privileges.

This difference in perception is the essence of the terrazzo gap. There is an apparent rift between the 75 percent of cadets who live most of their life on and around the central area called the terrazzo, and the other 25 percent, the intercollegiate athletes who spend a large number of hours away from the terrazzo—in the gym, on the athletic fields, and traveling to games and matches.

The perception that athletes have too many privileges, despite how jam-packed their days are, exists not only within the cadet wing but also among some of the faculty and staff. One athlete explains, "Their perception is that I *don't care* [about military training]; the reality is I *can't* participate as much militarily, because of the demands of athletics."

It is true that athletes and other cadets, especially doolies, have two different Academy experiences. That difference is unavoidable. Cadet athletes cope with this phenomenon in one of two ways. Some try to minimize the differences by doing as much as they can militarily. As doolies, they work hard to learn their knowledge, keep an extra-sharp uniform, and spend as much time as they can with their roommates and squadron mates. As upperclassmen, they take on leadership positions during summer training or in the off season.

Some intercollegiate athletes take a "separate but equal" approach. They feel that they are working just as hard, if not harder, than their non-athlete classmates. The only difference is that they are practicing instead of doing military training, all while taking the same academic course load and wearing the same uniform as every other cadet. They may live with their squadron, but their true friends and comrades are the teammates on their sports team. These athletes take the position that if other cadets are resentful, that is their problem.

Coaches may help or aggravate the terrazzo gap, depending on the coach. Some cadet athletes report that if they request time off from practice for a particularly important military activity, their coaches will support them. Others have a different experience.

The off-season tends to aggravate the terrazzo gap. Non-athletes may view off-season athletics as down time, with less intense practices and no travel. Athletes view it quite differently. They say that off-season practice focuses on conditioning, strength, and endurance, and is "ten times harder than on-season, even though the other cadets think it's easier." Off-season practice lacks the change of scenery provided by travel, or the motivation and excitement that comes with gearing up for and participating in games and matches.

An athlete's cadet experience will be different from that of other cadets.

A doolie gymnast reported that once her season started and she could invite her squadron mates to meets, their relationship improved. She was grateful they came to cheer her on, and they were impressed by the difficulty of her sport and the skill she had to have to be competitive.

Most cadet athletes make a conscious effort to close the terrazzo gap. For example, one cadet athlete who had been to the Prep School tried to be especially helpful during BCT, teaching his classmates to prepare their rooms for inspection or shine their shoes. Then once football season started, his classmates remembered what he had contributed before. By participating in as much military training as they can, making sure they stay out of trouble, and trying to explain their demands to their classmates, athletes remain part of their sports teams *and* the larger team that is the Cadet Wing.

One additional caveat: If you are being recruited as an athlete, be careful. Your recruiter is *selling* the Academy experience, and may downplay the role of military training and the added stress it causes. Be sure to talk to a cadet athlete or recent graduate you trust, ideally one who played your sport, to get an additional perspective.

ADVICE FROM ATHLETES

In addition to the interviews in Chapter 3 with San Antonio Spurs coach Gregg Popovich and former Dallas Cowboy Chad Hennings, I interviewed dozens of other cadet and graduate athletes who played a variety of sports. Nearly all of them said the Academy offered them athletic opportunities they would not have had at another school. And they all said that the added challenge of juggling athletics and the other demands of cadet life left them better prepared for the future.

Major General Michelle Johnson, class of 1981, was an Academic All-American basketball player, served as Cadet Wing Commander her senior year, and was a Rhodes Scholar after graduation. She has been a flying squadron, group, and wing commander, and is now stationed at NATO headquarters in Belgium.

On leadership: The lessons that were forged in team sports have been invaluable to me as a pilot, an officer, and a leader. If you thrive on team leadership, on working toward a common goal, go to the Academy. That same teamwork and leadership are why I'm still in the Air Force. I enjoy working in an environment where I can trust people to come to work, get things done—even if they're hard—and live by our core values. Whether you're playing basketball or people are shooting at you [in combat], integrity and an honest effort are what matter.

On success: You may have been the star athlete and the valedictorian in high school and find you're not the star at the Academy. It's hard to get this perspective while you're at the Academy, but remember it's not all or nothing. Don't give up on yourself. You can still contribute and make a difference. As an athlete, you're always trying to be the best *you* can be. That helps the whole institution. Victory isn't just what's on the scoreboard; it's the intangibles—helping each other through, teamwork and camaraderie—that you'll remember.

Colonel Bart Weiss, class of 1986, was an All-American quarterback as well as Western Athletic Conference Player of the Year in 1985, leading the football team to a #8 final AP ranking. He served as a cadet squadron commander during his final semester. On active duty, he has commanded a KC-135 flying squadron, and is currently vice director of athletics at the Air Force Academy.

On academics: I breezed through high school, even taking four Advanced Placement classes. At the Academy, academics and football together were rough. I got a 1.98 my first semester before I learned time management. I figured out how to prioritize. I learned you can't do it all—you have to focus on what's important, especially your weak areas. Eventually, I struck a good balance. I took advantage of the tutors on the road. The Athletic Director helped me a lot. I also leaned on my physics instructor and my Spanish instructor for support.

On the terrazzo gap: I had a good relationship with my squadron—there was no resentment. I never used football as an excuse to get out of training. Some of my teammates used football to get out of things, but I tried to do everything with my classmates; I felt obligated to do it all. You get lifelong lessons from both the good and the bad experiences. You have to keep an open mind, and learn from your mistakes. Remember, just because it's not always fun doesn't mean the Academy is the wrong place for you.

On professional sports opportunities: I was invited to training camp by the Atlanta Falcons, so I thought I might be able to do two or three years on active duty and then go play professional football. My parents were hoping for a big contract! But I decided that the Air Force had stood by me, so I felt obligated to stand by the Air Force; I felt connected.

Jacob Burtschi, class of 2007, *was a starting basketball forward for the varsity team,*

Cadet Jacob Burtschi was a leading scorer for Falcon basketball.　　　　　　　　*Courtesy USAFA*

averaging over 13 point per game and contributing to the team's best season ever. He played in two NCAA tournament games and the 2007 National Invitation Tournament semi-finals in Madison Square Gardens. He also set an Academy basketball record for the most varsity games played. He is currently playing professional basketball in Europe.

On the terrazzo gap: I came on a recruiting trip after recognition [when most of the intense training has ended for the year], so I had no idea what it was really like to be a four degree. I just knew they wore uniforms, had short hair, and did pushups—that's all I really knew about the military piece. And I really didn't think about the service commitment afterward. It was all kind of shocking to me at first.

My freshman classmates are still close to each other. We still talk to each other online and go out on weekends. We had athletes, smart kids, military buffs—we all looked out for each other, and no one gave each other a hard time. After our four degree year, we switched squadrons, and it was a whole new ballgame. People start judging you a little bit more. The terrazzo gap has gotten better, but there's still a terrazzo gap. Whenever I could be around [the squadron], I would. Now senior year, we all respect each other. We know where everyone is coming from. And we're not afraid to get on one another if someone is slacking off.

My advice is to make friends with everyone, not just other athletes. The military guys can help you out in so many ways; the academic guys can help you out with your studies. Don't think you're hot stuff and better than everyone else. Don't fall into the trap of not going to all the mandatory military training—you get greater respect from your peers if you participate when you can.

On the decision to stay at the Academy: The sophomore year in my opinion is the toughest year. There were so many times sophomore year that I thought it was time to move on. Our second coach in two years left. It was the toughest year [academically]. You're taking all the core classes at once. Looking back, I'm so glad I didn't make the decision to leave. It was a time I was getting tested. I talked to my dad, and he told me I'd have to start with a new coach, and that there are always times in life when things are tough.

So I stuck it out, and he was right. It was the best decision I've ever made in my life. I made it through a tough place, I'm getting a great education, I'm experiencing the world. And I have a guaranteed job for five years—I have friends who went to college who are now struggling to find a decent job. If you're having trouble, go talk to one of your friends or your parents back home. Get it all out, and refocus on what you're doing. You have to roll with the punches. There will be highs and lows, but things will turn around and get better. Stick with it. You'll find out who you are and what you're made of. And you'll make friends for life.

Cadet Katherine Moorkamp, class of 2013, *is a thrower on the Academy track team. She elected to attend the Air Force Academy because she was impressed by the track program and the coach, and because it provided her best option for participating at the Division I level.*

On BCT: I wasn't aware of the military aspect of the Academy before I got here, but I think if they tell you everything that's going to happen, they'll lose a lot of athletes. They don't tell the recruits about the hard parts.

I hated BCT, because I hated being told what to do. I was used to being independent, figuring out a lot of things on my own, relying on myself. But physically it was easier than I expected. I think athletes have a tough mindset that makes it easier, and they're tougher physically. To get through it, try to find one or two things each day that are good. Write them down.

Cadet Moorkamp throws for the USAFA track team.
Courtesy Katherine Moorkamp

On the terrazzo gap: Everyone thinks it's easier being an athlete. Some of the people in my squad would say we don't deserve respect. We might miss a few hours of training a week, but we put in hours of [athletic] training every day. As a four degree, I would rush up from practice to try and participate in the last part of a training session, and that got me respect.

I would talk to my classmates about practice and competitions, so they can understand the hard work. But you can't do that with the upperclassmen. Fortunately both my roommates have been intercollegiate athletes. We understood each other more.

On asking for help: Academics were the hardest part for me. You have to go to your teachers and ask for help. I had to fail a class to learn that. You can also take an academic day from practice once in awhile to get caught up. Better to do that than get thrown off the team.

On deciding to stay: I almost quit three times. But I see the lifestyle, the structure, the discipline as good things. I just had to adapt. And I love the people here. That's why I stayed—the friends, the classmates, my teammates, my sponsor.

If you want to know what you're really made of, come here. Looking back, I can see how much I've grown. You will be tested, and you will become more of a competitor. You will become a better, tougher, more capable version of yourself.

Cadet Lucus Duncavage, Class of 2015, *is a wide receiver on the varsity football team. The son of a Marine fighter pilot, Cadet Duncavage chose to attend the Air Force Academy as a path to pilot training.*

On academics: Don't underestimate it, whether you're an athlete or not! They put me in a study skills class and I said ,"I don't belong here. I don't need it." I thought I could easily make a 3.5 with the classes I had. But I was on academic probation at prog. I went back to my study skills instructor and said, "I will listen to you now." I went from a 1.4 at prog to a 2.5 by the end of the semester. Get Extra Instruction and use all the resources the Academy offers.

My advice is to stay on top of things. The little things will get you. Don't turn anything in late; always start early. The homework and projects give you a chance to pad your grade for the tests and lessen your stress level, because you can take your time with them and get the answers right.

Be organized; have a planner and use it. Sometimes you may have to sacrifice a subject. For example, you skip a reading in history and go to class unprepared because you need to study for a GR [exam] in physics. You have to maintain a balance.

On the terrazzo gap: There's some tension, but I didn't see it too much in my squadron. Athletes have about six hours less in every day to get things done, with the same course load and most of the same military duties as everyone else. Some people notice and respect that. But some think we get out of stuff and there is animosity.

I tried to be good in the squadron, get good scores on the knowledge tests, and not use lame excuses to get out of calling minutes. When recognition came [several days of intense training that marks the end of the doolie experience], I gave a 100% effort. I tried to help my classmates as much as I could. That really helped—I got more respect after that.

As a 3 degree [sophomore], I'm doing military things in the squadron as much as I can. That goes a long way. I think it's easier now, because you have more control over how you project your image [than doolies do].

On deciding to attend the Academy: This school is one of the best; it's world renowned. The lessons you learn here are invaluable—leadership, developing yourself as a person—you become better in general.

The payoffs outweigh the challenges. You will find a group of friends who will be your friends for life. You'll support them when they need it, and be able to lean on them.

The Academy is not for everyone. It takes a certain caliber of person to be here for four years. Consider the military side along with the sports—is it something you want to do? If so, accept the challenge and go for it. Deciding to come doesn't mean signing your life away. You have two years to decide before you make a commitment.

A final note: On the whole, research shows that cadet athletes tend to perform the same as other cadets in overall order of merit—combined military, academic, and athletic performance. They tend to graduate at about the same rate as well. In the Air Force, they tend to get promoted and earn command positions at the average rate.

They do bring discipline, teamwork, and resilience that are highly valued in an Air Force officer. Perhaps that explains the one statistic that breaks the pattern: In a study of the first 20 Academy classes, former recruited athletes were promoted to the rank of brigadier general at *twice* the rate of their non-athlete peers!

TWENTY-ONE
Diversity And Tolerance

If you look through an Air Force Academy yearbook from the 1960s, you will see the faces of a cadet wing that was very homogeneous. First, all of the cadets were men. Second, very few were black or Asian. Most were practicing Christians, or at least pretended to be every Sunday. If any of them were gay, they had to hide it with every fiber of their being, because if the fact were discovered, their Air Force career would have ended with humiliation, immediately.

Just as our society has evolved to be more appreciative of the gifts of a diverse population, the Air Force Academy has changed as well. Today, about 22% of cadets are women. Around 10% are Hispanic, 9% are black, and 7% are Asian. Approximately 15% are the first generation of their family to attend college, and 4% speak a language other than English at home.

Religious beliefs among cadets are as diverse as the nation's as a whole. The Academy now provides a place of worship for Buddhists, Muslims, and Wiccans. Agnostics and atheists are accepted as well.

As for sexual orientation, the Clinton-era policy known as "Don't Ask, Don't Tell" ended in 2012, so the Academy now admits openly-gay cadets.

Does this mean there is no more intolerance, disrespect, or prejudice among cadets? Of course not. But the Academy is working hard to promote a climate of mutual respect for several reasons. First, they are developing leaders of character. Good leaders are those who are understanding and respectful of everyone they lead. Second, the taxpayers who pay for the Academy expect it. And finally, they know it is the right thing to do.

If you grew up in an area where everyone looked, worshipped, and thought pretty much the same, the Academy may be a bit of a shock. Many cadets, however, really enjoy meeting and interacting with people whose experiences have been different from their own.

If you consider yourself part of any minority group, you may have concerns about how you will be treated or your chances for success. The best thing you can do is find a cadet or graduate and ask them about their experiences. The next best thing is to read the experiences of some of the people in this chapter.

Lieutenant Colonel Larry Card, Class of 1993, *is an A-10 instructor pilot who formerly served as an Air Officer Commanding. He is currently stationed at the Pentagon.*

Lieutenant Colonel Larry Card with his A-10 *Courtesy Larry Card*

I grew up in a lot of places. My dad was in the Air Force when I was little. I actually lived here [in Colorado Springs] when I was 5 and 6—my dad was stationed here at the Academy. I remember cadets coming over to our house. Even at 5 or 6 you can tell that these guys [cadets] really had what it took to be successful. You drive down the road, watch them parachute out of airplanes, or flying gliders around, and you say, "man!" When I was 9 or 10, my dad got out of the Air Force and from that point I lived in Alaska.

When I was little I just thought that would be really neat, and it never occurred to me that one day I could go if I wanted. Then about the time I was in junior high, I thought, "Wait a minute, if I want to be a pilot, all I have to do is go." I remember the transition from 6th grade to 7th grade: Instead of just goofing off all summer, I remember having my mom take me to this school supply store and buying all of these books to study over the summer, so when I hit 7th grade I would do very well. All of the sudden I had a goal in life that I wanted to achieve. I read up, saw the grades you had to get, the kind of classes you had to have, and did whatever it took to get here.

I always wanted to fly F-15s because I grew up in Anchorage, Alaska, right next to Elmendorf Air Force Base. So I grew up looking at those airplanes. But once I actually started looking at the type of flying I enjoyed and the different missions, the ones that meant the most to me, the A-10 was perfect.

The way I look at things, it's amazing how much difference you can make just by saving one life. I saved one of those 18-year-old kids' lives on the ground by going up there, doing my job, risking my life. Just think if your grandfather would have died at 18.

I think the number one thing we need to do is to treat everyone as individuals. Look at yourself as an individual, and look at the qualities you have, and focus on those—not the things that you think other people want you to be. When we do that, I think we start to move to an area that the military is kind of renowned for. You bring a bunch of people together with common beliefs, with common values. When I'm flying an airplane, those are the things that are important to me: a person's beliefs, a person's values, a person's skills. Nothing else. In the end, I don't think the kids come in here and separate themselves based on religious views, based on sex, based on race, or any of those things.

I think the Academy is just a microcosm of our society. So, is it possible he is going to see stereotyping? Probably. But that's part of American society and most societies. Is it going to be institutionalized? No, and it won't be tolerated by the institution if they know about it.

The fact of the matter is, you are going to see discrimination. You can't let that derail you from your dreams. I have never run into a person who I think had views like that or said anything, who meant any harm by it. The most common thing is a lack of knowledge. One way to get over the ignorance is for people to express themselves instead of overreacting. The only way they are going to learn is from actually sitting down and talking with people.

I make the analogy of the car. Some people jump in the back seat and wait to see where the car is going to take them. It's probably not going to be where they want to go. Some people have realized in order to get where you need to go, you need to hold onto the wheel and steer. That may be hard for some people. They think, I grew up in the inner city, schools aren't great, opportunities aren't there. It's going to be really tough. The only one who is going to make it happen is you, and we have to be able to instill in them, "Hey, it's *all* up to you." Every roadblock that you have ever been told about is probably there to some extent. But it's a roadblock; it's not an infinite wall that extends from one end of the earth to the other. What does that mean? You *can* get there, but you may have to work harder than the average kid out there who doesn't have those roadblocks in the way.

The [minority] kids who are qualified, the kids who need to come here, have either never heard of the Air Force Academy, or when they hear about it they've never been around the military and they say, "Why would I want to do that? I can go to Harvard and get a full scholarship." They really don't know what this place offers.

I'd say for the kids out there who want to make a difference, this is the place to be. I don't do my job because I am going to be a millionaire one day. I don't do my job because it's easy. I do my job because I want to make a difference. When you leave here, if you apply yourself, you're going to be an outstanding leader. Maybe nobody will ever read your name in a history book, but your legacy will live on, the impact that you made, even though nobody may know who left that legacy.

The number one thing the Academy does is give you opportunities. Some directly relate to leadership. Every year that you're here, you will be put in some position of responsibility. As a fourthclassman, your position of responsibility will be to take care of yourself and your classmates and probably some chores around the squadron. As a sophomore, they give you a little bit more. By the time you're a junior or senior, as an element leader, you actually have ten people you are responsible for across the board. If a cadet is having problems academically, you need to find a way to make sure he is getting the appropriate help. And our cadet squadron commander has all 120 people he or she is responsible for. Those are things that you're not going to get at Harvard.

Remember, you aren't here because this is an enjoyable place to be. You are here because it's going to give you the skills you need to go out there and be competent and successful in the career field that you want to have.

Lieutenant Colonel Nicole Malachowski, class of 1996,
A glider instructor pilot as a cadet, and was Cadet-in-Charge of the soaring (glider) program her senior year. After graduation she attended pilot training and was selected to fly the F-15E Strike Eagle. She logged nearly 200 combat hours in Iraq and Afghanistan before being selected to fly F-16s with the Air Force Air Demonstration Squadron—the Thunderbirds. She then served in the elite White House Fellows program, and is now an F-15E squadron commander.

From the age of five I knew I wanted to be a pilot, after I saw an F-4 at an air show. I came from a patriotic family with a culture of serving our country—many of my relatives, including my dad, had served in the Army or the Navy. But I fell in love with aircraft—the power, technology and grace—so the Air Force became the obvious choice for me. I wanted to be a fighter pilot, but I found out when I was 12 that women couldn't fly fighters. Fortunately, that changed while I was a cadet. I chose the Air Force Academy because I knew it gave me the highest chance of becoming a pilot, compared to ROTC or OTS [Officer Training School].

In high school, I was in Civil Air Patrol and Junior ROTC. I was the cadet corps commander in JROTC. Those programs helped teach me about Air Force history, customs and courtesies, marching, honoring the flag, and wearing the uniform, as well as aerospace science. They also taught me how to communicate and work with my peers, people from all different backgrounds. Most importantly I learned about leadership, to hold everyone accountable—even my peers and myself. I really liked being around people with the same goals, enthusiasm, and positive attitude. That reinforced my dream [of becoming an Air Force pilot], and the belief that I could do it.

BCT was an easy transition, a lot like CAP and JROTC encampments, just longer. I looked at BCT pretty logically—it's just something you have to go through, and they wouldn't have picked you if you didn't have the ability to get through it. Thousands of other people before me had survived it. I did realize that the only way to get through was by working together. After being in CAP and JROTC, that teamwork came naturally.

Once academics started, the hardest thing was task prioritization and time allocation. Some cadets can do 100% of the tasks they're given, but very few. Most have to apportion the weight of their efforts. They have to pick and choose what's most important—it's a lot like choosing the hottest threat on the radar when you're flying in combat. You have to wake up and decide "what am I going to do today." Most cadets feel bad about themselves because they can't do it all, but it's like life in the Air Force—you always have to figure out where to put your effort.

> *"95% of the Air Force judges you solely on your abilities."*

You need to have someone to vent to. I called my parents every Sunday for four years. They knew I was doing my best, and they always validated my efforts. You also have to maintain balance. Take a break on the weekend to go get some ice cream, go to a concert, have dinner with your sponsors. Working out is a good release, too. And keep your sense of humor; try to laugh at the silly things.

Flying gliders was how I relaxed and escaped. I had the opportunity to be the Cadet-in-Charge, leading a large group of my peers. It was a good leadership experience, especially because it involved what I was passionate about. Being a soaring instructor helped a ton in pilot training. It gave me a head start, a comfort level and appreciation for the three-dimensional world. It also gave me confidence when facing risks, and the ability to help other students in my class.

You have to remember that getting through all four years of the Academy requires patience. Even as you get more freedom and privileges as an upperclassman, it requires patience. Keep your eyes on the prize: the privilege of becoming an Air Force officer.

My advice to women is to assure you that 95 percent of the Air Force judges you solely on your abilities, so don't waste time worrying about the 5 percent who think women shouldn't be at the Academy or flying. It does you no good. At the end of the day, I hold *myself* accountable for my own actions and reactions. It's *my* dream. My aircraft only does what I make it do, so I don't let the naysayers detract from my experiences or my goals.

Also, you don't have to lose yourself or become one of the guys; it's ok to be feminine. You're a better part of the team if you're true to yourself. I think women bring very valuable qualities to a team. They're often good at bringing people together, resolving confrontation, and sensing others' strengths or weaknesses and helping them out. So be yourself. Let your capabilities speak for you.

Work hard, do well, and you can succeed. And have fun.

Cadet Lydia Hill, Class of 2015

Cadet Hill was recruited by the Academy fencing team, but soon turned her attention to forming a support group for LGBT cadets called Spectrum. The Defense Department policy change that allows gay military members to serve openly was implemented in September of her freshman year.

Cadet Hill as a doolie.
Courtesy Lydia Hill

When I graduated from a private prep school in Massachusetts, I wanted to be done with school and travel and do something. I was going to enlist and go back to school later. But I knew I would be financially stable if I came to the Academy. I had visited in March of my senior year, before recognition, so I felt I knew exactly what I was getting into.

BCT was hard, because I hadn't learned to deal with stress in constructive ways. I was having physical reactions to the stress, panic attacks. I wasn't the strongest girl, but the mental stress was the worst, just making it through each day. Plus being in the closet weighs on you every day. It takes a lot of effort to hide it every day. I'm supposed to be able to trust people but they don't really even know who I am.

The academic year was better. I'm a lot better at academics than anything else here. It gave me something I could focus on. Still I felt isolated. There aren't many people here who look like me. Fencing helped because I got to be removed from the squadron for awhile, and get out of some of the military training. But I realized I just wasn't into it anymore; it was something I felt I had to do because I was recruited.

The best way to cope is to find something to get involved in and be passionate about. I wanted to get the LGBT club formed and working on that helped a lot. I'm the co-cadet-in-charge. We just had club day, and afterward I got an email from a four degree who said he walked by our booth several times but was embarrassed to stop because his roommate was with him. That's exactly what we wanted to provide—it's a support group for whatever support LGBT cadets may need.

I feel like I'm accepted fairly well. If someone is not going to accept me, they just don't talk to me. I don't see anyone who is outwardly homophobic. Many cadets don't put [their sexual orientation] out there; they see it as a personal issue. There's a range of how out people want to be. Gay cadets date, and have the same issues as straight cadets. There's some drama. But most people haven't had any really bad experiences.

I think there's more under the table, subtle discrimination against women than gay cadets. It's more obvious. Guys make comments, like using "womanly" as a term that means weak. But you have to take a moment to be proud to be a woman. Find woman mentors. My sponsor mom is an '81 grad and she has helped me a lot.

If you come here, remember that people will yell at you. You're a four degree and that's the system. People will say things, but don't take it personally. Make the place fun. There are lots of ways to do that. Find the people you click with. It may take time. There are days that suck here. But talk to a friend and they'll make you laugh, and you'll be fine. You have to laugh about things.

My advice to candidates is if you think you can do it, don't let your fears hold you back. If you're gay, you're probably safer here than any civilian college in terms of hate crimes. The people who don't accept you will eventually fall away. Find another gay cadet who's older than you, who's been through it and can look out for you. Maybe you're dealing with problems at home or other stress. As a four degree you can't really speak out but someone older can point you in the right direction.

People are professional here. They know me more for my work ethic. I'm just as much a cadet as any straight cadet. You're defined more by what you do here than the fact that you're gay.

Cadet Monique Pal, Class of 2013

Cadet Pal was raised in a close-knit family of Fijian descent in Savannah, Georgia. She chose to attend the Academy because she wanted to serve in the military. She is president of the USAFA Interfaith Council, an organization that brings together cadets from different religions to resolve issues and learn about one another's beliefs.

I went to an arts academy for high school, and many of my teachers had military backgrounds and got me interested in serving. My liaison officer got me in touch with a woman West Point grad who told me a lot about what to expect.

BCT was miserable for me. I had never been away from home or away from my parents for a long period of time before. I knew what to expect physically, but not emotionally. I had trained with a personal trainer and done martial arts before BCT, but the altitude still got me. Then I got swine flu and was put in quarantine. What got me through it was the close bond I had with my roommate; she had the flu too. The first year is challenging for everyone, so finding common ground and bonding with your classmates is very helpful. It can make it funny. When I was a four degree, the women in my squad would have slumber parties on the weekends. We'd buy nail polish and magazines at the cadet store, make popcorn and make up songs.

"My religion is a part of me."

Academically, I was used to being at the top of my class without having to do any homework or study. I had taken a lot of AP classes, and thought I'd be well prepared for college level work. But AP classes are still a high school environment and the expectations at the Academy are different. I had a 2.29 GPA at the end of my freshman year. I had to transition to working hard to get good grades, and I'm doing better now.

I thought about quitting every day. I wrote home, "I'm quitting and coming home" many times. My mom said ok, but my dad said, "Suck it up; I did not raise a quitter." But none of my classmates in my squadron quit, so I couldn't be that one—the first to quit.

Joining clubs really helps you cope with the stress. You gain a family environment, people who care about you. I'm in the Drum and Bugle Corps. It gave me something I was more used to, something artsy. They also provided academic tutorials, fitness test workouts, and recreational events.

My roommate planned day but day, but I looked about a week ahead. I figured tomorrow was going to be as bad as today, but later it will be better. I would look for small things to look forward to—Parents' Weekend, the next Drum and Bugle Corps trip. I think day by day isn't a helpful strategy because you don't see an exam you have three days from now. You have to plan ahead, allocate your free time, and make time for fun.

As a woman, I feel respected by the guys here. They act as older brothers; they're helpful and supportive. My best friend is a guy. We became friends my four degree year, and he's still my best friend. Some guys make jokes about the girls, but not with malicious intent. It's all meant to be in good humor.

I'm Hindu, and we're a very small minority here—maybe 12 cadets in the whole wing. The chaplains have been very helpful; they're so willing to talk with you and help you out. They got us a room to meet in, and coordinated with the scheduling committee so we could go to services off base for major holidays. Practicing my faith here is no more difficult than any other religion—you just have to make time for yourself.

Some cadets are unaware about other people's religions or cultures. For example, in my culture, it's bad to step over someone. So when I make them aware, they will say, "Please move your legs so I can go around you." We have events with presentations and question and answer sessions about different religions and beliefs.

I have attended all different services at the chapel, just to be part of the religious atmosphere. The chaplains always explained things to me about what was going on in the service; cadets would too. If you approach the differences with interest, it's better.

My religion is a part of me, and I share it with people not to convert them, but to share and promote understanding of the differences. I discuss religion with my Catholic friend all the time—it's really helpful to find common ground in other religions. You find we have common morals and lessons. It helps you relate better to people, which will be really important as an Air Force officer.

TWENTY-TWO
Have Fun

By now you have grasped the message that succeeding at the Academy requires a lot of hard work, and it will often be stressful, difficult, frustrating, and exhausting. Most of the survival tips in this book, so far, have focused on how to meet these difficulties successfully and overcome the challenges by using your efforts as efficiently and effectively as possible, and asking for help along the way.

You may think that having fun is not part of the Academy experience. You may think, "If every minute of the day is so precious, how could there be *time* for fun?" However, nearly every cadet and graduate interviewed offered this piece of survival advice: do something for fun, something you love, something that relaxes you or makes you feel confident or just plain happy.

You may be wondering, given the highly structured military life at the Academy, "How does a cadet have fun?" This chapter will give examples of the many enjoyable clubs and activities the Academy offers to help balance the rigors of cadet life and make the time pass more quickly.

CLUBS

Like most colleges, the Academy offers a wide variety of clubs for sports, hobbies, and other special interests. Some clubs are competitive, including cycling, rodeo, rugby, and judo. Many colleges have a number of sports that lack NCAA status, but still have rigorous practice and competition schedules. Club athletes do not have all the same challenges and privileges of NCAA intercollegiate athletes, but their experiences

The singing group "In the Stairwell" gives a Christmas concert.
Courtesy USAFA

are quite similar.

Other clubs are focused on hobbies, special interests, and community service, such as chess, paintball or show choir. Still other relate to an academic area or an Air Force mission, such as Cyber Warfare, Chemistry, Spanish, or the Sabre Drill Team.

Clubs provide you an opportunity to explore your interests and relate to other cadets in a more relaxed environment than the typical doolie day. You will interact with upperclassmen without getting yelled at, and they in turn will mentor you in a comfortable environment. You will also get to know an officer or NCO who can share experiences about life in the Air Force as well.

Clubs also can give you the opportunity to travel, which provides a much-needed change of scenery and a new perspective on life as a doolie. If you have some talent or expertise, clubs offer a chance to show off your abilities and gain some confidence. For example, a talented fourthclass actor and singer can be a shining star in a Bluebards drama production, even if he or she is struggling in chemistry or doolie knowledge.

A third-year cadet who plays club rugby explains, "It's a chance to get away from the hill and run around, to relieve stress and do what you love. It is an additional time commitment, but in the end it helps to go do your own thing."

Women's rugby is one of many club sports. *Courtesy Emily Raney*

RECREATION

The Academy offers many opportunities for recreational activities. For example, you can sign up for a ski trip, and even rent your gear at the Outdoor Recreation Center. Many doolies will use a Colorado blue-sky day to go hiking right on the Academy's 18,000 acres, which allows them to feel like they are leaving the cadet area even if they do not have

The Rodeo Club is one of a wide variety of activities offered at the Academy.
Courtesy USAFA

a pass to leave the base itself. The Academy has its own riding stables, 36 hole golf course, and bowling alley.

Many cadets say a good workout is the best way to relieve doolie stress. If you find athletic activities relaxing, the cadet gym has racquetball, tennis, a pool, basketball courts, nearly anything you can imagine. Bikers and runners have miles and miles of roads and trails; in fact, civilians come to the Academy just to take advantage of them.

Arnold Hall, which is roughly the equivalent of a civilian college's student center, has a movie theater, big-screen televisions, and fast food. Even if you are taking advantage of the weekend to catch up on your studies, a short break at Arnold Hall can be very beneficial.

OTHER OPPORTUNITIES TO GET AWAY

A doolie urged, "Don't stay in your room all weekend doing homework. Take a break or you'll get too stressed out." Even if you do not want to sign up for a club, you will have other ways to get a change of scenery.

The previous chapter mentioned sponsor families. Many squadrons will restrict their fourthclassmen from going downtown when their military performance is not up to speed, yet they sometimes will still allow sponsor family visits. Just being in a real house can be very relaxing.

Colorado Springs, Denver, and the surrounding mountains offer plenty of activities. While doolies (and thirdclass cadets) are not allowed to own cars, they often can borrow one from an upperclassman who is busy studying or perhaps their sponsor family.

Chapel passes are another way to get off base. While the Academy has a chapel with some wonderful programs, cadets are also allowed to worship off base. Some churches will help with transportation, some upperclassmen will take you along if you attend the same church, and some cadets worship with their sponsor families. You may find it more renewing to practice your faith in a non-military setting.

What you do for fun matters less than the fact that you do *something*

Doolies take a break at a frozen yogurt shop.   Sue Ross

for fun. As one doolie explained, "Don't get so regimented with your time management that you get stressed out. You can get physically and mentally exhausted."

Cadets are notorious for their intelligent sense of humor and creative pranks, which may be evidence of that need for fun trying to express itself. Especially during Army or Navy football weeks, the practical jokes played on cadets and officers from the opponent service are ingenious. You can go to YouTube and find plenty of funny videos cadets made to lighten up their day.

Many of the doolies cautioned that social media—Facebook, texting, email, etc.—does not count as socializing. You need to get out of your room and do something fun. Said one doolie, "Facebook is not a substitute for time with your friends."

Another word of caution from a doolie: "You can't take too much free time. You have to find the balance." Many cadets are so excited about all the interesting opportunities at the Academy, they want to sign up for everything. These overenthusiastic participators often find themselves on academic probation or facing an Academic Review Committee, so do not go overboard.

A doolie who was halfway through his second semester, and only weeks away from recognition and spring break, remarked, "It's essential to have something [to do for fun] or you'll go crazy." Even at a regimented place like the Air Force Academy, you can find plenty of opportunities to have (a little) fun.

TWENTY-THREE
Living With The Honor Code

SCENE. It is your final month in high school and you are walking down the hall with your friend Sarah, who is a junior. She has just left Mr. Carter's third period class in American History where she had taken a test on World War II. Her friend, Kevin, is coming down the hall. Kevin is in fifth period American History and will be taking the test after lunch. Sarah greets him and you listen to the conversation.

Kevin: "How was the test?"

Sarah: "Not too bad. You gotta know all that stuff about the beaches they landed on."

Kevin: "Omaha and that stuff."

Sarah: "Yeah, and where the British landed. I didn't get any of them; didn't think he would ask them."

Kevin: "What about dates?"

Sarah: "Yeah, there were a bunch...there was one I missed, the Battle of Britain. I didn't even know what that was."

Kevin: "Yeah, the Spitfires and all that. Anything on the Germans?"

Sarah: "Couple of questions. Who was that guy they called the Desert Fox?"

Kevin: "Rommel?"

Sarah: "Yeah. One question is four choices on how he died. I said he was killed with a bomb."

Kevin: "No, he took poison. He killed himself. Didn't Carter make a big deal of that in your class?"

Sarah: "I didn't remember it." END OF SCENE

How many times in your high school career have you witnessed or participated in a scene such as the one above?

Once? Twice? Many times?

What do you think would happen to Kevin and Sarah if another student had overheard that conversation?

To most high school students that might seem like a weird question. Nothing would happen, of course. In many, if not most high schools, such conversations are as routine as talk about Friday night's football game.

The outcome would be drastically different if that conversation had occurred at the Air Force Academy. Why? Because every cadet has sworn to live by the Academy's Honor Code:

WE WILL NOT LIE, STEAL, OR CHEAT, NOR TOLERATE AMONG US ANYONE WHO DOES.

At the Academy, if such a conversation had occurred and Kevin and Sarah had gone on about their business and said nothing more about it, they <u>could</u> end up being expelled for cheating.

And if you had overheard them, you could be expelled, too, because you tolerated the cheating by not reporting them.

At the end of BCT, cadets take an oath to live by the honor code. *Courtesy USAF*

Why? Because all cadets, after finishing Basic Cadet Training, take the Honor Oath that they subsequently must live by. The Oath includes the words of the honor code, and is followed with a second sentence:

FURTHERMORE, I RESOLVE TO DO MY DUTY AND LIVE HONORABLY, SO HELP ME GOD.

Kevin and Sarah were not living honorably when they discussed questions on a test because they took unfair advantage over other students who had no such knowledge. That is how cheating is defined.

You would not be living honorably if you allowed Kevin and Sarah to take that unfair advantage. At the Academy it is dishonorable behavior to tolerate cheating.

Does all of this seem intimidating, frightening, or just plain odd?

It should not. The hypothetical scene with Kevin, Sarah, and you is presented in order to alert you to the fact that the behavior which may be commonplace in your high school is UNACCEPTABLE at the Air Force Academy.

You should know that before you get there. And you should practice changing your habits now, so that living under the honor code becomes second nature that much more easily.

LEARNING TO LIVE HONORABLY

You are not expected to walk out of a high school, where cheating is probably common, and a month later suddenly be able to live successfully under a totally new system.

The philosophy at the Academy is one that has descended from Aristotle, the Greek natural philosopher. Aristotle said that honorable behavior must be learned, and that the practice of living honorably over a period of time will lead to honorable behavior becoming a habit. Likewise, habits of dishonorable living are often carried into cadet life and impede honorable living.

When appointees arrive at the Academy, they are not expected to know anything about the Honor Code or what it means to live by it. The concept and practical advice on living with it are introduced gradually through many hours of formal instruction during BCT.

This instruction is designed to make basic cadets knowledgeable enough to know whether or not they want to take the Honor Oath at the end of BCT. Many more hours of Honor Code instruction will follow in subsequent years to help cadets understand what it means to lead an honorable life.

Honorable behavior must be learned.

This can be a big change for many cadets. A number of recent nation-wide studies reveal that most high school students—70-80%—have cheated at least once. Some believe it is harder to uphold the Honor Code today because of changes in the society from which cadets are drawn.

But according to a 1971 graduate who now supervises honor education, there is a misperception that today's cadets are less committed to the code than their predecessors. "In 1965, there was an honor scandal involving cadets who *broke into* the academic building at night, *stole* copies of tests, and then *sold* them to other cadets to *cheat* from! This is the same American culture as always. Every generation of Academy cadets has been challenged to do the right thing."

In fact, the number of honor cases reported has been holding steady over at least the last ten years, at about 160 per year. Of those, about half are violations—either the cadet admits to committing a violation or is found guilty by a board. Fewer than 30 cadets per year are disenrolled or resign after committing an honor violation.

The Honor Code is administered by the cadets themselves, under the supervision of officers. When a potential violation of the code comes to light, they perform an investigation. If the investigation indicates a possible violation, the cadets will convene an honor board to determine if a violation did occur. The cadets will make a recommendation to the Academy leadership as to whether the cadet should be disenrolled or given a chance at rehabilitation.

Disenrollment is often the punishment. But some cadets are offered a probation program instead. Probation means being restricted to the Academy, attending counseling sessions, and doing mandatory reading, reports, and presentations on the subject of honor. The probation period usually lasts six months, and is intended to make the violator think very hard about the Honor Code and what it means for his or her life. Upperclassmen who serve honor probation equate it to being a doolie again because of the increased supervision and loss of freedom.

Factors that determine whether probation is granted instead of disenrollment include whether the cadet admitted to the violation when he or she was confronted, the nature of the violation, and the seniority of the cadet. This last criterion is important because seniors who have been living under the Honor Code for four years are expected to have learned, understood, and internalized the code. They are judged harshly because they are about to become lieutenants in the Air Force, where the lives of others could depend on their integrity in many cases.

Such as this one:

A former cadet is now a second lieutenant stationed in Germany as an F-16 maintenance officer. His job: to make sure his assigned aircraft are ready for whatever mission they are ordered to fly.

One early morning, an airman on a crew the lieutenant is supervising forgets to make a routine test of the aircraft's electronic navigation system. The airman is not aware of the mistake and just as the lieutenant discovers it, there is an alert, then the squadron is scrambled. All planes must be airborne immediately.

 The lieutenant is in a dilemma. Holding back the airplane because of a dumb mistake will bring on the wrath of his commander and possibly a career-damaging comment on his record. Signing off the plane and take the slight chance that there could be something wrong with the navigation system is an attractive alternative. The equipment is reliable and nothing ever seems to happen to it. Moreover, if something did happen, the lieutenant feels sure that he could successfully claim that the malfunction occurred after the aircraft departed.

The solution to the problem looks foolproof. The lieutenant now makes the decision and rationalizes it in his mind. He will sign off the plane. He is not going to risk damaging his career this early, especially after he has put in four gut-busting years at the Air Force Academy to get where he is.

The pilot takes off in the F-16 and starts boring through heavy clouds toward Italy where he is to meet a tanker and replenish his fuel supply. But on his departure his heading indicator is off fifty degrees and as he thinks he is climbing on a safe heading the plane hits a mountain and explodes.

After the accident, investigators cannot find enough of the plane to determine what happened. The lieutenant is questioned but without evidence no blame is assessed. He escapes harm and his record remains clean.

And a pilot has died. Also a mission that might have been critical in saving hundreds or thousands of lives failed and a vital aircraft, irreplaceable in the days or weeks that a war might last, is lost.

So what about a cadet who cheats on a physics test, or lies to his squadron commander about why he was late to training on Saturday? Would his fellow cadets want to serve with this cadet, perhaps entrust their lives to him, if he became an officer? Does lying about "small" issues mean a cadet will lie about big issues later?

The point is that habits of dishonorable living usually continue—often with very bad outcomes.

Honor violations are not always clear cut to young cadets, so a large portion of the Honor Code instruction that the cadets receive is designed to help them interpret honorable and dishonorable behavior.

Here is an example of a simple case that illustrates the difficulty new cadets might have in practicing honorable behavior. What is your judgment?

One Sunday night a fourthclass cadet came back to the Academy from a weekend leave and arrived late—twenty minutes past the time when he was required to return. He sneaked into the dormitory but was caught by an upperclassman. The upperclassman confronted him and asked him the question, "Where have you been?"

The fourthclassman, who had stopped briefly in Arnold Hall to buy a snack while on his way to the dorm, answered the upperclassman by saying, "I have been in Arnold Hall."

Is the fourthclassman guilty of lying?

In their instruction on the Honor Code, cadets learn that such an answer comes under the category of "quibbling," which is defined as "giving a deliberately evasive answer."

The giving of a deliberately evasive answer is the same as lying under the Honor Code. Therefore, the cadet who said he had been in Arnold Hall, even though that was true in a narrow sense, was quibbling. He was quibbling because, in a broader sense, he was trying to evade the upperclassman's question and protect himself from discovery of a rule violation. So, yes, the fourthclassman was guilty of lying. The cadet has behaved dishonorably and has not had the courage or virtue to face his misbehavior.

New cadets also learn the finer points between rule violations and breaches in the Honor Code. If cadets are caught with beer in their room, they are guilty of breaking a rule prohibiting possession or consumption of alcoholic beverages in the dorm—a very serious offense. They will be punished, but will not be accused of an honor violation.

But, suppose there is some evidence that a cadet has taken beer into his room and an upperclassman asks the suspected cadet if he did that. If he says that he did not have beer in his room, that cadet is guilty of lying. This is an honor violation, and far more serious than rule breaking. Cadets grasp that distinction pretty quickly. One fourthclassman said, "You can get in trouble for a lot of things, but don't mess with honor."

The Honor Code is a proud and honorable tradition at the Academy.

Academy leadership tries to present the Honor Code not as a guillotine hanging over the heads of cadets, but as a proud and honorable tradition that binds them to one another and to all those who graduated before them. "We try to focus on the positive aspects of character development, provide cadets with roles models, examples, and a chance to reflect on their choices. The foundation of this character development is the Honor Code. But honorable behavior goes beyond the code. It's doing your duty, and living honorably."

WHAT CADETS THINK ABOUT THE HONOR CODE

What do the cadets at the Academy think of that system? Most who commented on it say that one aspect of the Honor Code is easy to accept—the part that governs their own actions.

Said one cadet, "It makes you feel good about yourself when you say that you won't lie, steal or cheat. And it's good to know that you can trust people and don't have to lock your doors like you would in a regular college."

Another said, "It's a good system. We need to be able to trust people, to know everyone is responsible. You can borrow a car, you can trust each other, even someone you don't know. We wouldn't want to jeopardize what we have—it's a brotherhood of trust."

A firstclassman remembered, "My freshman year in chemistry, I sat by my roommate, and we did our homework and labs together [which was permitted]. We took a test, and our answers were similar because we had studied together. The professor asked if we cheated. We said no, and the professor trusted and believed us. That says a lot about this institution. They say, 'Every time you take a test, you're really taking two tests: one on the material, and one on your integrity. If you can only get an A on one, it should be the test on your integrity.' Cheating was never an option for me."

The other aspect of the code—no cadet will tolerate any other cadet who lies, steals or cheats—is more difficult for many cadets to accept. This part of the code requires a cadet who witnesses what appears to be a violation to confront the offender and see that he takes action to address the problem or turn the offender in to a proper authority.

Said one cadet, "Everything here is teamwork, teamwork, teamwork. They stress teamwork here from the minute you arrive, and they hammer it into you day after day. You must learn to depend upon others, you can't do it alone, you must make the team more important than the individuals who are on it—all this stuff you hear over and over until it becomes a part of your thinking. That's good, it's easy to accept, it makes you feel good, it gives you strength...it's powerful."

Most cadets want everyone to be held accountable.

"But then there's the Honor Code that says, 'Hey, if I see one of these guys who is my buddy, who I've been depending on to get me through all this—and who I've helped, too. If I see him doing something wrong [a possible honor violation], I suddenly have to turn on him, I have to turn him in … rat on him. That's hard for me, very hard."

Some of the other cadets admitted that the non-toleration aspect of the code was difficult, but they readily defended it.

One said, "If he is cheating and is a friend, what kind of a friend is he? That's what I always ask myself."

Another said, "I don't want a person for a friend if he is going to cheat. If he cheats here, he will cheat later. It snowballs. From asking for two questions on a physics test, it will go on and potentially kill somebody."

Another cadet put a hypothetical friend's cheating into a different perspective. He said, "I am ready in my mind to turn in such a person. His action puts me in a compromising position. It's HIS fault that I have to turn him in, not mine. It [the blame] is on his shoulders. They teach, and I believe, that the mission comes before the friendship. I have to be ready in my mind to look somebody in the eye someday and send him out on a mission to die. You can't let friendship enter into such a decision."

Most cadets interviewed have faith that the system can be trusted, and they expect that if their classmates have violated the code, they will be disenrolled—they want everyone to be held accountable.

One fourthclassman was facing an honor board just a few days after our interview. He had been accused of cheating on a homework assignment. He said he was innocent, and trusted the board would agree. "I expect the system will work. You have to trust the system to work. We're taught that in BCT: Don't fear the Honor Code; it's not a witch hunt."

BE PREPARED TO LIVE UNDER THE CODE

What can a candidate for the Air Force Academy do to prepare for life with the Honor Code? That question was asked of an officer who administered the Academy program.

"I think," the officer replied after a thoughtful interlude, "that the best thing young people can do is to stop making excuses for their mistakes. Let me explain.

"In many cases it is the very conscientious cadet who commits the honor violation. Often it is a cadet who will not admit that he cannot get the grade he wants, or one who is such a perfectionist that he cannot admit that he has made mistakes for which he is to blame. A mistake to that kind of person is equated with failure and that is something he will not tolerate for himself.

"So he rationalizes the mistake and makes excuses—so that the blame falls on somebody else—a professor who he thinks is doing a bad job of teaching, for example. That type of self-deception, which is a form of internal lying, can ultimately lead to deception in one's behavior, often in the form of cheating.

"My advice to young people who want to come here and live with our Honor Code is to practice being honest with themselves. If they make a mistake, they should let their own conscience take the blame—even if it hurts.

"Admit the mistake; then try to learn from it. And, if they find themselves making excuses or looking for a scapegoat, they should recognize that behavior for what it is: self-deception. They are lying to themselves when they do that, and it is not a big step to cross the line and begin lying to others."

Another suggestion comes from an Admissions Liaison Officer with many years of experience dealing with candidates. He strongly recommends "that all potential candidates, when they get a chance to sit down and talk with cadets about the Academy, should get them to describe their experiences with the Honor Code.

"It's something that the cadets take very seriously and when they talk about it, they won't mince words. By doing this, the prospective cadet will know a lot more about what to expect and isn't so likely to blunder into something that he's mentally unprepared to accept."

So be prepared mentally to live by the Code, and look for opportunities to practice honorable behavior *now*. The Assistant Director of Honor, who is also a graduate, emphasized the importance of developing honorable habits. "I'd encourage candidates to *practice* this before USAFA. While acknowledging the pressure of high school peer groups, the candidates can be encouraged that living honorably is more often satisfying than painful (or ostracizing.) And, by practicing now, they gain the confidence, competence, and commitment that will enable them to act and live honorably once they arrive here."

A final suggestion comes from a former Vice-Commandant of Cadets, who remembers the advice of the late Major General Bud Breckner, a former POW who often spoke to cadets about honor. "General Breckner had many opportunities to measure the character and integrity of his comrades, as well as his own. He stressed that, 'One's integrity can never be taken away; it can only be given away.'

"If you come here and then go on to become an Air Force Officer, we want you to keep your integrity at all times. That is what the Honor Code is really all about. Its purpose is to teach you to keep your integrity and to hold you accountable when you give it away. So, if a young person can come here, keep his integrity and not give it away, he will have no problem living with the Honor Code."

CHAPTER TWENTY-FOUR
After Graduation: Air, Space, And Cyberspace

For decades, graduation from the Academy meant heading off to pilot or navigator training. The great majority of Air Force Academy graduates would be expected to fly. Many graduates tell stories of cadets who were physically qualified to fly but chose not to, and were summoned to the hallowed halls of the commandant's office to defend such foolish thinking!

In the past, being physically qualified for flight training made you more competitive for admission, since the Air Force Academy wanted to graduate as many pilots as possible. The doolie response to the question, "What is the mission of the United States Air Force?" was "To Fly, Fight, and Win…and Don't You Forget It!"

Because the Air Force's mission has changed so much over the last decade or so, career options have changed as well. Air Force Academy graduates serve and contribute in a very wide variety of career fields.

Change, however, often causes confusion or misinformation. Many candidates have heard rumors about these changes that are incorrect. We will examine some of these misconceptions.

- *Myth #1: The Air Force Academy does not send graduates to pilot training anymore.* Reality: For many years now, just over 50% of each graduating class goes to pilot training. True, this could change while you are a cadet, but for now this is reality. One candidate at a senator's nomination interview was asked why he put his academy preferences in the order he did, with Air Force last. He answered, "Because I want to fly, and you can't do that in the Air Force anymore." He was wrong!
- *Myth #2: Pilot training slots are so competitive that you have to be a superstar to get one.* Reality: For the past several years, just over 50% of cadets in each graduating class are physically qualified and want to go to pilot training. The math works out well—that is the same number for whom slots have typically been available.
- *Myth #3: If you want to fly, you need to come to the Academy with a private pilot's license.* Reality: Leaders in the flying programs will tell you that all you really need, besides the physical qualifications, is a good attitude and the willingness to work hard and learn. If you do have the resources to fly before you come to the Academy, it may help you decide for sure if flying is for you. But it is not necessary, and if you learn bad habits or decide you already know it all, it may actually hurt.

- *Myth #4: Even if you go to pilot training, you will fly an Unmanned Aerial System (UAS).* Reality: the Air Force has now established a separate training program to fill the growing demand for UAS pilots.
- *Myth #5: If you do not fly, you have limited opportunities for advancement in the Air Force.* Reality: As the Air Force mission becomes more diverse, the leadership reflects that change. You do not have to be a pilot to be a commander or a general.

YOU CAN STILL FLY AIRPLANES

The Air Force Academy is still a great way to have a career in aviation. As mentioned above, currently every physically qualified cadet who wants a pilot training slot can expect to get one. The Air Force Academy will even help you succeed in pilot training by giving you flying experience as a cadet, based out of their own airfield located right on Academy grounds.

Nearly half of cadets will have the opportunity to fly and possibly solo a glider. This program takes place either during the second summer or second year as a cadet. The gliders are launched from the Academy's own airfield, towed aloft by single-engine tow planes.

The soaring students are taught to fly by upperclass cadets who have successfully completed the program themselves, and were selected and trained to become instructors. They also perform demonstrations and enter competitions.

Soaring provides an opportunity to explore your interest in flying.   *Courtesy USAFA*

The cadet soaring instructors have an enormous advantage if they go on to pilot training, having learned by teaching, the best way possible.

Said one soaring instructor, "You gain judgment, maturity, and courage by flying in bad conditions with a brand new student." They also learn leadership skills that are helpful beyond the flightline: communications skills, patience, confidence, and how to teach. Another cadet soaring instructor remarked, "If you're the type of kid who stares up when a plane flies over, this is it!"

Cadets can also take part in the powered flight program, usually during their senior year. Cadets fly brand new Cirrus SR20 aircraft, dubbed the T-53A by the Air Force. This aircraft has two seats and a glass cockpit, and can cruise at 130 knots. All the instructors are experienced Air Force pilots.

Cadets who participate in powered flight gain valuable exposure to the operational Air Force flying environment, including the disciplined processes used for reviewing weather conditions and safety procedures and planning flights. Powered flight students receive nine flights, and most will solo at least once.

The powered flight program is not required for future pilots, but it will help them become more familiar with the culture and environment they will be part of. For those who struggle with airsickness, the program gives them a chance to overcome that. Most of all, it may stoke the passion they have to fly.

You may still have one burning question: Do I have the right stuff? The same attributes that will help you succeed in any of the Academy's aviation programs will also help you succeed in pilot training. As one cadet said, "Attitude is everything. You have to have a willingness to learn. We don't want to force feed them."

According to the fighter pilot who commands the powered flight program, "You get out what you put in. Be prepared, have a positive attitude, and don't be cocky."

NEW FRONTIERS: UNMANNED AERIAL SYSTEMS, SPACE, AND CYBERSPACE

Three growing career fields present opportunities for graduates to participate in cutting edge technology and develop brand new strategies and tactics. The Air Force Academy provides a variety of opportunities to explore all three.

Unmanned Aerial Systems

Also called Remotely Piloted Aircraft, Unmanned Aerial Vehicles, and even drones, UASs are basically airplanes operated via remote communications by a pilot on the ground. You may be familiar with UASs in the news for their contributions in Iraq and Afghanistan, such as the Predator, Reaper, or Global Hawk.

UASs were first used primarily in a reconnaissance role, passing images of the battlefield to combat and intelligence personnel. Their role is expanding, with many now able to drop bombs or launch missiles. They may someday be used for air refueling and other roles as well.

UAS pilots are usually based in the United States, but sometimes they operate from a deployed location instead. While the Air Force's pilot force is likely to shrink because of the high cost of acquiring, maintaining, and operating a large fleet of aircraft, the UAS force is growing and in high demand. UAS operators are trained at Randolph Air Force Base, Texas.

The Academy offers several airmanship courses that allow cadets to learn about and pilot UASs. They sometimes work with personnel at Fort Carson, a nearby Army base, to learn how the UAS is used in joint combat operations. Cadets also use the UASs as part of the cadet survival training program.

Like the powered flight program, the UAS airmanship classes are not required for those who will fly UASs after graduation. But the program does allow cadets to pursue their interest and get ahead of their peers in terms of knowledge and experience. While UASs were viewed in the past as a distant second place choice to manned aircraft, that is changing. Because of their increasing role in combat, and the opportunity to become familiar with their capabilities, many of today's technology-savvy cadets eagerly look forward to a career in UASs. You can get paid to play video games all day!

Space Operations

Space operations have long been the domain of the Air Force. On any given day, space operations personnel are launching and controlling satellites, monitoring for signs of attack, and keeping our communications and navigation systems functioning. Many Academy graduates will have the chance to participate in the Air Force's space mission.

The Academy has offered core courses and an academic major in Astronautical Engineering for years. Now, however, cadets can choose to major in Space Operations, taking courses such as Upper Atmospheric and Geo-Space Physics, A History of Space Power, and Remote Sensing and Imagery Analysis.

Cadets and faculty members watch the successful launch of FalconSat-5
Courtesy USAFA

Cadets can also participate in the FalconSat program, an interdepartmental, multi-year program to design and actually launch a satellite into space. FalconSat-5 successfully launched from Alaska in the fall of 2010 carrying a variety of experiments. Future versions are now in various stages of development.

Once again, if you are interested in the space aspect of the Air Force, the Academy offers opportunities to explore that interest.

Cyberspace

Playing Xbox Live, surfing YouTube, checking your grade on the last history test...we take for granted that the domain of cyberspace is ours to use as we like. The Air Force has acquired the job of defending cyberspace so it is available to the warfighter, and to explore ways to use it for military advantage.

Not surprisingly, the Air Force Academy's computer science major offers the option to take courses in Cyber Warfare, including Cryptography and Network Security.

Also not surprisingly, the Academy offers opportunities for cadets to pursue their interest in Cyber Operations beyond the classroom. Cadets can belong to a Cyber Warfare Club, which participates in exercises and competitions around the country. In April of 2012, for instance, they competed at (and won) a competition run by the top-secret National Security Agency, defending and maintaining a computer network against experts posing as the enemy. That same month, the Cyber Warfare Club also competed in the National Collegiate Cyber Defense Competition and came in second.

CHOOSING POST GRADUATION CAREERS

How will your career be determined? The Air Force will provide some limitations on how many graduates can go into each of literally dozens of different career fields. Then, based on their class ranking, (determined by academic, military, and athletic performance), cadets will select their specialty. The vast majority get one of their top choices, if not their first choice. As already mentioned, in recent years nearly every cadet who wanted to fly had a pilot slot available.

You will have lots of exposure to various career fields through academic courses, military training programs, and interacting with officers and NCOs who represent the whole spectrum of Air Force careers. If you are not sure what you want to do, you simply have to take the initiative to find out more about your options. By the time you select your specialty during your senior year, you will be able to make a very informed decision.

What careers did recent graduates choose?

Half became aviators, mostly pilots. Some become Combat Systems Operators—navigators, electronic warfare officers, weapons systems operators—air crew members other than pilots. And some go on to fly UASs.

The next most popular career field is acquisition, which involves managing the complex process of how the Air Force develops and buys new systems. Space, missiles, cyberspace, intelligence, and engineering are also popular choices.

Other career specialties are as varied as aircraft maintenance, special tactics, and medicine. Without taking the time to list all the options, realize that you will surely find a place where your interests and talents can be put to use.

This chapter has given you a small taste of the many academic courses and extracurricular activities you can explore at the Academy. There are many, many more. All of them will give you a chance to explore a potential future Air Force career, pursue your passion, and get a head start on your peers.

You may come to the Academy certain that you know what you want to study and what job you want after graduation. If not, or if you change your mind once or twice along the way, that is fine. Just realize that the phrase "the sky's the limit" has new meaning for today's Air Force cadets and officers.

TWENTY-FIVE
Advice For Parents

Over fifty parents were interviewed during the research for this chapter. Most had one son or daughter at the Academy, but some had two and one had three!

Some of the other parents had sons or daughters who were recent graduates and who are now serving in the Air Force. A few were parents of former cadets who had either dropped out of the Academy or who had been expelled.

Most of the parents were middle-class Americans; however, some were poor and a few were first-generation immigrants. Some were Academy graduates themselves, and some had no experience at all with anything connected to the military. They represented a wide variety of attitudes, especially about the military and their child's decision to serve.

At one extreme were the military officers, both active-duty and retired, who were very enthusiastic about their cadet's choice of careers. At the other extreme was a mother who "joined every peace organization I could find" in an attempt to counter the effectiveness that her B-52 navigator son might have as a brainwashed "militarist."

Despite their diversity, all shared the belief that parents of Air Force Academy candidates need advice on a variety of problems they will encounter. This chapter is a collection of advice from all those parents, and from cadets, graduates, staff, and faculty members as well.

Just as important as the "what to do" advice is the "what not to do" advice, because you will want to avoid certain missteps that would make life *more* difficult for your son or daughter.

The advice covers a lot of territory and steps through the cadet experience sequentially, beginning with the application process.

THE PROSPECTIVE CANDIDATE
- Apply for the Right Reasons

During all the interviews one bit of advice was heard over and over and over, and it was strongly recommended that it should be the first advice parents of a prospective candidate should hear. The advice is this: **Make absolutely sure that going to the Air Force Academy is your son or daughter's idea, not your idea or someone else's.**

Nearly everyone had a story to tell about a young man or woman who went to the Academy because it was someone else's idea. None of those stories ended happily.

Typically, they ended with the cadet quitting, then going home to the emotional trauma of facing relatives, friends and admirers who all believed that he had once had the "right stuff" but threw it away for some reason. The emotional scars that damage the family relationship, even in an otherwise healthy family, take a long time to heal. Everyone involved feels betrayed or ashamed or damaged.

Another typical ending was for the cadet to be expelled for poor academic or military performance. Often this is the face-saving tactic of a poorly motivated cadet who knows he will have to face a zealous, angry parent when he goes home. When he is expelled, he can say, "Dad, I tried as hard as I could but I just couldn't hack the math." That excuse is hard to rebut.

The ending can be worse, both for the cadet and the parents. A West Virginia father whose son was expelled for a rule violation during his senior year asked to be interviewed so other parents might learn from his mistake.

He said, "My son really didn't want to be there, but he put up a good front for a long time. He knew we were very proud of him and he just toughed it out to keep from hurting us—to keep from letting us down. And what hurts is that if I had been a good listener during the first years, I would have realized that. He tried to tell us how unhappy he was and it just didn't get through. Now he's home and it's been very hard for all of us. But at least we are communicating now and I believe that he is going to do all right. As parents we are wiser, but that is not going to get rid of the guilt we feel for causing so much misery for him."

A Georgia father said, when commenting on the importance of self-motivation, "It requires an incredible amount of determination to survive at the Air Force Academy, and cadets who are not 100 percent motivated for reasons of their own are not likely to survive."

The mother of a cadet from Massachusetts probably summed up the advice most succinctly. She said, "If a kid goes there sitting on the fence, he is going to get knocked off."

Saddest of all is the story many cadets tell of friends and classmates whose parents said, "If you quit, don't come home." What a terrible burden to bear, on top of all that doolies must endure already. Every so often a cadet leaves the Academy with a few boxes of personal possessions and no money, nowhere to go, and no plan. These cadets are proof that even the most intense pressure from home is not enough to keep them at the Academy if their heart is not in it.[1]

---

1. *My own father, who had taught at the Academy during my elementary school years, tried to talk me out of going, just to be absolutely sure I really wanted to go for my own reasons and not to please my parents. The last thing he said before he took me to the airport was, "If the Academy isn't for you, just call. We'll send you a plane ticket home." These words were a wonderful gift that I never needed to take advantage of.*

Another bit of advice is a logical extension of the preceding: make sure that your son or daughter wants to go to the Academy for the *right* reasons.

According to many who evaluate colleges and universities, the Air Force Academy gives young people an excellent academic education. But if that is all that your son or daughter wants, it would be a mistake to go there.

The goal of the Air Force Academy is to produce high quality Air Force officers, many of whom will become pilots. They will work long hours in the service of their country, and most will endure separations from their families on deployments to austere locations.

The academic education that young people get there is like the entree of a full-course dinner. A high quality college education lies at the heart of the Academy program, but a whole lot more goes along with it.

The Air Force Academy education is above all a four-year officer training program. It is rigorous and demanding and requires young men and women to make great personal sacrifices, especially of their personal freedom. Prospective candidates should have firm goals that are in concert with the Academy's mission. If they want to become Air Force officers after proving and improving themselves in a high-stress environment, then they stand a chance of succeeding. It all depends upon how badly they want to achieve their goal.

However, if they are going for ANY other reason, or if their goal is not clear, perhaps they should look elsewhere. There are hundreds of high quality civilian colleges and universities where they can get an excellent education without enduring all of the misery that they will suffer at the Air Force Academy. And by avoiding that misery they also will avoid the emotional trauma that comes from being branded as a quitter, or the guilt and feelings of failure that come with being expelled.

- Know What They Are Getting Into

Other words of wisdom come from Air Force Academy Admissions Liaison Officers (ALOs) who function somewhat like talent scouts. There are about 1500 of them scattered about the country, and their duty is to find talented youngsters and assist and evaluate those who have the ability and desire to attend the Academy. One who has been in the business almost thirty years claims that, "The kids who know the most about the Academy before they go there are the ones who are most likely to survive when they get there."

This same conclusion was repeated many times. So parents are advised to do everything they can to enable a candidate to learn as much as much as possible about the Academy. The following is a variety of suggestions on how to achieve that goal.

"The Academy puts on a program every summer called the Summer Seminar," said a father from Georgia. "It is available to high school kids who have completed their junior year and I think it is imperative that kids attend it—if the parent can afford the cost of transportation, of course. Both my sons went and they learned a lot about the Academy. The oldest really became gung ho after the visit and he is doing well there. The youngest got his eyes opened and decided, even though he, too, wanted to be a pilot, that ROTC at Georgia Tech was better for him. It is well worth the money."

The father was commenting on a one-week program that allows high school students to attend classes at the Academy, sleep in the cadet dorms, and eat in the cadet dining hall.

Throughout the program the students are escorted and supervised by cadets and there are many opportunities for frank discussions on Academy life. To find out more have your son or daughter contact a high school counselor, or visit the web site at www.academyadmissions.com/admissions/outreach-programs/summer-seminar.

An alternative, which is available anytime during a high school student's junior or senior year, is an official visit to the Academy. Such a visit can be arranged by a telephone call 1-800-443-3864 (10 days' advance notice is needed), which will arrange an admissions briefing for the family and a cadet-escorted tour for the candidate. This tour includes visits to the different buildings, observation of cadet classes and a lunch with the cadets. Family members will receive a separate tour.

Tours are available in the summer, but there are no cadets available to conduct them and little can be observed except the buildings. It is MUCH BETTER to go during the academic year when cadet life is at its normal high intensity.

Students not yet into their junior year can also receive the admissions briefing if they visit the Academy. But if they take a tour, it will have to be self-guided and they will not have as many opportunities to ask questions.

A third alternative is to attend a sports camp. These week-long camps are offered in some 15 different sports, from football to cheerleading to water polo. You will have to fund the travel expenses and registration fees. While not specifically geared for potential candidates, the camps provide a chance to interact and talk with cadets, and see the Academy up close. Schedules and registration information can be found at www.goairforcefalcons.com.

The bottom line is that every option should be pursued to learn more about the Academy beforehand. Prospective candidates should speak with as many different cadets as possible. If they are asked, Admissions Liaison Officers will try to arrange for candidates to speak with cadets who are home during vacations. In addition, many areas of the country have active Air Force Academy Parents' Clubs and their officers understand the importance of prospective candidates getting advice from cadets. They, too, will help arrange meetings. (More information on parents' clubs is presented later in this chapter.)

Prospective candidates must also have a realistic knowledge of what it means to be an Air Force officer. Parents can help by locating an active duty or retired officer and by making sure that their candidate gets an appointment and discusses the many aspects of life in the Air Force. Young people are not always aware of the negative aspects of such a career. An officer can round out the picture, which may turn out to be something less attractive.

THE ADMISSIONS PROCESS

The admissions process is long and complicated, and if your son or daughter completes all the steps, you will no doubt be exhausted and relieved. There are many things parents can do to assist their candidate. First, familiarize yourself with the admissions web site, www.academyadmissions.com. You will find a tab for parents and mentors with information just for you.

Most of the parents who were interviewed believed, prior to getting involved in the admissions process, that for a candidate to be appointed to a service academy, one had to have political pull with a congressman or senator.

All but one changed their mind after they got involved with the admissions process and heard the experiences of other candidates—both winners and losers. A father who was a brand new resident of Louisiana gave a typical comment: "When my son decided where he wanted to go, I thought, boy we're dead; we don't know anybody and this is a political state. Now, after seeing what he and others went through, I am convinced that the system is basically fair and not political."

Parents' club presidents who commented on the matter agreed. The Michigan president said, "In my four years as an officer in this club, complaints about the process are conspicuous by their absence."

The New York City president said, "Believe me, in a city like this with all the political things going on, you can bet I would have heard some negative comments. I don't remember hearing even one."

The one parent who believed differently said that her family's good connections may have had an influence on her son's appointment. However, that son was also interviewed by the author at the Academy and he was a highly motivated, successful cadet. He was certainly not JUST a political appointment.

Admissions officials also stress the fact that ALL appointees must be fully qualified. U.S. Senators and Representatives cannot get unqualified candidates into the Air Force Academy, they assert.

The actual details of the admissions process are explained in the Section Two of this book, and you will probably learn a few important things if you read through it. What parents should know is what they can do to help with the process, and what they should NOT do.

- Parents Should Stay in the Background

Most parents believe that their proper role is that of a supervisor. They say this because of the mass of paperwork that is required and because of the many deadlines and appointments that are critical in the process. In addition, the types of young people who are applying are typically those who have many irons in the fire and, while they are good at the things they are doing, have had little or no experience juggling forms and scheduling multiple deadlines, conferences and interviews.

Several parents recommended that the candidate and parents make a master schedule on a calendar—a schedule that includes every phase of the process. Following such a schedule will then be like following the pre-takeoff checklist for an airplane; everything will get done and nothing will be missed.

Other parents think their best role is that of a secretary. They believe that the candidate should be helped with the letters and forms, proofreading and other miscellaneous chores that the candidate may not have time to do.

Just about everyone, including congressional staffers, Liaison Officers, and parents, agreed that parents SHOULD NOT get involved in other aspects of the admissions process.

Most say that the candidates themselves should make the phone calls that are a necessary part of the process. They give two reasons.

First, Liaison Officers, admissions counselors, and congressional staffers all know there are parents who tend to push kids into applying for the Academy. And usually they begin worrying about that when they start getting phone calls from parents, which means that an excessive amount of communication with you, the parent, will actually hurt your candidate's chances for an appointment. Said one veteran Liaison Officer, "Just the moment I detect any attempt by parents to push a son or daughter, immediately my antennae go up. From that time on I am very cautious and if I continue to suspect those parents after an interview, I become very cautious in grading the candidate."

Since the Liaison Officer's recommendation counts toward the candidate's overall admissions score, the parent should think seriously about any phone call that the candidate could make for himself.

The other argument for the candidate making all the phone calls was best made by a congressional staffer:

"Basically, each cadet is selling himself during all phases of the admissions process. Why not use phone calls as opportunities to do that? When I get a call from a candidate who sounds self-assured, particularly if he or she is polite and is following up to check on the arrival of some document, I'm impressed. I am not impressed when parents call and I wonder why they are taking away this opportunity for the child to sell himself."

- Preparing for Interviews

Many candidates have to be interviewed by one or more panels before they can be nominated. Often the candidate's first interview is the FIRST EVER interview before adults.

Guidelines for interviews are presented in the candidate section of this book, but one of the recommendations can be enhanced with parent support. This is the recommendation for candidates to locate one or more retired military officers and have them conduct a practice interview with the candidate.

Even just one exposure to an officer asking questions will give the candidate invaluable experience. Performance invariably improves with practice, and who knows but what the candidate's first real interview might be the most critical one in the whole admissions process.

Parents can also serve as an interview coach. One Air Force Academy graduate shared the questions she had been asked at her *own* nomination interview with her daughter as she was preparing. Most parents, military or civilian, have been through a competitive interview at some point and have good advice to share.

- Other Steps in the Admissions Process

Another thing that parents should know is that the candidate's score on the SAT or ACT tests is a very important part of the overall evaluation. In a recent class, the average cadet entered with an SAT over 1300 and ACT scores of 30 in every area. Realize that the BEST score on either of the tests that will be used by the Academy. Therefore, do not be surprised if the candidate wants to take both tests or wants to repeat them. The tests cost money, but it is not wasted. On the contrary, the fee paid for repeating those tests might pay off with an appointment that otherwise might not have been obtained.

Parents also are urged to investigate the medical and physical requirements of the Academy. They are spelled out in detail on the web site. There is no point in a candidate building his hopes when he is clearly disqualified for medical or physical reasons.

All candidates must take a Candidate Fitness Test as a part of the admissions process. Parents may want to check the specific requirements on the web site. The parent can help supervise and assist with some of the candidate's physical conditioning, particularly with girls who lack upper-body strength. A father from North Carolina who had done this told of seven girls who accompanied his daughter to one of the Candidate Fitness Tests. "Of the seven who went with us, five got so discouraged that they just completely gave up and dropped out. My daughter was prepared and she did fine."

One final tip came from an Arizona mother. While discussing teenagers and the typical way many of them procrastinate when it comes to admissions paperwork, she said, "It is a good idea to ask yourself WHY the child is procrastinating. It may be that by procrastinating he is subconsciously trying to get himself out of a situation that he does not want to be in. He may think he wants to go to the Academy and may even verbalize it if you ask him. But you may want to step in at this point and try to get him to look more deeply at his motives and be completely honest. He really may not want to go and by finding this out now, he can save everyone a lot of headaches and heartaches."

AFTER THE APPOINTMENT

The appointment is an offer of admission by the Air Force Academy. If the candidate accepts the appointment, then he or she will join the next class, which will enter about the end of June.

- Orientation

During the spring months, the Academy offers an optional orientation program for appointees. The appointees live with a cadet and observe many of the things that doolies (first-year cadets) are put through by upperclassmen. They also attend classes and get a feel for the amount of work required for success in the academic program.

Most parents felt the orientation program was important and well worth the cost, which involves transportation, meals, and at least one night's lodging in Colorado Springs. (One night will be spent free at the Academy.)

"My daughter went to the orientation program and she came back more excited than ever," said a New York father. "But my son went later and he decided not to take his appointment after seeing what the cadets had to go through. He was also admitted to Notre Dame and he felt he would be happier there. So it's a good deal for the kids and for the Academy. The kids avoid the hassle of going, then finding out it's not for them. It's good for the Academy because they get to appoint someone else who might stick out the whole four years."

- Physical Conditioning

When appointees attend one of the orientation sessions, it is recommended that they get fitted and purchase a pair of combat boots. That way they can bring them home, break them in and get their feet conditioned for the rigors of basic training. And encourage them to BREAK THEM IN THOROUGHLY. Those who do not often end up with blisters that can keep them on the sidelines—an undesirable situation for a basic cadet.

Appointees should arrive at the Academy as physically fit as they can be. They should continue to condition by running and doing pushups, pullups, and flutter kicks. You do not need a gym membership, a personal trainer, or any special equipment. Just commitment.

SUPPORT

All appointees report to the Air Force Academy around the end of June. When they first step off the bus that takes them to the cadet area, they will be "greeted" with loud, critical, in-your-face guidance from the upperclassmen. Life as they knew it has just ended. In fact, one doolie we interviewed remembered one of the appointees on his bus turned right back around and got on the bus. But if they stay, they will have to endure the "doolie year," which will probably be the roughest eleven months of their lives.

One mother from Colorado advised preparing mentally for the goodbye if you bring your son or daughter to check in on the first day. The last thing they need, right before that in-your-face greeting from the upperclassmen, is a tearful mom or dad or sister. You can cry on the drive home.

If you bring your son or daughter to inprocessing, be emotionally prepared for the goodbye.
Courtesy USAFA

Many cadets will say goodbye at home, then fly to the Academy by themselves. The Academy and the Association of Graduates will help them find lodging and transportation to in-processing. Some cadets who arrived this way said it made it easier not having to say goodbye on in-processing day.

Life will not be easy for the parents, either, especially when the full impact of what has happened begins to sink in. "You don't realize it at the time," said a mother from Mississippi, "but you are losing your child forever when he steps on that plane. The next time you see him he will be a different person. That's when it will hit you. You realize then that his childhood is gone forever."

Your cadet will pay a price to mature that rapidly. It is paid during Basic Cadet Training, abbreviated BCT and pronounced, for good reason, "beast." In the short time of six weeks every fiber of the cadet's body will be tested and challenged. (After BCT is over, they will be formally accepted into the cadet wing and earn a few—very few—privileges.)

Within that short time, young men and women who reigned as kings and queens of their high schools are suddenly thrust into a social caste lower than the untouchables.

The in-your-face criticism starts on day one. *Courtesy USAFA*

Those who have heard nothing but accolades over the years for their grand accomplishments suddenly hear nothing but shouts and taunts from ubiquitous and imperious upperclassmen ringing in their ears.

And all this is happening during hot summer days, at a temperature-adjusted altitude (density altitude) of about 11,000 feet above sea level, while their bodies are straining for oxygen and the chemicals of stress and fatigue are languishing in their muscles and brain. This is no serious challenge to their health and they will shortly adapt to the new altitude. However, until they do, even athletes who have always relied upon their stamina to haul them out of previous experiences with physical stress may suffer frustrating bouts of fatigue that can exacerbate the mental stress that is upon them every waking minute.

In short, your cadet is undergoing what seems to be a mental and physical crisis.

To the Air Force, the cadet is undergoing a necessary character test.

It is a test to see if the cadet has the strength of character to become an Air Force Officer—one who can be trusted to fly fifty million dollar airplanes loaded with nuclear bombs or sit with fingers on the control switches for deadly nuclear missiles.

And while all this is going on, Mom and Dad are sitting at home, growing more anxious as each day passes. Is he holding up under the strain? Is she getting blisters in those boots? Is he adapting to the altitude? Is she going to call and say she is at the airport and on her way home? These and a hundred other questions torture their minds. The constant contact and feedback you had before is gone.

Then there is the guilt that many parents talked about during the interviews. Did I give him too much encouragement? Is she there because she wants to save us the financial hardship of sending her to a civilian college? Should I have tried harder to keep him from going off and maybe someday killing himself in an airplane? Is she staying out there just because she knows how proud we are of her? These are the kinds of questions that haunt parents as feelings of guilt rise in their souls.

According to a Florida mother who has had two sons graduate from the Academy, "This is hold-your-breath time...a time for heavy praying... it's a time when the kid is unsure he can make it, a time when parents are unsure that he can make it, and a time when parents are unsure they even WANT the kid to make it."

Neither the anxiety nor the guilt is likely to be relieved by the one hastily scribbled letter that parents typically receive sometime while the cadet is going through BCT. Often the letter is written just before bedtime, at the direct order of an upperclassman, and while the cadet is so tired the simple act of holding a pen is a chore.

So what do you do? Some parents will spend hours poring through pictures posted by the Association of Graduates' "Web Guy." There will be dozens and dozens of close up and group action shots of the new basic cadets doing every activity.

You may succeed in finding your son or daughter in a lot of pictures, or you may not—they all look surprisingly alike. Your child may look dirty, sweaty, exhausted, or just generally miserable. Do not worry. These pictures do not tell you how well they are doing.

What else can you do? Over and over parents and cadets stressed that you should do everything possible to make your cadet feel that he has your love and support.

- Mail Call

In the words of one doolie, when asked what advice this book should give to parents, "Tell them to write letters before [their son or daughters] even leave home. This is huge. Then keep it coming. From friends and relatives too."

"One of the best ways to [support them]," said an Arizona father who has three sons at the Academy, "is to make sure they never have an empty mailbox. I made it my goal to write every night. Anyone who has been in service knows how devastating it is to go to mail call and see everybody else getting letters and you getting nothing. Also, from my own experience at the Naval Academy I knew what they were going through, especially that first year. You have to treat that doolie year very carefully...very tenderly. It's their first time away from home and I don't care how sophisticated they are, they need to know that you are thinking of them."

"I wrote every day," said a mother from Mississippi, "and I gave the coach and our son's friends stamped, addressed postcards so they could write, too. Later, I sent him stamped, addressed postcards, too, and I wish I had thought of it sooner. They have so little time, anything like that will help them."

A father from New York who also is co-president of a parents' club stresses that parents should use their creativity when thinking of ways to support their cadet. "In my own case, for example," he said, "my daughter has had her eyes on the stars for many years. Her goal in going to the Academy is to become an astronaut so to give her a little boost after she arrived, I had written to Sally Ride and Judy Resnik, the astronauts, and to Arthur C. Clarke and Isaac Asimov, two science-fiction writers she admired. In the letters I told them about her and asked if they would write her a note just to bolster her at a difficult time. You know what? All four wrote to her! And I know that those letters meant a lot and probably helped her through some rough times when she was doubting herself."

A father from Florida seconded the need to think in unconventional terms. "We wrote several letters before our son even left," he said, "because we wanted them to be there when he arrived. As it turned out, he didn't get them for about a week, but then there were ten or fifteen of them. I think we got our message across, which was that we really care."

A similarly creative mother from California generated a number of interesting letters for her son just by putting up a card with his name and address on the bulletin board of her church. "He even got some letters from teenagers, which was a surprise," she said.

Several parents also offered advice on what to put in letters and what not to say. "They need positive reinforcement at this time," said a parents' club president from Illinois who has two sons at the Academy. "So write positive things and keep negative things to yourself."

CELL PHONES AND E-MAIL

In decades past, cadets lined up on Sunday afternoons to use the squadron phones to call home. Parents could only call the cadets in emergencies. And ordinary "snail mail" was the primary means of sharing information.

Now, after BCT is over and the academic year begins, the information highway is open wide to parents who wish to communicate with their cadets. Cadets live for contact from home, "So, by all means," say parents and cadets who regularly use e-mail, "Keep the messages coming."

But there is one caveat and it was best expressed by a firstclassman. She said, "It is great to get to your room and sit down to an e-mail message from Dad. But please, please get it in the parents' chapter of your book that e-mail does not take the place of real letters. It means so much to walk down to the mailroom, peek in the window to see if there is mail, then turn the combination and discover a letter from Mom and Dad. It is an expression of love and it puts a smile on your face."

Use e-mail regularly; your cadet will love it. But also write letters regularly, even if you constantly repeat yourself. It is the expression of love that counts as much as the message. And don't expect an answer the same day you send your cadet an e-mail. They get literally hundreds of e-mails a day, so many have disciplined themselves to take care of critical things first—doing homework, shining shoes, etc. They may be too busy to answer you today, tomorrow, or this week. Do not be hurt.

Cell phones are a great way to stay connected as well. Depending on the squadron, your cadet may not have cell phone privileges for part or most of the first year. Again, when they do, they will probably develop a regimen for using the phone that keeps them from getting distracted from their to-do lists. Many cadets schedule a regular time, perhaps Sunday afternoon, to talk to Mom and Dad. The rest of the time they may leave it turned off.

"And don't tell them enticing things that they are missing at home," said a Florida father. "They're missing home enough as it is. Also, I don't think it is a good idea for them to be hearing how much you miss them. Be positive when you write or talk on the phone. Think it out before you blurt it out."

Another father, from Georgia, said, "Don't bug them for details of what is going on. They're not used to that altitude. They're beat. It isn't like a summer camp—they're going through hell and they don't want to talk about it."

The doolies also give some cautionary words on how to send letters. During BCT, they will visit the mailroom as a group, under the supervision of the upperclassmen. Letters on pink stationary decorated with stickers, hearts and flowers, singing cards, or perfumed stationary will earn the recipient some extra harassment and pushups. As with everything a doolie has or does, standing out is a bad thing. As one doolie succinctly put it, "It will be bad." Best to use only plain white envelopes, and put the embellishments inside the letter, not *on* the envelope.

Several parents suggested giving the cadet a subscription to the hometown newspaper—and making sure that you subscribe early enough for it to arrive at the Academy with the cadet. Said a mother from Mississippi, "Our son never read the paper before he left, but now he reads it word for word and page for page...he is hungry to hear things from home, more than I ever would have thought."

Equally important as letters and newspapers is the care package, say parents. Their advice is to send them as often as you can and it doesn't matter much what is in them—cookies, salami, vanilla wafers—even a faded old jersey was welcomed, said one parent. The important thing to remember is to send more than enough for just your cadet. He or she will always share and your cadet may end up with far less than you expect.

With care packages parents have the opportunity to use the creative input of all members of the family, including little brothers and sisters. "I would never have thought of putting in Gummy Bears," said a Louisiana mother, "but our daughter thought of it."

Also, try to include things that are difficult for the cadet to get. A Mississippi mother said, "We had to laugh when we got this request for Froot Loops—he never ate them at home. But in the dining hall the upperclassmen would not let the doolies have them. So he asked for them and we sent them. Then he and his friends got a big laugh out of just having them. It's a little thing but it was a morale booster."

You can also send "Cadet Treats" baskets to your cadet. Located in Arnold Hall, the cadet recreation center, Cadet Treats will prepare special baskets such as get well baskets with juice, soup, pudding and hot chocolate; or birthday baskets with cake, candy, and birthday plates; study baskets; and even balloon bouquets. The baskets are delivered right to the squadron. You can contact Cadet Treats at 877-9CADETS, or visit their website at www.usafasupport.com/cadet-activities/cadet-treats.

Care packages are not allowed during BCT, but several parents told of smuggling treats in by letter. "Gum is worth its weight in gold," said a California mother and parents' club president. "Just tape it to a card and the worst that can happen is that an upperclassman might see it and take it for himself."

A Georgia father and parents' club president said, "We smuggled in fruit roll-ups—they lie flat enough to go into a letter. Beef jerky also is flat and a good thing to send."

- Lend a Sympathetic Ear

Almost all parents agreed on what you are likely to hear when your cadet does call, e-mail, or write. They will likely complain about school or the upperclassmen being too tough, or they may go into great detail about an experience that makes no sense to you but was traumatic to them. Many cadets we interviewed answered the question, "What did you do when you were feeling down," with, "I called home." Your cadet may seem discouraged *every* time you talk to them—that

> *Expect downer phone calls from your cadet.*

is *why* they call home, but it does not mean that they are miserable all the time. They instinctively call home looking for encouragement and validation—they need you to tell them they are great kids and you know they can make it, positive words that are in very short supply during an average doolie day.

"It's a real roller coaster ride," said a North Carolina father and president of the state parents' club. "One week they will call and really be down. You give them encouragement, of course, but you spend the whole next week worrying and feeling guilty. Then, when they call again and you expect they're going to tell you that they're coming home, they're just fine. This is something all parents have to expect and be ready for; they have to understand that this is normal behavior."

A father and president of a Michigan parents' club added: "What really creates anxiety for parents is when the cadet begins hinting around or even outright says that he might quit and come home. What both parents have to realize is that practically every cadet thinks about quitting at some time, and many think about it often. In my experience, both as a parent and hearing other parents tell of their experiences, it is unusual for a cadet NOT to say he is going to quit and come home at least two or three times. If all cadets who said that actually quit, the Academy would have a 60 or 70 percent attrition rate."

So what do you say when the cadet talks about quitting? Here are some typical responses of parents who were asked that question.

A father from Florida whose son is in his second year at the Academy: "The worst thing you can say is, 'Yes, come on home.' That makes it too easy. I have said, 'I don't think you have given it enough time. After all, this is what you chose as your life career. Go talk to a counselor or your chaplain before you do anything rash; it took you twelve years to get there and you have only been there ___ weeks. You need to give it more time."

A mother from New Mexico whose son is about to finish his doolie year: "You must listen to kids. Let them talk, let them say that maybe the place isn't for them. It's important for them to vent that frustration—they're in something they've never been in before. My husband was great on the phone. He'd always say, 'Now let's think about this.' Then he would use an analogy of any army group in battle that is being attacked and about to be defeated. He'd say, 'Are they going to let themselves be defeated? No. They will pull back and regroup; then take another look at it. You have been in a battle and I think you need to do the same thing: back up and regroup and just think what you really want to get out of this.' Conversations like that have helped our son so much. He would go do what his father suggested and the next time we talked to him everything would be all right.

Listen to them if they talk about quitting.

"The main thing is to try to keep the kid from acting on the emotions of the moment. Try not to let them throw a tremendous opportunity away on a moment's whim. Of course, you can't say, you're there and you're going to stay there—parents can't give them an ultimatum because we're not the ones who have to go through all of that."

A mother from Louisiana whose son is in his third year: "When they call home and they say 'I've had it,' you say, 'You made it this far, you can make it farther.' I knew I had to do it even though that first year he was up there I was questioning *myself* constantly, saying, 'Am I doing the right thing?' Now I know it was the right thing. I saw that when I saw how he was growing and maturing."

A father and parents' club president from Virginia whose son is about to graduate: "My son was very determined not to quit, partly because when he was in high school, a counselor objected to him listing the Air Force Academy as his first choice for a college—she told him to put down something more realistic for his goal. He still went through the phases of wondering if it was worth it. I think parents should be good listeners and keep reminding cadets of the goals they have set for themselves. On days he was particularly down, I would ask, 'Is it worth giving up your goals when the going gets tough?' He would say, 'Yes, I still really want to do it but I just don't want to go through all this stuff.' But then, the next day he would be better and by the next week whatever was dragging him down was behind him and he would be fine. You have to help them keep their goals foremost in their mind. Keep them from changing their goals when the going gets tough or when they have a downer day."

What about the fine line between being a good listener and supporter and wrongly encouraging a cadet to stay where he really does not want to be?

An Air Force colonel who has had both a son and daughter graduate from the Academy and who knows intimately the kinds of problems cadets encounter says, "After all the encouragement, and all the 'hang in there, kid, we're behind you' types of support, you have to be ready—and I think the parent will know it if he is truly listening—to hear the child say, 'I do not want to stay here.' You ultimately have to let him go and you should be there with open arms. If that child shows up on the doorstep, you have to take him in your heart and help him work out the next step."

On the same subject a California mother said, "You don't have to worry if the kid knows that the door at home opens both ways. He will be much more secure; and if he truly believes that you are supporting him, he won't stay if it isn't something he really wants."

A Florida mother with two recent graduates added another perspective to the problem. She said, "You have to encourage them and be the devil's advocate when they want to quit. Just make sure it isn't your own emotions that you're trying to protect while you're doing it. Ask yourself if you are trying to keep the kid in there so your own pride will not suffer, then you'll know which side of that line you're on."

"You don't have to worry if the kid knows that the door at home opens both ways."

While your cadet is struggling through the stresses of the doolie year, life goes on outside the Academy. Parents sometimes get sick or get divorced, grandparents die, and other bad things happen. You will have decide how to pass on that bad news. Resist the temptation to shelter your cadet. One Air Officer Commanding (an officer who supervises a cadet squadron) gives this advice: "Call if you have issues.

Don't hide the big issues, or it will cause a rift. You know your kids and what they can handle. You have to trust your kids."

PARENTS' WEEKEND
"Get a second mortgage on your house if you have to."
"Take an extra job if necessary."
"I don't care if they have to borrow the money..."
"I think it is almost a duty..."
"Do it even if you have to beg or borrow..."

The preceding are excerpts taken from interviews with parents who were giving advice about Parents' Weekend, held each year over Labor Day weekend. Perhaps those excerpts will help convey the strength of the convictions which go along with their advice: do not fail to attend Parents' Weekend, especially during the cadet's first year.

Said an Academy professor who also has the reputation of being an outstanding cadet sponsor, "You have no idea how it tears kids up when their parents don't show up for the first Parents' Weekend. Here they are [the doolies], they've just come through the most rigorous two months of their lives...they have made it through BCT. They have had a glimpse of the rigorous academic schedule they're going to have to cope with and the upperclassmen in their new squadrons have just begun to tighten the screws...but they have survived so far and they are proud of themselves for having done so. At this time they badly need for their parents to see them in their uniform and to share that pride, especially when thousands of other cadets are walking around with their parents, getting love and sympathy and declarations of support. It is very hard on a teenager who is already homesick to cope with such a disappointment. Parents who don't show up should be prepared for the cadet to come home for Christmas and announce that he is not going back."

If you agree with the preceding advice and are financially able to go to the first Parents' Weekend, here is a variety of information that you may find useful.

A mother from Mississippi: "The day your child accepts that appointment, start working on getting motel reservations for the Labor Day Weekend. Colorado Springs is loaded that weekend with other activities—an international hot-air balloon meet, bicycle races—you name it. Later, you'll get a list of motels from the Academy, but don't wait on them." (You can contact the Colorado Springs Convention and Visitors Bureau at www.visitcos.com or 877-PIKESPEAK and get lodging information.)

A mother from Florida: "If you have to take off from work, make arrangements early so you can be sure and have vacation time approved."

Be prepared for the fact that your son or daughter will seem amazingly different from the kid you hugged goodbye a few months earlier. BCT has changed them; it is supposed to. They will look different and act different. They may not want to tell you much in specific about their experience, either because they do not want to think about it, or it is just too hard to describe.

A father of two cadets and a parents' club president from Illinois: "Be ready for a shock when you see your child. My son weighed 190 when he left home and about 160 when we saw him. He looked emaciated and sad but we found out that he was just lean and healthy. It was really depressing for us at first."

And said a North Carolina mother, "He looked like he just came out of a POW camp; he seemed to be all bones. But we laughed about it and I kidded him about how he would be a good model now with his cheekbones showing."

Parents will also greet a child who will be in a behavior mode they might not expect. Said a father and parents' club president from New York, "Don't be surprised if all they want to do is sleep. It happened to our daughter...it happens to all of them...they're beat when you first see them but they liven up after they've had a little rest."

A father from Utah: "We got there all cranked up to sightsee and all our daughter wanted was to sleep. We let her sleep and the rest of the family went sightseeing and it worked out well. She was fine the next day."

A mother from Mississippi: "They've got a schedule all outlined for you, Tour A, Tour B, etc. We were anxious to see everything but our son just wanted to get away. The state fair was going on in Pueblo so we went down there and he loved it...he was like a kid again, seeing the show animals and having fun on the rides. He didn't want to talk about anything at the Academy until later. Then he took us on a personal tour of the Obstacle Course and Jack's Valley where they had part of their BCT. He was enthusiastic and proud and this was much better than any group tour. My advice is don't plan anything. See what your cadet wants, then adapt to it. You can go early or stay another day if sightseeing is important."

A father and parents' club president from Georgia: "I had initially thought, since he had been gone for only eight weeks, that going out there was an unnecessary expense. But I got some good advice and we went, and now I know that it is a must if you want your cadet to survive that first year. But do not expect anything much from them for awhile. Our son just wanted to get away, so we drove to the Keystone Resort west of Denver. He slept all the way in the car, but when he revived, he was fine. He played golf with his brother, laughed a lot, and we had a wonderful time. I would recommend getting away like

Do whatever you can to make sure you attend Parents' Weekend. Courtesy Sandy Langston.

this if you can afford it and if the cadet needs it. You can always tour the Academy later."

A father and parents' club president from Ohio: "All our son wanted to do was go to a motel and crash. Then he wanted to just lie around in the room without his uniform and watch television. Fast food was also a high priority. We have heard from several parents who were disappointed because their kids behave that way. I advise new parents that this is normal behavior. I tell them that the kid will brighten up after a day of rest."

A father and retired officer from Georgia: "Don't ask them how they like it. That system isn't made for them to like–it is made to challenge them. If they answer truthfully, they will have to say that they hate it, especially at this point. For your sake and for the sake of the cadet, such negative things are better left unsaid. Also, don't take sides against the system. Don't condemn it because the kid has to live and survive in it—you don't. You leave and go back home and he has all he can handle without more negative thoughts dragging him down."

A wing vice-commander from South Carolina, whose daughter is a graduate and three-time All-American track star, and whose son is also a recent graduate and varsity football player, explained, "Expect to see a change in them—a dramatic change both physically and emotionally. They are dogbeat tired and fall asleep almost every time they sit down. Also they may exhibit typical manifestations of the stress and conditioning that they are going through. Expect emotional outbursts, periods of crying, periods of childlike withdrawal, and any number of other emotional displays...they're just getting an insight into what is in store for them and keep in mind that their fear of failure can be staggering at this point. Also realize that the first two years are tough, grueling, gut-busting years for which most of them are ill prepared. Keep reminding yourself of this if you feel your support flagging."

Several parents spoke of the problems of saying goodbye at the end of Parents' Weekend.

"It's very hard," said a Wisconsin mother and co-president of a parents' club. "You see him walk across that parade ground with his head down and he hears through open windows the upperclassmen playing 'I'll Be Home For Christmas' and 'Leaving on a Jet Plane' loudly on their stereos. The upperclassmen are doing that deliberately to make it harder on the doolies, so be ready for it. It can make you mad or make you want to cry."

"I practiced and did everything I could to psych myself into not crying when I said goodbye," said a Kentucky mother. "I think it is important to be an actress sometimes. You don't want them to see you crying. They have enough to make them feel badly when they head back to their squadron."

"Don't let the goodbyes linger," cautioned an Arizona mother and former co-president of the state parents' club. "When it comes time, smile if you can, cry if you have to, but get it over fast. They feel badly enough already without parents making it worse."

"The hardest thing for me in the almost three years our son has been there," said a Mississippi father, "was to say goodbye at the end of that first Parents' Weekend. My advice is to be prepared for a very sad experience, but, for your cadet's sake, try not to let the depth of those feelings show through."

Said a Mississippi mother: "I was brave when we said goodbye, but I cried all the way from Colorado Springs to Jackson and the next time he called I was ready to tell him to come home. But he was fine and in good spirits, and I felt much better knowing that we had gone there. There were two doolies in his squadron whose parents didn't come and he felt real bad for them."

One controversial issue cropped up during several of the discussions about Parents' Weekend. The subject was girlfriends: should they accompany the parents that first year? (None of the parents with daughters spoke of any problem with boyfriends.) Following is a sampling of opinion along with a compromise that many parents felt was a good one.

Said an Illinois father with two sons at the Academy: "We had a problem with one of our son's girlfriends. We didn't want her to go along and we said, 'Hey, it's called Parents' Weekend, not Girlfriend's Weekend.' But don't not go if the girlfriend has to go along."

"She went and I really didn't want her to go," said a Georgia mother. "But he felt that he needed that. It was definitely not quality time because he was torn between spending time with both of us. They broke up later so I don't know if it was a good idea or a bad idea to take her."

"We were thankful it could not work itself in the first year," said a father from Florida. "The second year our daughter had been scheduled to go and something came up and he suggested that his girlfriend go instead and we took her. I do not recommend it unless you cannot avoid it—unless everyone gets along very well. We didn't know her that well...they were with us and then they weren't. I don't want to be totally negative because every girlfriend is different, and she might be very important in a cadet's life."

"Our son's girlfriend is an extremely smart and lovely girl and we encouraged her to go along," said a mother from Mississippi. "We encouraged them to go off on their own, but they wanted to stay together. She was a very important part of his support system at that time. Since then they have begun dating others and it may not last."

"We had no problem with our son's girlfriend," said a Georgia father. "If you discourage something like that, you may have to live the rest of your life with the guilt if it turns out that he is really serious about the girl."

"I think there is more to be gained than lost," said a Michigan father. "If there is a loving, supporting relationship in the family, it will work out all right. However, I can see where there would be exceptions."

A California mother and president of a parents' club suggested a compromise that, when presented by the author to other parents, received mostly favorable support.

She said, "We have seen some bad experiences, like parents sitting around in their hotel room feeling depressed while the son and girlfriend are off somewhere. Free, family-type discussions are inhibited, too, when a stranger is around. To get around this I suggest that they use Parents' Weekend for themselves and the immediate family, and that they encourage the girlfriend to go to Colorado Springs in October for the Autumn Ball. That way the parents can have the cadet to themselves and the girlfriend can have her exclusive time. An additional advantage is that the cadet has something to look forward to in October, and doesn't have that long period between the first of September and Thanksgiving or Christmas without seeing someone he knows."

There is an element of risk involved with this compromise. The girl might travel all the way to Colorado Springs and discover that her cadet has been put on restriction for that weekend. In addition, she should realize the cadet is not likely to have as much free time that weekend as he would have during Parents' Weekend.

LETTING GO

Note that Parents' Weekend is not strictly the first chance you have to see your cadet. At the end of BCT, the cadets all march in an Acceptance Parade, honoring the doolies' change in status from basic cadet to fourthclass cadet. Often the doolies will be given a few hours after the parade to meet with their families if they come. While most of the visiting families at the Academy that day are those who live in Colorado, some enthusiastic parents fly from California or Florida just to spend this short time with their cadet.

Even more extreme, every summer a few parents will camp out on the chapel wall throughout BCT, holding up signs and shouting to their basic cadet. They visit the athletic fields or other routes the cadets transit, hovering like the proverbial helicopter, happy to catch a mere glimpse of their beloved child. This can only have a negative impact on the cadet. They will not be allowed to speak to (or even look at) their parent, they will be ridiculed by the upperclassmen, and they will be reminded of home when they should be concentrating on their new responsibilities.

Parents who hover around the Academy are a distraction to their cadet.

Said one graduate/mom, "Some parents are just *too* involved. They want to know what their kids are doing every minute of the day. They want to be involved as if they were experiencing it themselves. Don't live vicariously through them. Don't get a condo here!"

If you know you are a helicopter parent, start rehearsing in your mind the decision to back off and let your son or daughter go, and grow.

VISITS HOME

Some cadets are able to get home during the short Thanksgiving break; many get home for the one-week spring break; practically all get home for Christmas. In any case, the cadet's behavior may surprise parents who are not ready for it. For example:

"He came home the first Christmas, dropped off his bags, said 'Hi Mom, hi Dad,' and took off to go see his friends—mostly his old teammates," said a Georgia father. "We didn't see much of him for four days and were really hurt. So was his girlfriend. Then we found out from other parents that this is not unusual."

"There are some definite don'ts that I try to pass on," said a North Carolina father and president of the state parents' club. "One is don't schedule your cadet for any appointments or visits. It is real tempting to say, 'Oh you look so nice in your uniform you just have to put it on and go visit Aunt Sally and Uncle Jim.' My advice is to get out of as much of that as possible—they've been in a pressure cooker and they need to get out of that uniform and unwind—that is the most important thing. Let Aunt Sally and Uncle Jim visit your home if necessary and make the visit as painless as you can.

Do not bug your child to show off his uniform or tell you everything she is going through.

"Another one is don't tease them or hound them about the way they keep their room. When it is a mess, it is easy to say, 'Oh, I thought they were going to teach you neat habits at the Academy.' What parents have to realize is that they need the opposite of what they've had at the Academy. They need to be sloppy for a change. And don't worry; they'll probably get neater as the vacation proceeds, and definitely they will improve over the years."

A Mississippi father added another don't to the list. "When the kid gets home, don't bug him to tell everything that he has gone through. I know it is tempting because the parent is genuinely interested, but think of how it is when you are on vacation. You don't want to talk about your job."

Do not be surprised if your cadet experiences some awkwardness in the family, or disappointment when they get together with old friends. A Texas mother explained that when her daughter came home that first Christmas, "it was hard for you to tell her anything. She sees herself as an adult now, and her standards for everyone around her went up. That creates a distance. It's almost like she's a part of a world we could never understand." In the short six months since they started BCT, they have been through experiences that have changed them. They may have less in common with their old high school buddies, and less patience with everyone.

Most parents dread the last days of the Christmas vacation because the cadets typically become morose about going back. Even if they have not yet experienced it, they all know of the "Dark Ages," the dismal, cold months of January and February when they go to class in the dark and return to their room in the dark.

Also, they know that the upperclassmen will bear down right after Christmas because they want to rid the doolies of any independent habits or thoughts that they might have picked up while away.

"In addition," said a Massachusetts mother and co-president of a parents' club, "you may have to contend with the problem of one who will not go back. We had two sons out there, but despite all of our encouragement, the younger one decided to punch out."

"They say they're going back to the 'black hole'," said a mother from West Virginia. "They don't want to go back but they do and if there is any little thing you can do to perk up their spirits, that is the time to do it. They can really get down at that time of the year."

You can help them through these dark ages with lots of mail and encouragement when they get back to the Academy.

SPONSORS

Every doolie is assigned to a family in the Colorado Springs area who has volunteered to become a cadet sponsor. The purpose is to provide a home away from home where the cadet can go during off-duty time and relax, do laundry, watch a movie and perhaps enjoy a home-cooked meal. Most sponsors also provide transportation to and from their homes, at least during the years when car ownership is prohibited.

Often the cadet-sponsor relationship becomes very close during the four years that the cadet is at the Academy. In addition, parents of cadets sometimes become good friends of the sponsors and may even stay in the sponsors' home during visits to the Academy.

Several parents credited sponsors for helping their sons and daughters survive at the Academy. Said a Pennsylvania mother, "Frankly, I was a bit worried about our daughter being so far away but our worries ended when she got her sponsor. They were wonderful to her. They treated her like a daughter and when we were out there they were very nice to us. We have to give them a lot of credit for helping get her through the four years."

A North Carolina father was even more enthusiastic. "I'll say it outright; I don't think either my daughter or I could have survived without her sponsor. They watched over her like she was one of their own. And when I was worried and couldn't call her at the squadron, I could call the sponsor and get information about her—things that she would never pass on in a telephone call. This is an important communication link that many parents do not appreciate."

Not all cadet-sponsor relationships are as ideal and sometimes the cadet will get discouraged and give up the relationship. If this happens to your cadet, urge him to go to the office in Arnold Hall where the sponsor program is administered. There he can request a new sponsor, and the new one may work out much better.

In interviews with sponsors, some have expressed disappointments with cadets and their parents. Cadets are faulted most for taking their sponsor family for granted. Typically they are criticized for not writing thank-you notes after the sponsor has prepared a special meal or done something out of the ordinary for the cadet's birthday.

Parents are encouraged to communicate with the sponsor. A graduate whose son recently graduated said, "Contact the sponsors. They will appreciate the contact. They can also help alleviate your fears [about your child's state of mind]. This is a valuable connection, a relationship that can be very helpful for parents." Said a retired colonel who sponsors eight cadets and has two of his own sons at the Academy, "My wife makes it a point to write to each of the cadet's families just as soon as we adopt them. It is always hard for us to believe, but over the years that we have been doing this, we only hear back from about half of the parents. This is discouraging and hard for us to understand."

SPECIAL PROBLEMS
- Spending Money

Various concerns were expressed by parents as they were interviewed. One of them concerns cadet spending money—or the lack of it.

"They end up with about fifteen dollars a week during that first year," said a mother from Massachusetts. "You can't do much with that, so I try to slip a twenty-dollar bill in my letters when I can afford it. They aren't required to eat their evening meal in the dining hall and if they have the money, they can order in pizza and use that time for studying. I don't look on giving them money as babying them like some parents might. I see it as just another way to help them and also to let them know that we care."

As a Mississippi mother said, "The education is free but fun costs money. They need to have some fun once in awhile."

The same mother also had a suggestion that other parents thought was a good idea. "I recommend that parents open a special savings account starting in July when their cadet first leaves home. Put twenty dollars in that account each month then, near the end of the junior year, when the cadet discovers that his class ring is going to cost about 900 dollars, you will have most of that saved and you can buy the ring for him. We did that and it was a surprise our son really appreciated. You're very proud of them by this time and I think it is a good way for a parent to express appreciation for what the boy or girl has accomplished."

Parents should not feel guilty if they cannot afford such luxuries for their cadets. Said an Illinois single mother with five children, "My oldest is a second degree [junior] and when he comes home, we laugh about the cookies and cakes that are delivered to the cadets. We laugh because I can't even afford such luxuries at home on my salary as a secretary. I do feel guilty all the time and wish I could do those things but my son grew up very independent and I think he is proud of the fact that he is getting by on his own."

> *The education is free but fun costs money.*

- Finding Out How Your Cadet Is Doing

Another concern parents expressed was the way the privacy laws affect information flow from the Academy. Said a New York father and co-president of a parents' club, "It really bothers parents when they discover that their daughter is in the hospital out there. Then when they call, frantic to find out something, the voice over the phone says, 'Just a moment, I will have to check with the cadet before I can release that information.' Parents just don't realize that the law prohibits them from releasing information unless a waiver is granted by the child. The same thing applies to grades. The Academy will not send grades to parents unless the child signs a waiver. I hear complaints about this all the time at parents' club meetings."

In response to that parent's comments, the Academy Hospital official responsible for patient administration was asked what parents should do to get information if their cadet ends up in the hospital.

He said, "It is true that we do have to conform to the Privacy Act when it comes to releasing information. However, if a cadet has a problem that we think is serious, we immediately contact the parents and we find a legal way to let them know what is going on."

The official also wanted to inform parents of the unique position of basic cadets who might be admitted to the hospital. "When the basic comes into the hospital—which is usually for a minor problem such as an ankle sprain or fluid dehydration—we have to try to maintain the same environment that exists for the other basics. For example, they are not allowed to watch television or speak on the phone with anyone, including parents."

If parents should learn that their cadet is in the hospital, or you have any other issue or emergency, call your cadet's Air Officer Commanding (AOC). This is an officer, usually a major, who is directly responsible for the safety and health of about one hundred cadets. It is the AOC's responsibility to check out the serious concerns of parents, and you can expect them to listen carefully to what you have to say.

The former vice commandant explained that your child will have the opportunity to fill out a form indicating what kind of information can be shared with the parent. She suggested you discuss the pros and cons of releasing information before your child leaves, and agree on what your role will be as a parent.

She went on to say, "If you are seriously concerned, call the AOC. It's not bothersome if you call." Just be prepare for the AOC to tell you he or she must talk to your cadet first, either because the AOC does not know anything about your area of concern, or because your cadet has not given permission to release information to you as parents.

Parents also should realize that the AOC's are charged with overseeing a process that weans new cadets away from dependency upon their parents—a process that is supposed to transform cadets into independent adults and military officers. Consequently, it is reasonable to expect that AOC's will try to minimize parent involvement. It is possible that a parent's concern about things like stress might fall into what the AOC might see as the "so what else is new" category. The result might be a perception on the part of the parent that his concerns have fallen on unreceptive ears.

Occasionally such differences in perspective cloud the understanding between a parent and the AOC. If this should happen to you and you believe that you should persist with the inquiry, the chain of command moves to the Group AOC and you should contact that officer. If the problem is not resolved at that level, you can go up the chain of command until you are satisfied.

What about personal matters that a parent would not want to discuss with an AOC? There are two other options.

One is the Counseling Center, which has a staff of trained, certified counselors who will respect the confidentiality of any communication that does not involve the breaking of a law or an Air Force regulation.

The counselors are there for just one purpose: to help cadets solve personal problems while they are at the Academy. If a parent feels the need to discuss a delicate matter that might affect the cadet's well being, yet one deemed inappropriate for the AOC's ears, a call to one of the counselors would be an appropriate course of action.

The other option is to consult with one of the Academy chaplains. Handling matters of a personal nature are routine for them and they have been cited by parents for being extremely helpful and sympathetic. One bonus in dealing with a chaplain: they enjoy the privilege of being able to maintain COMPLETE confidentiality on any matter.

Be assured that if your son or daughter got an appointment to the Academy, he or she has what it takes to succeed, and in four years you will be in the stadium witnessing a scene like this. *Courtesy USAFA*

A final word of consolation: While cadets may complain or struggle, they usually cope with the stresses of the Academy just fine. You can worry yourself crazy, or relax and realize that if there is a crisis someone will call and let you know. During the author's own graduation banquet, my father said, "I want you to know that the last four years were a lot harder on your mother than they were on you." He may have been right.

But you can take this assurance with 100% certainty: If your son or daughter got an appointment to the Air Force Academy, then he or she has what it takes to succeed. It might not be fun, but those who are truly motivated, ask for help when they need it, and stay determined CAN succeed.

One additional point of certainty: your job is (mostly) done. It is up to them now.

PARENTS' CLUBS

The final suggestion in this chapter is to seek out and join an Air Force Academy Parents' Club. Actually, you should try to locate members of your club even before your cadet receives an appointment and you become eligible to join. The club members are excellent advisors who can help you and your candidate with the admissions process. They have been through the process and have had success. Other than the local Liaison Officer, they are the next best authorities.

What do parents' clubs do? It would take another chapter to describe all of their many activities. In general terms they are a support group for parents and their cadets.

Some clubs have committees or individuals who adopt the parents of doolies and provide a "soft shoulder" service. Normally the doolie parents are called regularly so that while they are undergoing the typical first-year anxiety, they will have a sympathetic and experienced ear to hear their problems.

Parents' clubs also hold informative meetings where, for example, new appointees get to meet with Academy cadets on leave while parents are briefed by a visiting Academy Official.

Some parents' clubs are very active in rounding up members for an all-out assault on Colorado Springs during Parents' Weekend. The Wisconsin group is one of the most active in that regard. They arrive *en masse* with "doolie bags" loaded with combs, index cards, pens, lollipops and a host of other little goodies that doolies might need or enjoy. Many of the items are "freebies" solicited from sympathetic businesses.

The Maine Club also descends upon Colorado Springs as a group and the members take great pride in having maintained 100 percent parent participation for the last several years.

One of the social functions of a club may be a Christmas Ball where cadets, parents and dates can mingle during the holiday vacation. Arizona and Eastern Michigan are two places where this event has matured into an All-Academies Ball where cadets and midshipmen share the limelight and the festivities.

Parents' clubs are not for everyone. Some parents do not want or need a larger group to be part of their relationship with their son or daughter. And some cadets, when they are home on leave, want absolutely nothing to do with anything "Academy." But if you enjoy the strength and cameradie that come with large numbers, parents' clubs are for you.

The parents' clubs are always experimenting with new ideas and new ways to support the cadets. For example, the one club is trying the idea of having every member send a birthday card to each cadet from the state. "If that works," said the club president excitedly, "think of how a cadet's eyes are going to pop when he sees all those cards in his mailbox!" How does a parent find out more about a parents' club that might be available? Call either your local Liaison Officer or the Parents' Club Coordinator in the Admissions Office of the Academy. Either person can put you in touch with club officers who, in turn, can help you locate the members who live closest to you.

It is now time for a final word.

Without exception, every parent who was interviewed, including those of Academy dropouts, believed that their sons and daughters had received, or were receiving, an outstanding education at the Academy.

Also, the parents spoke with feeling when they described how the Academy experience had strengthened and matured their sons and daughters, and how they became better people because of that experience. Several of the parents admitted they were initially opposed or very skeptical about having a son or daughter go to the Academy—as you may be right now. However, those parents all said that they have changed their minds and now believe strongly that their sons and daughters did the right thing.

Even the pacifist mother who is strongly opposed to what her "militarist" son is doing as a B-52 navigator said without reservation that she is glad he went to the Air Force Academy.

For the young man or woman who is strongly self-motivated and qualified, the U.S. Air Force Academy offers an outstanding opportunity to get an excellent education and to develop into a mature, responsible adult, the best possible version of himself or herself.

If attending the Air Force Academy happens to become the choice of your own son or daughter, it is highly probable you will grow to support that decision with conviction and enthusiasm.

And to the parents who end up doing that:

BEST WISHES AND GOOD LUCK!
SCR

ACKNOWLEDGMENTS

Hundreds and hundreds of people helped with the first four editions of this candidate book, and dozens more helped with this fifth edition. To all the administrators, professors, cadets, congressional staffers and panelists, liaison officers, and parents who offered their time and insights: Thank you.

As always, a number of people gave an extraordinary amount of their time and effort. First is Phil Prosseda (Class of '80) from Admissions, who gave me a lot of his time answering questions in person and via email. Mr. Brad Milliman in Cadet Wing Media, who was a wizard at supplying the great majority of the pictures in the book—and as you can see there were many. Thanks also to Gary Howe (Class of '69) from the Association of Graduates for connecting me with some amazing grads.

A heartfelt thank you to all the cadets and graduates who shared their stories—their pain and struggles as well as their triumphs and joys. Though I cannot list you all by name, I value your stories and insights.

This book is full of graduates and cadets who say that one of the best things about going to the Academy is the people you get to meet, and that your classmates will become your friends for life. This book is a testament to that fact.

Way back in 1983 when we marched into the football stadium and tossed our hats in the air, my class's #1 graduate was Rich Fullerton—and he's as nice as he is smart. Twenty-nine years later, he has just finished a term as the Academy's vice dean and returned to his permanent professor position in the Department of Economics and Geosciences. Colonel Fullerton was so generous with his time as he set up faculty panels, chased down information for me, and answered questions about the academic side of the Academy.

Next is Billy Walker, who in our cadet days was an intercollegiate wrestler. He has returned to the cadet gym where he spent so many hours working out, overseeing 23 Division I sports teams and PE and fitness testing for 4,000 cadets. As deputy director of athletics, Colonel Walker answered many questions for me; set up interviews with staff members, grads, and cadet athletes; and helped track down pictures.

And finally, my roommate from BCT and two years in Cadet Squadron 12, Tamra Rank. We muddled through together, making hospital corners on our beds, doing pull-ups, learning all the verses to the national anthem, laughing a lot and crying a little along the way.

After graduation, we went to pilot training and served as instructor pilots together in Texas. As lieutenant colonels, we were UPT squadron commanders together at Columbus AFB, and we'd spend Saturday mornings walking and talking shop with our daughters in strollers. She is my daughter's godmother and the world's best example of a true friend. As Vice Superintendent of the Air Force Academy, Colonel Rank put me in touch with countless experts, tracked down information, answered questions, and kept all the doors open for me. Without her, this book absolutely could not have been written.

Your Academy classmates truly become friends for life.

A final thank you: I have learned so much from this book's original author, Bill Smallwood, whose passion for helping young men and women find their path to success is the driving force behind this work. Thank you for trusting me to continue your legacy.

Sue Ross

INDEX

ACT/ SAT 13, 27, 45, 58, 81, 83, 96, 104, 113-115, 120, 157, 161, 163, 176, 221

Admissions Liaison Officer 37-39, 42, 43, 79, 81-83, 85, 86, 88, 91, 101, 107, 108, 111, 114, 131

Advance Placement Classes 46, 49, 54, 56, 67, 163, 182, 194

Air Officer Commanding 12, 18, 171-173, 187, 231, 242, 243

Burtschi, Jacob 182-184

Candidate Fitness Assessment 69, 83

Campbell, Kim 26-28

Card, Larry 187-190

Cell Phones 123, 227

Civil Air Patrol 28, 72-74, 83, 190, 191

Contrails 75, 139

Counseling Center 170, 171, 242

Crawford, Barry 31-33

Duncavage, Lucas 185-186

Extra Instruction (EI) 3, 28, 29, 60, 65, 66, 164, 165, 178, 185

Grayson, Adam 28-30

Hennings, Chad 19-22

Hesterman, John 14-17

Honor Code 7, 16, 21, 30, 49, 104, 200-206

Howard, Christopher 22-24

Intercollegiate Athletes 37, 126, 164, 174-186

Interviews 42. 43. 81. 82. 88. 95. 97-99, 101-113

Junior ROTC 22, 23, 72, 74, 81, 83, 88, 190, 191

Johnson, Michelle 181

Kobayashi, Ky 24-26

Malachowski, Nicole 190-192

Pal, Monique 193-195

Parents' Clubs 244, 245

Parents Weekend 232-237

Physical Fitness Test (PFT) 28, 68, 69, 70

Pilot Training 36, 40, 143, 191, 209-211

Precandidate Questionnaire 84

Prep School 31, 98, 117-120, 171, 176, 180

Popovich, Gregg 10-12

Rank, Tamra 17-19

Rice, Edward 12-14

ROTC 40, 88, 104, 115, 118, 190, 218

Saturday Morning Inspections 21, 124, 125, 136, 137, 155

Sailplanes (Gliders) 1, 188, 191, 210

Sijan, Lance 130

Summer Seminar 42, 218

Sponsors 28, 160, 167-170, 185, 193, 198, 232, 239, 240

T-53 Aircraft 211

Unmanned Aerial Systems 210-212, 214

Weiss, Bart 181-182

Other titles by Silver Horn Books

The Naval Academy Candidate Book: How to Prepare, How to Get In, How to Survive, 3d ed. By Sue Ross. $18.95
Available at navyonline.com and amazon.com

The West Point Candidate Book: How to Prepare, How to Get In, How to Survive, 3d ed. By Sue Ross with Randy Lee. $18.95
Available at amazon.com

What is a Midshipman: All about Life at the United States Naval Academy. By Sue Ross
Available at the US Naval Academy Gift Shop